Doug Cannell.

THE MONUMENTS AND
INSCRIPTIONS OF
CARACOL, BELIZE

A. Hamilton Anderson
1901 - 1967

UNIVERSITY MUSEUM MONOGRAPH 45

THE MONUMENTS AND INSCRIPTIONS OF CARACOL, BELIZE

Carl P. Beetz
Linton Satterthwaite

Published by
THE UNIVERSITY MUSEUM
University of Pennsylvania
1981

Library of Congress Cataloging in Publication Data

Beetz, Carl P., 1953-
    The monuments and inscriptions of Caracol, Belize.

    (University Museum monograph; 45)
    Bibliography: p.
    1. Caracol site (Belize)   2. Mayas—Writing.
3. Stele (Archaeology)—Belize.   4. Indians of Central
America—Belize—Writing.   I. Satterthwaite, Linton,
1897-   .   II. Title. III. Series.
F1435.1.C37B43   972.82′2   81-16344
ISBN 0-934718-41-5   AACR2

CONTENTS

PREFACE
William R. Coe and Christopher Jones xi

I. INTRODUCTION 1
   Terms and Abbreviations 5

II. THE STELAE AND THEIR ASSOCIATED ALTARS 7
   Stela 1/Altar 1 7
   Stela 2 11
   Stela 3 12
   Stela 4 23
   Stela 5 26
   Stela 6 31
   Stela 7 36
   Stela 8 37
   Stela 9/Altar 4 40
   Stela 10 42
   Stela 11/Altar 19 44
   Stela 12 47
   Stela 13 48
   Stela 14/Altar 7 52
   Stela 15 56
   Stela 16 62
   Stela 17/Altar 10 64
   Stela 18 68
   Stela 19 69
   Stela 20 72
   Stela 21 74

III. THE ALTARS 77
   Altar 1 77
   Altar 2 77
   Altar 3 80
   Altar 4 81
   Altar 5 82
   Altar 6 84
   Altar 7 84
   Altar 8 85
   Altar 9 86
   Altar 10 86

Altar 11 87
Altar 12 89
Altar 13 93
Altar 14 96
Altar 15 97
Altar 16 98
Altar 17 99
Altar 18 101
Altar 19 102
Stone 28 103

IV. SUMMARY: STELA AND ALTAR PLACEMENT AND PAIRING.... 104
Table 1, Synopses of Stelae 108
Table 2, Synopses of Caracol Great Glyph Altars by
    suggested LC positions 110
Table 3, Long Count positions by katun ends for
    Caracol stelae and altars 112

V. THE RULERS OF CARACOL 114
Altar 4, Stela 13 and Stela 16 116
Stela 6 and Stela 14 117
Stela 1 and Stela 3 120
Stela 21 124
Stela 8, Stela 9 and Stela 11 124
Stela 19, Altar 12 and Altar 13 124
Stela 17, Altar 10 and Stela 10 127
Summary 128

BIBLIOGRAPHY 131

ILLUSTRATIONS 133

ILLUSTRATIONS

DRAWINGS

Figure 1, Stela 1, front 135
Figure 2, Stela 2, front, upper half 136
Figure 3, Stela 3, front 137
Figure 4, Stela 3, back 139
Figure 5a, Stela 4, front 141
      b, Stela 4, back
Figure 6a, Stela 5, front 143
      b, Stela 5, lower right glyph panel
Figure 7a, Stela 6, front 145
      b, Stela 6, right side
Figure 8, Stela 6, back 147
Figure 9, Stela 8, front 149
Figure 10, Stela 9, front 150
Figure 11, Stela 10, front 151
Figure 12, Stela 11, front 153
Figure 13a, Stela 13, front 155
      b, Stela 13, back
Figure 14a, Stela 14, front 156
      b, Stela 15, front
Figure 15a, Stela 16, front 157
      b, Stela 16, back
Figure 16a, Stela 17, front 158
      b, Stela 18, front
Figure 17a, Stela 19, front 159
      b, Stela 19, right side
Figure 18a, Stela 19, left side 161
      b, Stela 20, front
      c, Schematic diagram of positions of Stela 4 fragments as found
Figure 19, Stela 21, front 163
Figure 20a, Altar 1 164
      b, Altar 2
      c, Altar 3
      d, Altar 4
Figure 21a, Altar 5 165
      b, Altar 6
      c, Altar 7
      d, Altar 11

Figure 22, Altar 10 166
Figure 23, Altar 12 167
Figure 24, Altar 13 168
Figure 25a, Altar 14 169
      b, Altar 15
      c, Altar 16
      d, Altar 17
Figure 26a, Altar 18 170
      b, Altar 19
Figure 27a, Stone Group 46, reconstructed fragment 1 171
      b, Stone Group 46/50, reconstructed fragment 2
      c, Stela 4 fragment
      d, Stone Group 46, reconstructed fragment 3, front
      e, Stone Group 46, reconstructed fragment 3, back
Figure 28a, Stone 28, top 172
      b, Stone 28, right side
      c, Stone 28, front

PHOTOGRAPHS

A. Hamilton Anderson: 1901—1967 ii
Linton Satterthwaite oversees removal of Stela 1 and
      Altar 1 at Caracol in 1951 x
Figure 29a, Stela 1, front 173
      b, Stela 2, front
      c, Stela 4, front
      d, Stela 4, back
Figure 30a, Stela 3, front 174
      b, Stela 3, back
Figure 31a, Stela 5, front 175
      b, Stela 5, lower right side glyph panel
Figure 32a, Stela 6, front 176
      b, Stela 6, right side
      c, Stela 6, back
Figure 33a, Stela 7, *in situ* 177
      b, Stela 8, front, upper half
      c, Stela 8, front, lower half
Figure 34a, Stela 9, front 178
      b, Stela 10, front, upper half
      c, Stela 10, front, lower half
Figure 35a, Stela 11, front, upper half 179
      b, Stela 11, front, lower half
      c, Stela 14, front (cast)
Figure 36a, Stela 13, front, upper half 180
      b, Stela 13, back, upper half
      c, Stela 15, front
Figure 37a, Stela 16, front 181
      b, Stela 16, back
Figure 38a, Stela 17, front 182
      b, Stela 18, front

Figure 39a, Stela 19, front, lower half 183
      b, Stela 19, Frame "IV"
      c, Stela 20, front
      d, Stela 21, front
Figure 40a, Altar 1 184
      b, Altar 2
      c, Altar 3
      d, Altar 4
Figure 41a, Altar 5 185
      b, Altar 6
      c, Altar 7
      d, Altar 10
Figure 42a, Altar 12 186
      b, Altar 13
      c, Altar 14 and Altar 15 fragment
Figure 43a, Altar 16 187
      b, Altar 17
      c, Altar 19
      d, Stone 28

MAP

    Figure 44, Map of Caracol, Belize ....Pocket, back cover

Linton Satterthwaite oversees removal of Stela 1 and Altar 1 at Caracol in 1951

PREFACE

Often just a commendatory prelude, a preface seems worthwhile here in order to explain certain matters of the background and framework of the study which follows. Foremost is the fact of Linton Satterthwaite's heavy responsibility for research concerning the monuments and epigraphy of Tikal, Guatemala from 1956 onwards. As one might expect, this involvement prevented his continuation of the processing of the Caracol data even after considerable progress in both his text and its illustration. Throughout later years, his hope remained to return to the Caracol corpus once the far larger task of his share of Tikal analysis had reached a conclusion. On neither count did his life suffice.

Linton Satterthwaite's death in March of 1978 followed that of his wife early the previous year during a period of his own faltering health. At that time many friends contributed to a Margaret E. Satterthwaite Memorial Fund, the objective of which was to promote the completion of her husband's Caracol and Tikal researches. Towards this purpose, we acknowledge here with gratitude a major supplementary gift by Mrs. Francis Boyer.

Among other decades-old, never fully processed projects of the American Section, Caracol had come to be a well-nigh archival item; yet it was one we were convinced too important to languish endlessly in the form of cabineted raw field data and our mentor's preliminary manuscripts. That the material should be "salvaged" and put expeditiously into print with only the most requisite additions and conscientiously limited effort was our goal. But who was to do the job? Recalling Linton Satterthwaite's frequent caveat that we ourselves must not jump from project to project with the first undone, the thought was rejected of shelving personal Tikal obligations to the benefit of Caracol, even as bounded as we judged the effort should be.

The solution lay in the presence of Carl Beetz, two years along in graduate studies in Anthropology. He entered the field with the keenest interest in Maya epigraphy, a fascination needless to say that was not overlooked in the American Section. After much discussion of what the condition of speedy "salvage" might be, he undertook what we could not, and with, we add, assurances of an honorarium to be paid from the Fund on the task's termination. Linton Satterthwaite at the time was in the last months of life, but, despite his increasing difficulties, assuredly he understood and welcomed what had been agreed upon.

Those perusing this volume will encounter a product hardly reckonable as the once proposed "salvage." Instead, they will find a work not only expanded in calendric concerns but also responsive within stated limits to intriguing material couched in the inscriptions, now recognized to be relevant to history. It became far more than elementary reclamation, the original intent, and how such transpired could be of interest. In retrospect, all might have been predicted had we only taken into account the membership of Carl Beetz in that odd species called "scholar."

A first inkling that basics were being exceeded grew from glimpses of his assigned office space wherein the walls seemed progressively to disappear behind tacked-up drawings of purported clauses, rulers' name glyphs and other products of an unrelenting pursuit of meaning far beyond his mandate. Nothing could serve except to urge him to constrain these clandestine departures. In effect, a sparse addendum was after all thinkable, one designed to telegraph the inherent potentials of Caracol inscriptions. Still, as the months passed, each week seemed inexorably to produce more insights and interpretive possibilities from Carl Beetz' cubbyhole. Minimally to maintain rapport, we finally and reluctantly capitulated to the reality of an increasingly burgeoning Caracol report. And so it went, until one day not far back when he announced that comprehensive additions to and refinement of the whole, long-ago executed body of line illustration were essential. He could see numerous deficiencies in glyphic rendering, let alone myriad shortcomings in the past inked figural delineations. True, we had long been aware that certain sculpted bracelets and other regalia had been misconstrued within the photographic sources. (Yet, consistent with "salvage," and provided proper note were made textually, we thought a majority of readers would be forgiving.) Ineluctably, drafting began anew and of course via the pen and eye of Carl Beetz. Thus it was that mere rescue from a so-to-speak archival deep-freeze came to be replaced by laudably something else.

This volume is jointly authored, and, to be candid, from its just described beginnings what we had in mind was credit along the lines, say, of "Satterthwaite, with supplementary data by Beetz." Strictly dual authorship happens in print to convey ambiguously either senior and junior contributions or equivalent input. Rarely can one knowledgeably quantify a matter of this sort. However, we do take the stand that the individual first cited is the one to take the full future brunt of inquiry and criticism. For obvious reasons Carl Beetz is that person today. Aware of scholarly delicacies, nonetheless we remember Linton Satterthwaite's limitless generosity and, more germanely, his ingrained need to recognize each man's contribution.

In recent discussions of the volume's format, the question of a possible frontispiece arose, which is to say, a primary page available for a photograph. This led us to think of a dedication, not on any of our parts, but an acknowledgment Dr. Satterthwaite himself would have wished to make. While he deeply admired many Mayanists of his generation, we cannot believe that, had he been here to choose, his gratitude in the whole enterprise of Caracol would not have gone to the late A. Hamilton Anderson. Serving as the first Archaeological Commissioner of then

British Honduras (Belize), he was instrumental to and a frequent participant in the program of Caracol excavations. A plethora of letters attest both to their perennial friendship and their collaborative concerns for the ancient Maya world so exuberantly present in that country. Understandably, Mr. Anderson's photograph appears as the frontispiece.

Supporters of the orinigal effort to "reclaim" Caracol offered more than financial help. In memory of both Dr. and Mrs. Satterthwaite, Geraldine Bruckner undertook the editorial responsibility for this volume from its beginning to end. She has done so with an expertise that long benefited all University Museum publications prior to her retirement. In this work she was assisted by Barbara Allyn Wilson. As somewhat peripheral players, we extend to them our appreciation on behalf of all.

Finally, we excuse Carl Beetz from an account of how press charges have been met for what lies between these covers. While the greater amount stems from the American Section Research Fund, a nevertheless substantial shortfall has in part been most generously fulfilled by Mr. Alfred Zantzinger and by Mr. Brandon Barringer. Particularly crucial has been a gift by Mr. Horace Willcox in memory of his mother, in life a long-term contributor to American Section efforts and needs. Requisite additional funds come from the Research and Publication Committee of the Museum's Board of Managers. Because printing bills continue to grow more onerous in productions of this kind, support from these individuals and sources is commensurately ever more appreciated.

WILLIAM R. COE
CHRISTOPHER JONES

I: INTRODUCTION

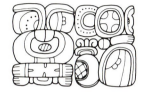

Research at Caracol, Belize began with the discovery of the site in 1938 by the mahogany cutter Rosa Mai. Later that same year, the site was visited by Mr. A. H. Anderson and Mr. H. B. Jex. At that time, eight pieces of monuments were located. For over a decade thereafter the site slumbered in relative abandon in the forest. Travel was so restricted by jungle that only loggers or a passing chiclero might visit the ancient buildings.

Heavy logging carried out in the area in the late 1940s led to the construction of roads for truck access. This made the site more accessible so that Satterthwaite was able to visit the ruins as a part of a general Museum archaeological reconnaissance of western British Honduras in 1950. During the two weeks that the University Museum expedition stayed at the site, twenty-four new monuments were discovered. Such a quantity of inscribed stone led Satterthwaite to return to the ruins for further exploration and recording in 1951 and again in 1953. During these latter two seasons several of the stelae and altars were shipped to Belize City or to Philadelphia for conservation and exhibition. The Government of British Honduras chose to keep only whole monuments since they lacked the capacity to deal with the reconstruction of broken pieces. On the other hand the Museum transported mostly broken stones which were subsequently rebuilt. At the end of the final Museum trip to Caracol the monument count stood at thirty-nine: twenty stelae and nineteen altars.

Anderson, as the Archaeological Commis-sioner, returned in 1955 and 1958 to complete excavation of some tombs he had located. In the course of work during the latter season he came across the surviving fragment of the slate Stela 21. The monument was buried at that time to hide it from looters. Satterthwaite made a quick visit to Caracol in 1958 to record the stone which was then re-hidden. Instructions as to its location were retained both in Philadelphia and in Belize.

Work at Caracol since 1958 has been desultory. Following the destruction wreaked by Hurricane Hattie in 1961, Anderson had to cut his way back to the ruins in 1966 to check for damage. The jungle again rapidly blocked access to the site. In 1978 the Archaeological Commissioner, Elizabeth Graham, sent a team into Caracol to recover Stela 21. The monument was boxed and flown by helicopter to Belmopan.

The 1950s fieldwork related to the Caracol monuments produced field sketches and latex molds of each stone. Additionally, some fifty-five hundred photographs, both day and night, were taken. Excavation around each monument yielded quantities of sherds and two caches. Two chambered burials, Burials 1 and 2, were explored during the 1953 University Museum expedition. A third tomb, Burial 3, was found directly below Burial 2 but was flooded and therefore not immediately excavated. In 1955 and 1958 Anderson excavated other interments, Burials 3-5 (Anderson 1958, 1959). All the material from these latter tombs, along with all of Anderson's notes, was swept out to sea in the destruction brought by the hurricane in 1961. A final result of the early Caracol fieldwork was the construction of a site core map by Jeremiah Epstein which is presented here.

Satterthwaite began to study the Caracol inscriptions almost as soon as he saw them at the site. He began work on the present volume and prepared notes of varying depth on the calendric transcription of each monument. However, with the advent of the Museum's involvement in the enormous Tikal Project, Satterthwaite found himself in 1956 compelled to set aside study of the Caracol texts in favor of those from Tikal.

In 1977, Beetz accepted responsibility for finishing the text of the Caracol monuments volume and of preparing it for publication. An honorarium was provided by the Margaret Satterthwaite Memorial Fund to assist in the development of the book. Although Beetz met once with Satterthwaite before his death in early 1978, Beetz was compelled to rely upon Satterthwaite's notes and the original field records to finish the work. The original intent was to complete the text by using as much of Satterthwaite's own writing as possible, even where it might be slightly out-of-date. By December of 1978 this task was completed. However, during this work Beetz noted that there were weaknesses in the text because of advances that had occurred in the field of Maya epigraphy since the early 1950s. Thus, with the encouragement of Drs. Coe and Jones of the University Museum, he undertook the task of completely overhauling the manuscript to bring it into line with contemporary studies. For this reason, the final text is a thorough amalgam of that of the two authors. Beetz' work has provided the final form, most of the conclusions and a new section (V) dealing with dynastic history. The historical data has given insights on the calendric readings of the monuments, which in turn have led to new interpretations and adjustments in the text. Details of excavations and special deposits are for the most part not presented in this volume. Reference is made to this information where it appears to be important to an understanding of the placement of a monument.

The line drawings of monuments are intended as the basic visual record of a stone. It is difficult to find a single photograph which can convey as much as a line drawing made with consultation of many photographs taken under a variety of lighting. Thus the photographs reproduced here are not intended to display much more than the condition of the stone, its shape and the depth of relief. All photographs presented in this volume were taken by the University Museum.

The process of making the drawings began with the taking of field photographs by Satterthwaite. After a set of initial shots that recorded the circumstances of discovery, the fragments were laid out in rough orientation for daylight photographs. Day work consisted of overall shots with reference scales and some detail shots. Night photographs made with the aid of flood lamps powered by a gasoline generator then concentrated on detail. To bring this detail out, each set of night photographs consisted of several shots of the same area utilizing light directed from at least three different directions.

To supplement field photography, latex molds were made of the stones. In Philadelphia, plaster casts made from the molds and the few original monuments that had been shipped were photographed under studio conditions by Reuben Goldberg. This work was again done with flood lamps directed from at least three different angles.

Satterthwaite studied the monuments, casts and photographs to determine the outlines of carving, which he then sketched. These sketches and the reference photographs were consulted by the illustrators to draw the first drafts over quarter-scale blowups of monument photographs. A process of correction by Satterthwaite with subsequent redrawing followed until the final version was inked. The illustrators for the various Caracol monuments are:

Stela 1 Carl Beetz
Stela 2 Carl Beetz
Stela 3 Carl Beetz
Stela 4 Carl Beetz
Stela 5 Carl Beetz
Stela 6 Carl Beetz (front and back), Betsy Roosen (side)
Stela 7 Undrawn
Stela 8 LaBerta Ehman
Stela 9 Betsy Roosen
Stela 10 LaBerta Ehman
Stela 11 Carl Beetz
Stela 12 Undrawn
Stela 13 Betsy Roosen (front), LaBerta Ehman (back)

Stela 14 Virginia Greene
Stela 15 LaBerta Ehman
Stela 16 Carl Beetz (front),
  LaBerta Ehman (back)
Stela 17 LaBerta Ehman
Stela 18 Carl Beetz
Stela 19 Betsy Roosen
Stela 20 Carl Beetz
Stela 21 Carl Beetz
Altar 10 Betsy Roosen
Altar 12 LaBerta Ehman
Altar 13 LaBerta Ehman
Giant Glyph Altars Betsy Roosen
Stone 28 Carl Beetz
Slate stelae fragments Carl Beetz

Recently Beetz reviewed the entire set of drawings; many were seen to need severe correction and modification because the entire process of creating the representations was only irregularly applied in actuality. In some cases, inadequate field photographs were taken. In others, some casts proved not to cover the entire area of carving. A major difficulty was that several of the illustrators had little familiarity with Maya art or hieroglyphic writing and were thus prone to misread the preserved detail. Also, the number of photographs available to an illustrator varied dramatically—from around sixteen for Stela 11 to around one thousand for Stela 14. As a result, Beetz has undertaken the task of correcting and re-drawing many of the stones.

Accuracy of representation varies from stone to stone. The most precise stelae drawings in this report are those of Stelae 1, 2, 3, 5, 6, 14, 16, 18, 20 and 21. Stelae 4, 8, 9, 10, 11, 13, 15, 17 and 19 and Altars 10, 12 and 13 are well represented but confused as to details of human figures and hieroglyphs in the drawings. Of this group Stelae 8 and 10 were perhaps the most poorly done. Stela 11 had to be drawn from an incomplete record of glyph panel casts and oblique photographs. Thus it was impossible to depict the full amount of preserved detail with complete accuracy. As drawn, the figural work of Stela 11 represents something of an artistic rendering rather than a precise copy. Giant Glyph Altars received scant attention in the field in many cases. However, owing to their rather simple subject matter, they are all well represented in the drawings.

This volume opens with the individual monument descriptions numerically presented in their order of discovery and identification. Stelae are the first stones presented. Where they exist, altars found in close spatial association to stelae are presented in a common discussion. It should be noted that not all the altars described as spatial pairs with stelae actually formed functional pairs when originally erected. Descriptions of each of the remaining altars and Stone 28 follow the stelae and their accompanying altars. The delineative portion of the volume closes with a general discussion of the relative temporal positions of the monuments and their possible original pairings and locations. This is followed by a section which deals with the historical content of the known Caracol inscriptions.

Descriptions of the individual (or spatially paired) monuments use a standard format derived from the presentation in *Tikal Report No. 4* (Satterthwaite 1958). The format is the same for the altars as for the stelae although it is abbreviated in many instances. A monument description opens with a synopsis of salient information. Style dates given in many of these synopses were calculated by Tatiana Proskouriakoff who had kindly allowed us to use her results in this volume. Under the heading "Other References" on these same tables, advertence is frequently made to the earlier Caracol reports that appeared in the *Bulletin of the University Museum* (Satterthwaite 1951, 1954; Willcox 1954). However, actual page number references for the given stones in these articles are not here detailed, since the reports tended to be general in nature. Finally, the stela and altar classifications are derived from *Tikal Report No. 4* (Satterthwaite 1958:136-141) although reference for the stelae is also made to the older Morley system of classification (Morley 1937-38:I, 152 and IV, 261-267).

The "General Remarks" that follow present information relating to the discovery of the monument, its position relative to other monuments and structures and its state of preservation. A pair of tables utilizing a format similar to that in *Tikal Report No. 4* for summarizing the calendric reading of the monument then precedes a section entitled "Comment on the Inscription." However, these two tables have been modified somewhat from their original format. The "Glyph Classification and Chronological Decipherment" table presents calendric data in a column immediately to the right of block designations. Further to the right, comments on both eroded or destroyed blocks and on non-calendrical information appear indented equally. Historical information that is referred to in this table is discussed in pages 114-130 of the volume. The subsequent "Comment on the Inscription" continues, to contain all discussion relative to calendric and chronological decipherment of the carving. In a case where a monument carries no readable text, the "Comment on the Inscription" has been omitted and any information relating to the number of glyph blocks, arrangement of text and possible chronological position has been incorporated into the "General Remarks."

Rules of block designation and block count are also derived from *Tikal Report No. 4*. A unit of text that appears to represent the major section (usually that immediately following an ISIG or opening CR date) is referred to as the main text. Continuous texts in disparate panels on different sides of a stone are considered to be part of the main text. Columns of a main text are lettered in sequence from left to right in accordance with the Maya order of reading. Rows of text are numbered in sequence from top to bottom. Separate units of text or inscription that cannot be connected with the main text with certainty are given letter designations in reverse order beginning with Z. Thus the first such designation for a monument would be "Panel Z." The second would be "Panel Y" and so on. In this manner it is hoped to avoid the mistake of assigning column labels which may later be demonstrated incorrect. The block count given in the "Glyph Classification" table is based on the number of whole blocks discerned. Where confusion exists, the minimum number of blocks is given. In this reckoning, no account is taken of divided blocks. Thus the actual number of glyphs on a monument is liable to be somewhat higher than the number of blocks. The "Scene" Altars 10, 12, and 13 are exceptions to the rules of block labels given

above. In the cases of the latter monuments, there are circumferential texts which run continuously. According to the above principles, these texts should be labeled A1, B1, C1, etc. However, for convenience, they are simply labeled as Blocks 1, 2, 3, etc.

It has taken almost thirty years to bring the present volume to the point of publication. The original fieldwork that led to its development was oriented entirely to the recovery of these inscriptions. As a result, little is known of the archaeology of the bulk of the site of Caracol. It can safely be predicted that further fieldwork at the ruins will bring to light new monuments and texts which, hopefully, will fill in the gaps of the present record and resolve many of the difficulties raised herein.

Particular gratitude must be given to the late A. H. Anderson for his warm cooperation and assistance. We would like to acknowledge the contributions of the field supervisors of 1951, Horace Willcox and Seymour Nuddle, and of 1953, Jeremiah Epstein. Appreciation is extended to the illustrators of some of the monuments, LaBerta Ehman, Betsy Roosen and Virginia Greene and also to the late Anna K. Stimson who helped to support this effort. Additional photographic work was provided by William Clough and Harmer Frederick Schoch. Similarly we would like to thank Geraldine Bruckner and Wendy Bacon for their work in editing and correction of the text. We are particularly grateful to Tatiana Proskouriakoff for her contributions to decipherment of the glyphs and especially for the calculations of style dates she has provided. Heinrich Berlin and the late Sir J. Eric S. Thompson corresponded with Satterthwaite and gave input into the calendrical and historical understanding of the Caracol inscriptions. Special thanks are given to William Coe and Christopher Jones who have supplied continual consultation and assistance in countless ways towards the publication of this volume.

TERMS AND ABBREVIATIONS

Most of the terminology and abbreviations are derived from *Tikal Report No. 4* (Satterthwaite 1958:91-92) and will not be discussed again here. Two new abbreviations utilized in the present work do require explanation. The first is "EG" as an abbreviation for Emblem Glyph. The definition of an emblem glyph was given by Berlin (1958) and is followed here. "PC" is used in place of the term "Provisional Character" which designates a character whose name can be demonstrated to exist on the monuments, but whose actual name phrase is not clear or cannot be read through erosion. The PC series begins with PCZ and runs backwards; PCZ, PCY, PCX . . . PCA. It is hoped that new texts and possibly further study of known inscriptions will eventually allow the replacement of a PC designation with a more descriptive label.

DD	Dedicatory Date
IS	Initial Series
ISIG	Initial Series Introductory Glyph
SR	Sacred Round
VYr	Vague Year
CR	Calendar Round
PE	Period End
SS	Secondary Series
SSIG	Secondary Series Introductory Glyph
LS	Lunar Series
MA	Moon Age
MN	Moon Number
MT	Moon Type
EG	Emblem Glyph
PC	Provisional Character

II: THE STELAE
AND THEIR ASSOCIATED ALTARS

STELA 1/ALTAR 1

Location:	In Corridor A2, between rear of Structure A1 and Structure A10. Stela 1 partially, and Altar 1 entirely covered with debris from Structure A1	
	Stela 1	**Altar 1**
Associations:	None evident	None evident
Dedicatory Date:	9.8.0.0.0 5 Ahau 3 Chen	(9.8.0.0.0) 5 Ahau (3 Chen)
Style Date:	9.5.0.0.0 (Uncertain; very flat curve)	
Condition:	Partially eroded, upper portion more than lower	Badly flaked on edges and eroded on upper surface
Photographs:	Fig. 29a Satterthwaite 1951:Pl. XIII Willcox 1954:Fig. 50	Fig. 40a Satterthwaite 1951:Pl. XIII
Drawings:	Fig. 1	Fig. 20a Satterthwaite 1954: Fig. 42
Other References:	Satterthwaite 1951, 1954 Willcox 1954 Riese 1980:3	Satterthwaite 1951, 1954 Willcox 1954 Riese 1980:14
Carved Areas:	Class 1: F (M7)	Altar Class 1: T
Material:	Limestone	Limestone
Shape:	Parallel sides, vertical in lower third, bending left for upper two-thirds; rounded top	Ovoid; flattened top and bottom; fairly symmetrical
Dimensions:	L: 2.40 m. HA: 2.08 m. W: 0.88 m. Th: 0.32 m. H above Floor: 2.10 m.	Max. W: 2.07 m. Max. Th: 0.48 m. Min. W: 1.70 m. Min. Th: 0.28 m.

GENERAL REMARKS

Stela 1 and Altar 1 form an apparently undisturbed stela-altar pair that marks the completion of Katun 5 Ahau at the LC position of 9.8.0.0.0. Unlike many of the Caracol stelae, Stela 1 was found standing and unfragmented. Altar 1 lay in front of the stela, 0.35 m. distant and in line with a low step or wall approximately 1.90 m. from the back face of the stela.

The stela was discovered in 1938 by Anderson

while investigating the then newly discovered site. At the time of discovery, Stela 1 was largely buried by rubble from Structure A1. Only the upper left corner of the monument could be seen above ground. The stela was fully excavated by the University Museum expedition in 1950. In the process of this excavation, Altar 1 was discovered, as was the plastered step of Structure A1. The stela was set into a hole through a plaster floor. Sometime later a second plaster floor was laid abutting the base of the stela. In 1951, Stela 1 was crated and shipped to the city of Belize for display in the Bliss Institute.

Carving on the monument is limited to the front face. The edges are plain and rough-hewn. The back is plain and possibly split off. The upper portion of the carving on the front is poorly preserved, probably because of the greater weathering it was subjected to during the period it was exposed above ground.

When found, the altar was oriented with the top of the design on the side closest to the stela, so that both stela and altar could be seen conveniently by an observer standing before the altar.

In outline, the altar is ovoid. It is laterally extended with flattened sides at the top and bottom. The flat upper surface bears a well weathered giant Ahau. The edges of the stone are uncarved and badly flaked. The bottom surface is irregular, ranging from a minimum of 0.28 m. to a maximum of 0.48 m. in thickness. The altar was set into the uppermost of two plaster floors, perhaps in order to level out its very irregular bottom profile. This same plaster floor abutted Stela 1. Thus the two monuments were set into (Stela 1) or onto (Altar 1) an existing earlier floor which was then covered by a new monument-abutting floor. The relationship of these features to the nearby Structure A1 cannot be determined from the existing field record. Altar 1 was shipped to the city of Belize in 1951 in company with Stela 1.

STELA 1/ALTAR 1: GLYPH CLASSIFICATION AND CHRONOLOGICAL DECIPHERMENT

(Order of reading: Main text, left-right and downward in double column;
Panel Z, presumably downward. Number of blocks: 24+12=36)

Main Text

	A1	ISIG (damaged variable not identified—probably a head with postfixed glyph)
	B1	9 baktuns (restoring 2 lost dots for symmetry)
	A2-B3	8 katuns, 0 tuns, 0 uinals, 0 kins
A 9. 8. 0. 0. 0	C1	5 Ahau, damaged prefix above coefficient (T53 "centipede" affix with circle of dots to right?)
	D1	3 Chen (damaged but certain; space for lost knot element above main sign)
	C2	Event glyph? (T181 postfix)
	D2-C3	Name phrase: Serpent-head (possibly a variant of Lord Water) followed by eroded but unmistakable Caracol Glyph
	D3-E1	2 non-calendrical glyphs
	F1	T710 "hand scattering" glyph
	E2	1 non-calendrical (possibly a part of the name at F2)
	F2-E3	Name phrase: Possible head-variant of Lord Water followed by Caracol Glyph
	F3	T606 female parent indicator (Jones 1977)
	G1-H1	Lady Jaguar
	G2	1 non-calendrical block, possibly divided
	H2a	Katun sign without coefficient; taken to indicate first katun of life for Lord Storm-water Moon at G3
	H2b	1 non-calendrical glyph
	G3-H3	Name phrase: Lord Storm-water Moon followed by Caracol Glyph

Panel X

	xA1-xB5	10 blocks (reconstructed; mere traces of carving survive)
	xA6	5 Ahau (partially reconstructed; presumably duplicating Date A of main text)
	xB6	Damaged glyph

Panel Y

	yA1-yA2?	Traces of 1 or 2 inscribed glyphs

Panel Z

	zA1	Traces of 1 inscribed glyph

Note: The terminal SR day of the IS on Stela 1 is repeated as a giant 5 Ahau on Altar 1, *in situ* in front of this stela

STELA 1: SUMMARY OF CHRONOLOGY

A1-D1   Date A   IS   9. 8. 0. 0. 0   5 Ahau 3 Chen

ALTAR 1: SUMMARY OF CHRONOLOGY

A1   Date A   CR   (9. 8. 0. 0. 0)   5 Ahau (3 Chen)

COMMENT ON THE INSCRIPTION

DEDICATORY DATE OF STELA 1

The IS 9.8.0.0.0 of Stela 1 may safely be taken as the DD since it is a katun ending and the only date. Proskouriakoff obtained a flat curve as a result of her efforts to assign a style date to the stela. Thus the style date was listed as "indeterminate." However, Proskouriakoff was able to say that it was "possibly about 9.5.0.0.0" with a very early position but with dress and scrolls of transitional type. It can be added that the profile pose of the "dwarf" is Late Classic, in which one leg and foot do not quite hide the back of the other.

If we take 9.5.0.0.0 as an approximate style date and allow a range of ±3 katuns, the epigraphic date is covered. There is certainly no guarantee that local changes were in precise agreement with the area-wide periods of Proskouriakoff's style system. An additional difficulty arises because Stela 16 and Stela 1, respectively, are dated to 9.5.0.0.0 and 9.8.0.0.0 (both by IS), which marks off a "hiatus" period between Early and Late Classic in the style dating scheme. Bracketing this "hiatus" period at Caracol is the 9.13.10.0.0 IS of Stela 21 which may be taken as definitely in the local Late Classic period, even if there was considerable local lag. Various features not considered in the style dating procedure confirm Stela 1 in an intermediate position between Stela 16 and Stela 21:

	Stela 16	Stela 1	Stela 21
Main text			
Position	Back	*Front	Front
ISIG size	Oversize	*Normal	Normal
Incision	Yes	Yes	No
Reading order	Normal	Normal	By rows
Ceremonial bar	Horizontal	*Angled	*Angled
Side borders?	No	No	Yes
Subsidiary figure(s)?	No	*Yes	*Yes

Stelae 16 and 21 differ in every one of these seven miscellaneous traits. On Stela 1, four traits agree with Stela 21 (marked with * on the table) and three with Stela 16. Not only does this endorse the intermediate position of Stela 1, but it tends to confirm that the IS date of each of the three monuments is not too late to be its DD.

GIANT GLYPH ALTAR KATUN-NAMING HYPOTHESIS; LC POSITION OF ALTAR 1

In this and succeeding discussions, the katun-naming hypothesis is used along with other controls to place Giant Glyph Altars at LC positions (Satterthwaite 1954:30-36). According to this hypothesis, the giant Ahau on an altar records the name of the katun during which the monument was dedicated. Thus such a stone could commemorate an LC position within an ongoing katun just as well as one on the final day of the katun. Altar 1 is the only Giant Glyph Altar at Caracol that can be firmly fixed into the LC. It was found in evident primary association with Stela 1 which bears only the single LC date of 9.8.0.0.0 5 Ahau 3 Chen. Since Altar 1 also bears a single large 5 Ahau, there is every reason to suppose that the two were originally paired.

STELA 2

Location:	In Corridor A2, between the south end of Platform A1 and Structure A9. Lying on the surface when discovered
Associations:	None evident
Dedicatory Date:	Unknown
Style Date:	Unknown
Condition:	Incomplete; seven fragments found in disturbed condition; butt missing; heavily eroded
Photographs:	Fig. 29b
Drawings:	Fig. 21
Other References:	Satterthwaite 1954 Riese 1980:3
Carved Areas:	Class 3: FLR (M3) ??
Material:	Limestone
Shape:	Uncertain. Parallel sides; top rounded or curved left; convex back
Dimensions:	L: min. 2.30 m. W: 0.86-0.90 m.? Th: 0.35-0.42 m.

GENERAL REMARKS

During the 1951 field season, Stela 2 was found lying on the surface of the ground just to the south of the end of Platform A1. The remains discovered consisted of seven fragments scattered over an area of 1.5 m. As reconstructed, only the top 1.5 m. of the stela and a piece 1.0 m. long out of the center of the shaft remain. A gap of indeterminable length exists between the two portions. The butt of Stela 2 was not found despite an inspection of the area around the monument. The fact that the pieces of the stela were found disturbed and scattered leads to a supposition either that only the top portion was re-erected at this locus in a manner similar to Stela 3 or that the top portion of the stela was in the process of being moved somewhere else but was forgotten and left behind like Stela 4.

The stone is heavily eroded, particularly on the lower portions. Despite damage the top portion allows the reconstruction of a figure holding a bar in its hands. The middle fragments show only vague tracings of carving on the front and, on one edge, the outline of what was apparently a glyph block. The middle fragments reveal a transverse convexity of the back surface reaching about 0.15 m. in depth. The upper fragments show a similar transverse convexity and a longitudinal slope toward the top.

The carved upper fragments reveal a general depth of relief of 1.0-1.5 cm. The whole of the figure displayed on the front stands out some 3.0-5.0 cm. from the background at the edges.

STELA 3

Location:	Upper Portion:	Semi-erect; 26 m. east of the base of Platform A1, 24 m. northwest of Altar 2 in Plaza A3
	Lower Portion:	Flat on the surface of the ground at the west edge of Reservoir B

Associations: None evident. Possibly Altar 7, found in front of Stela 14

Dedicatory Date: 9.11.0.0.0   12 Ahau 8 Ceh

Style Date: 9.6.0.0.0??

Condition: Upper portion eroded; face of figure on front missing. Lower portion well preserved; a large gap in the center of the stela from ancient breakage

Photographs: Fig. 30a, b
Satterthwaite 1951:Pl. XIV; 1954:Fig. 24
Beetz 1980:Figs. 9, 11

Drawings: Figs. 3, 4

Other References: Satterthwaite 1951; 1954
Berlin 1973:7
Marcus 1976:60-63
Kelley 1976:38, 41-42
Beetz 1980:9
Riese 1980:3-5

Carved Areas: Class 2: FB (M1)

Material: Limestone

Shape: Parallel sides at bottom, tapering slightly towards top

Dimensions: L. 3.46 m.   HA: 2.65 m.
W: 0.89 m.   Th: 0.42 m.
H above Floor: 3:10 m.

GENERAL REMARKS

When found, this monument was broken into two major portions. The upper portion was located in 1950 by a workman in Plaza A3. It had been re-erected in a pit dug into the limestone bedrock, facing southeast. In 1953, the lower fragment of the stela was discovered lying face up on the surface of the ground at the west edge of Reservoir B.

Before discovery, the upper portion of the monument had been fractured near ground level, apparently from the impact of a falling tree. It was in two major fragments and leaning back at an angle of 45°. Small pieces of limestone were packed into the pit with the stela when it was re-erected, possibly in order to stabilize it. One-third of the upper portion of Stela 3 came to be below ground level as a result of the re-erection, and suffered far less damage from erosion than did the rest.

The lower portion of the stela was immediately recognized as the complement to the previously excavated portion. There was no evidence for either erection or re-erection at the locus of discovery. This fragment of the stela was not associated with other monuments nor with floor construction. Possibly it was in the process of being moved when it was left and forgotten. The lower part of Stela 3 had fractured into two major fragments. It was moderately eroded on the front surface, but not so badly as the front of the separate upper portion. The back of the lower portion, with the hieroglyphic inscription, is in nearly perfect preservation.

The upper portion of Stela 3 was shipped to the University Museum in 1951. From there it was sent to the Denver Museum of Natural History in 1952. The lower half of the stela was shipped to Belize City in 1953. Later that year, at the request of A. H. Anderson, R. B. Renison Esq., the then Governor of the Colony, shipped the lower part of Stela 3 to Denver as a gift of the people of British Honduras to the people of Denver. After thirteen years, the reconstruction of the stela was completed in 1966 and the entire monument displayed in the Denver Museum.

STELA 3: GLYPH CLASSIFICATION AND CHRONOLOGICAL DECIPHERMENT
(Order of reading: Main text, left-right and downward in double column, reading from
back to front; Panel Z, presumably downward in single column
Number of blocks: 80+20=100. Minimum number of glyphs: 133+28=161 for
main text; an additional row of 3 glyphs in Panel Z)

		Back	
		A1-B2	ISIG, variable lost
		A3	9 baktuns (damaged head-variant period sign)
		B3	6, 8, 11 or 13 katuns (damaged head-variant period sign; coefficient of 6 preferred with a thick bar and fillers)
		A4	11-14 tuns (damaged head-variant period sign; 12 preferred with filler)
		B4	4 uinals (damaged head-variant period sign)
		A5	11-18 kins (damaged head-variant period sign; 16 preferred with fillers)
A	9. 6.12. 4.16	B5	5 Cib (reconstructed SR)
		A6a	Damaged glyph (with coefficient of 9 or 14??)
		A6b	Eroded glyph
		B6	6-18, with 11 preferred by inspection; damaged glyph (MA11?)
		A7a	6, damaged glyph (MN 6?)
		A7b	MT 9 or 10
		B7a-B7b	2 non-calendrical glyphs?
		A8a	14 Uo?
		A8b	T740 "birth" event glyph (Proskouriakoff 1960)
		B8a-A9b	Name phrase: 3 glyphs naming God C Star followed by an unidentified EG
		B9a	Female parent indicator? (eroded) (Jones 1977; Schele, Matthews and Lounsbury 1977)
		B9b-A10a	Lady Bird
		A10b u.h.-l.h.	Male name?, EG?
		B10a	Male parent indicator (Jones 1977; Schele, Matthews and Lounsbury 1977)
		B10b	Unidentified EG
		A11a	Lost glyph (SSIG?)
SS1	6. 7. 4	A11b-B11a	4 (kins), 7 uinals, 6 tuns
B	(9. 6.18.12. 0)	B11b	8, day sign mostly lost (read as Ahau)
		A12a	Lost except for trace at bottom (Mol?)
		A12b-B12	Lost
		A13a-A13b	2 non-calendrical glyphs
		B13a	SSIG
		B13b	Lost except for remnant of postfix (reconstructed as 8 kins, 4 uinals)
SS2	12. 4. 8	A14a	12 tuns
C	(9. 7.10.16. 8)	A14b-B14a	9 Lamat 16 Chen, Yax, Zac or Ceh (reconstructed as Chen)
		B14b	Unrecognized event glyph
		A15a-A16a	Name phrase: 4 glyphs naming God C Star followed by an unidentified EG
SS3	3.12. 0	A16b-B16b	SSIG, 0 (kins), 12 uinals, 3 tuns

D	(9. 7.14.10. 8)	A17a-A17b	3 Lamat 16 Uo
		B17a	T740 "birth" event glyph
		B17b-A18b	Name phrase: Yellow Storm followed by expanded version of the Caracol Glyph
SS4	5. 3. 4	B18a-A19a	SSIG, 4 (kins), 3 uinals, 5 tuns (ornamented misshapen bar with tun)
E	(9. 7.19.13.12)	A19b-B19a	8 Eb 15 Zotz
		B19b	1 non-calendrical
		A20a	Name glyph of Yellow Storm
		A20b	1 non-calendrical
		B20a	4 katuns (presumed to refer to katuns of life for a character whose name is eroded at C1-D1)
		B20b	1 non-calendrical
		C1a-D1b	4 non-calendricals, eroded
SS5	1. 5. 2.10	C2a-D2b	SSIG; 10 kins, 2 uinals, 5 tuns, 1 katun (SS reconstructed)
F	(9. 9. 4.16. 2)	C3a-C3b	10 Ik (preserved) 0 Pop (reconstructed)
		D3a-D3b	2 non-calendricals, eroded
		C4a	Name of Lord Storm-water Moon
		C4b	Name of Yellow Storm
		D4a-D6b	10 non-calendricals
SS6	15. 6	C7a-C7b	SSIG, 6 (kins), 15 uinals (damaged but readable)
G	(9. 9. 5.13. 8)	D7a-D7b	4 Lamat 6 Pax (reconstruction of badly damaged block)
		C8a-D8b	4 glyphs, mostly lost
		C9a-D9b	4 non-calendricals
SS7	3.14.17	C10a-D10a	SSIG, 17-19 (kins), 14 uinals, 2 tuns (17 preferred for kin coefficient)
H	(9. 9. 9.10. 5)	D10b-C11a	3 Chicchan 3 Ceh (unusual Chicchan glyph)
		C11b	Unidentified event glyph
		D11a-D12a	Name phrase: 4 glyphs naming God C Star followed by an unidentified EG
		D12b	T757, "rodent" introducing glyph (Proskouriakoff 1968)
		C13a	Lost
		C13b-D13a	Name phrases Lord Storm-water Moon followed by Caracol Glyph
		D13b-D14a	4 non-calendricals (partially reconstructed)
SS8	7.15	D14b	15 (kins), 7 uinals (no SSIG)
I	(9. 9.10. 0. 0)	C15a-D15a	2 Ahau 11-13 Pop; half-period glyph (13 required as the month coefficient)
		D15b	1 non-calendrical, eroded
		C16a-C16b	Name phrase: Lord Storm-water Moon followed by Caracol Glyph
SS9	3. 4. 4	D16a-D16b	4 (kins), 4 uinals, 3 tuns (no SSIG; only traces of the uinal coefficient)
J	(9. 9.13. 4. 4)	C17a-C17b	9 Kan 2 Zec
		D17a-C18a	4 non-calendricals (some forming part of the name phrase that follows?)
		C18b-D18a	Name phrase: Lord Storm-water Moon followed by Caracol Glyph

SS10	17. 1	D18b	1 (kin), 17 uinals (no SSIG; traces of a high uinal coefficient)
K	(9. 9.14. 3. 5)	C19a-C19b	7 Chicchan 18 Zip (Chicchan as in Date H)
		D19a-C20 u.h.	4 non-calendricals (some forming part of the name phrase that follows?)
		C20b l.h.-D20b	Name phrase: Lord Storm-water Moon, 2 un-recognized glyphs, the Caracol Glyph

Front

SS11	4.12.18	E1-E2	SSIG, 18 (kins), 12 uinals, 4 tuns (head-variant tun sign)
L	(9. 9.18.16. 3)	F2-E3	7 Akbal 15 Muan
		F3a-F3b	Non-calendrical clause identical to one following the same date on the Hieroglyphic Stairway at Naranjo
		E4-F5	4 to 6 non-calendricals in 4 blocks
SS12	1. 1.17	E6-F6	17-19 (kins), 1 uinal, 1 tun (no SSIG; reconstruction of damaged blocks; tun-head dubious by inspection)
M	(9.10. 0. 0. 0)	E7a-E7b	1 Ahau 8 Kayab (reconstruction of damaged blocks)
		F7a-E8	3 non-calendricals, damaged (middle one may be name of Lord Storm-water Moon)
SS13	4. 7. 0	F8-E9	0 (kins), 7-8 uinals, 4 tuns (damaged uinal coefficient reconstructed)
N	(9.10. 4. 7. 0)	F 9a-b, u.h.	8 Ahau 8 Zec (reconstruction of damaged glyphs)
SS14	− 19. 8.18	F9a-b, l.h.	18 (kins), 8 uinals, 19 tuns (no SSIG; reconstruction of damaged glyphs)
		E10a, u.h.	1 non-calendrical
		E10b, u.h.	Glyph with a possible coefficient of 6-8 (lost SR date ??)
		E10a, l.h.-F10	3 non-calendricals (closing text on the stela; final glyphs may be name of God C Star)
O	(9. 9. 4.16.2?)	− − − − − −	(presumed terminal date suppressed)

Panel Z

		zA1	2-3 non-calendricals (damaged and divided glyph block)

STELA 3: SUMMARY OF CHRONOLOGY

A1-A8a	Date A	IS	9. 6.12. 4.16	5 Cib, MA 11?, MN 6, MT 29-30, 14 Uo?
A11b-B11a		SS1	6. 7. 4	
B11b-A12a	Date B		(9. 6.18.12. 0)	8 Ahau 8 Mol
B13b-A14a		SS2	12. 4. 8	
A14b-B14b	Date C		(9. 7.10.16. 8)	9 Lamat 16 Chen
A16b-B16b		SS3	3.12. 0	
A17a-A17b	Date D		(9. 7.14.10. 8)	3 Lamat 16 Uo (same as Naranjo Lintel 1, A1-B1)
B18a-A19a		SS4	5. 3. 4	
A19b-B19b	Date E		(9. 7.19.13.12)	8 Eb 15 Zotz
C2a-D2b		SS5	1. 5. 2.10?	
C3a-C3b	Date F		(9. 9. 4.16. 2)?	10 Ik 0 Pop?
C7a-C7b		SS6	15. 6?	

D7a-D7b	Date G	(9. 9. 5.13. 8)	4 Lamat 6 Pax
C10a-D10a	SS7	3.14.17	
D10b-C11a	Date H	(9. 9. 9.10. 5)	3 Chicchan 3 Ceh
D14b	SS8	7.15	
C15a-D15a	Date I	(9. 9.10. 0. 0)	2 Ahau 13 Pop, half-period
D16a-D16b	SS9	3. 4. 4	
C17a-C17b	Date J	(9. 9.13. 4. 4)	9 Kan 2 Zec
D18b	SS10	17. 1	
C19a-C19b	Date K	(9. 9.14. 3. 5)	12 Chicchan 18 Zip
E1-E2	SS11	4.12.18	
F2-E3	Date L	(9. 9.18.16. 3)	7 Akbal 16 Muan (same as Naranjo Hieroglyphic Stairway, M1b-N1a)
E6-F6	SS12	1. 1.17	
E7a-E7b	Date M	(9.10. 0. 0. 0)?	1 Ahau 8 Kayab? (same as Naranjo Lintel 1, G2-H2)
F8-E9	SS13	4. 7. 0?	
F9a-b, u. h.	Date N	(9.10. 4. 7. 0)?	8 Ahau 3 Zec?
F9a-b, l. h.	SS14	− 19. 8.18?	
(suppressed)	Date 0	(9. 9. 4.16. 2)?	10 Ik 0 Pop?

Note: This table reflects numerous reconstructions of damaged date and SS elements in addition to a correction of the coefficient 13 to 3 in Date N. Single question marks suggest minimal doubts. Suggested alternatives for Date 0 are:

I   9.11. 3.15.18   6 Etznab 6 Chuen
II 9. 9. 4.16. 2   10 Ik 0 Pop

The latter alternative is favored.

COMMENT ON THE INSCRIPTION

DATE A AND THE RECONSTRUCTION OF THE B-C-D-E SEQUENCE OF SS DATES

Date A is a badly eroded IS and LS placed by analysis at the LC position 9.6.12.4.16. The baktun and uinal values are certain by inspection and the others are "preferred" readings of the coefficients. However, the result is not confirmed by mere inspection of terminal date elements or by an apparently recorded moon age. Accordingly, in the table of "Glyph Classification" limits for the not wholly certain coefficients are presented. The readings selected are justified below by a process of elimination. Limits for the coefficients are as follows:

Katun: 6, 8, 11 or 13 allows for the possibility of a now lost division of the bar into two bars, a certain center dot and possible upper and lower flanking dots rather than fillers.

Tun: 11, 12 or 13 allows for a sure two bars with three badly eroded dots or fillers to the left.

Kin: 11 or 16 allows for a possibly mistaken impression of three rather than two bars. A single central dot clearly has fillers above and below. A coefficient of 11 calls for the day Chuen, and 16 similarly for Cib. Neither of these days is recognizable by inspection.

It is certain that the IS was the base for a chain of SS which evidently counted forward. Therefore, we may attempt to work back to the IS value from Date D, the first of the chain of SS dates which is completely stated and legible. Alternative LC positions for Date D (3 Lamat 16 Uo) that yield katun values within the appropriate limits are:

I   9. 7.14.10. 8
II   9.13. 0. 0. 8

Counting back a distance equal to the sum of SS1, SS2 and SS3 should lead back to an LC value that agrees with the limits previously specified for the coefficients of the katun, tun and kin. Calculation shows that this distance must be 1.2.1.4 plus some value for the lost uinal and kin coefficients of SS2. The reconstructed value for that SS must be chosen to obtain 4 uinals and either 11 or 16 kins in the IS. With these factors in mind, calculations can be made that reach early and late pairs of IS values:

Date D	9. 7.14.10. 8	3 Lamat 16 Uo	Date D	9.13. 0. 0. 8	3 Lamat 16 Uo	
	− 1. 2. 1. 4			− 1. 2. 1. 4		
	9. 6.12. 9. 4			9.11.17.17. 4		
	− 4. 8			− 12. 8		
Ia	9. 6.12. 4.16	5 Cib 14 Uo	IIa	9.11.17. 4.16	1 Cib 19 Ceh	
	− . 5			− . 5		
Ib	9. 6.12. 4.11	13 Chuen 9 Uo	IIb	9.11.17. 4.11	9 Chuen 14 Ceh	

The late versions are ruled out by the necessity of a tun coefficient with three bars. The early versions (Ia and Ib) both pass all within-limits tests. They correspond respectively to reconstructing SS2 as 12.4.8 or 12.4.13. The choice thus becomes clear, since only the 12.4.8 of SS2 in alternative Ia connects the legible day coefficient of Date B with the legible coefficient 9 of Date C. In addition, it agrees with apparent traces of Mol as the month for Date B, and with 16 Chen as Date C. The latter date must be in Chen rather than Yax, Zac or Ceh, because SS3 connects it with Date D.

Any lingering doubt about this result disappears when it is noted that the 3 Lamat 16 Uo of Date D occurs also on Naranjo Lintel 1 where it is fixed at 9.7.14.10.8. Further confirmation comes from an examination of the Naranjo Hieroglyphic Stairway where it can be noted that Date L (7 Akbal 16 Muan) of Caracol Stela 3 is placed in agreement with our reading at 9.9.18.16.13.

It might be noted that T740, the "birth" event marker follows immediately after the VYr statement for Dates A and D. Following each of these occurrences of the "up-ended frog" glyph are series of glyphs that can be interpreted as nominative phrases.

Day Coefficient of Date A (B5)

The entry in the Glyph Classification table allows for the possibility of two bars to give the day coefficient a reading of 10 rather than the required reading of 5. Inspection alone indicates 5 to be the preferred reading. In this regard it can be noted that the left hand edge of the clear bar is defined by relief carving rather than by an incised line as it should be if serving only to separate two bars of a numerical prefix. The traces of carving in the position of the upper part of a second bar may be part of a non-numerical prefix rather than a mistake by the Maya sculptor. This supposed affix does not seem to be the T53 "centipede" prefix found on Stelae 1 and 6. It should also be noted that a coefficient of 10 would disagree with all four of the previously calculated within-limits alternative values for the IS number.

Day Name of Date A (B5)

Calculation signifies that this sign should be Cib. However, inspection reveals that it is actually a head with a large round eye and rather clear traces of bared upper teeth, as if the head was basically a skull. This would normally indicate a reading of Cimi or perhaps Eb. Neither of these two day names appears with any of the within-limits reconstructions of the LC value.

Thompson's discussion of various associations of ideas with the day Cib (1950:84-86, Fig. 9, 50-68) suggests that Stela 3 may be displaying a previously unknown head variant for Cib, rather than a rare Maya mistake. Only one previously noted head-variant is noted in his day-sign figure. In reference to this illustration, Thompson said:

"The symbolic variant of Cib is almost surely a section of a conch shell . . . and is almost the same and in the same position as the form of the glyph for south, which in turn is associated with the dead . . . The conch shell is a symbol of the underworld and darkness, although it has another association. The personified form of Cib has, as we have seen, features of the jaguar god, a deity of the underworld and darkness," After further discussion he concludes that "The case is not proved but it is a fair presumption that Cib was the day of the Bacabs, patrons of beekeeping who, converted into diverse creatures, merge with the earth-bound souls of the dead in insect form."

If this view of the day Cib is accepted the way seems open to viewing the skull-like head as an alternative for the previously known head with jaguar features rather than as a mistaken record of Cimi or Eb.

Month Position of Date A (A8a?)

The month position has been calculated to be 14 Uo. It could properly be suppressed without casting any doubt on the LC reading. If it was indeed given, the expected location is at B7a following Glyph A of a fairly clear LS. Nevertheless, there is good if not compelling evidence for seeing the correct coefficient and month sign at A8a, separated from Glyph A by 2 non-calendricals. At this spot, cross-hatching may be lost from the ovoid superfix, while traces within the ovoid main sign suggest crossed bands. The coefficient 14 here is fairly clear.

Lunar Series

A clear Glyph A (probably A9) is found at A7a preceded by two glyphs with coefficients and possible traces of the moon sign at the upper right. The glyph immediately preceding Glyph A carries a clear coefficient of 6, which is the maximum for Glyph C. The coefficient at the next glyph (working backward) seems best read as 11 with a thick bar divided by traces of a central incised line. There is one certain centrally placed dot flanked by what is probably a filler above and a now lost filler below. Thus the extreme limits for the coefficient are 11, 12 and 13. The arbitrary moon age at the IS position is 16.95 days. Even if the coefficient is taken at the dubious reading of thirteen, the deviation is −3.95 which is outside of Teeple's arbitrary limit (1930:53).

This raises the possibility that our reading is mistaken in finding only two bars instead of three, or that the Maya themselves may have erred. A reconstruction of the moon age as sixteen days would make the deviation from the arbitrary standard only .95 days.

By position Glyph G5 should fall at A6a and Glyph F at A6b. Instead of a single bar prefix, A6a seems to carry a superfix of one or two bars and four dots. Both of the main signs in these two spaces are too much eroded to give clues as to their readings. Possibly Glyphs G and F were not recorded at all, in which case the position of the LS is irregular.

The process of reconstructing the IS and SS2 numbers revealed no other comprehensively valid solution other than that presented in the "Summary" tabulation. Thus it appears there, with no question marks, as an established reading. Dates A-E appear in chronological order along with a running SS control at all points. The only irregularity occurs at SS4 where there is a considerable space between the tun sign and the thick superfixed ornamented bar. There is damage here, but plain background survives on the right between the two elements. The tun sign was drawn to the same height as the day sign next to it where space for dots as well as a bar was required.

RECONSTRUCTION OF THE SEQUENCE OF SS DATES F-G-H-I-J-K-L-M-N-O

This chain of SS dates can be reliably reconstructed by calculating from Date I, fixed at 9.9.10.0.0 by a clear CR with half-period glyph. A number of individual reconstructions of the SS numbers and CR dates are necessary but justifiable for the rebuilding of the sequence.

To judge whether inspection allows that badly damaged glyphs were or may have been period glyphs, it should be noted that well preserved examples in this text show variety in their postfixes, and that no sure use of the common "SS postfix" (T126) is made. From this, it can be seen that we cannot require that remains of a period glyph postfix indicate a certain number of elements, or that they formed a symmetrical or an asymmetrical grouping of elements. This is best illustrated in the tun postfixes of SS3 and SS7, both of which have the "quincunx" sign on the left. Also to be observed is the entire absence of surviving head-variant coefficients. It seems safe not to allow for that complicating theoretical possibility.

In the examination of eroded day signs it is clear that in nine cases with sufficient preservation for certainty there was a complete cartouche with a symmetrical three-element "pedestal" subfix (T125?), probably all with a miniature inverted Ahau sign between flanking scrolls (Dates C-E, G-L). In Date B only the upper portion of the border of the main sign is preserved, but it presumably also conformed. The day sign of Date A probably lacked a cartouche, but this is the case for Thompson's one head-variant Cib. It seems reasonable to expect the complete cartouche and pedestal in the two remaining SS dates. There seem to exist clear remnants of them in Date M, while in Date N the complete cartouche is clear with little space for an elaborated pedestal as in Dates C-E, G-L. This cartouche seems to have been symmetrical and in this case to display faint traces of Ahau markings in the interior under favorable lighting. Thus, only at Dates A and B is the complete cartouche test for existence of the dates lacking, the second of these probably because of damage. The symmetrical three-element pedestals were surely or probably present in all cases. On the other hand, where preservation permits sure identification, there are no other main signs with complete cartouches.

Date F, SS5, SS6

A clear 10 Ik appears as the day sign of Date F. The next block is too badly eroded for the month to be identified. Date G provides a bracketing "upper end" date at 9.9.5.13.8 which is fixed by calculation back from date I. The SS leading from Date F to Date G is not entirely clear but may be reliably read as 15 uinals and 5-9 kins. Calculation readily indicates that 15.6 is the only alternative that will lead back to a day of 10 Ik. Further confirmation of Date F as 9.9.4.16.2 might be gleaned from the calculation of Date 0. Two possibilities are offered for this repressed date, the second of which is also 9.9.4.16.2. If this reading is accepted as Date F, then SS5 must be 1.5.2.10 by calculation. A fairly clear SSIG at C2a opens an SS of three blocks in length before the 10 Ik of Date F. These blocks fit nicely for the expected SS, since the kin sign is regularly suppressed in these notations.

Dates G-H, SS7

We have only uncertain traces of 4 Lamat in Date G, but the 6 Pax seems to be certain in the next block. The month sign is a grotesque head with clear remains of one of the two narrow elements which branch out from the top of the head as in symbolic Pax signs and the one head-variant depicted by Thompson (1950:Fig. 18, 46-52). A break between two of the major fragments of Stela 3 runs through SS7 with a partial loss of the kin coefficient. That coefficient surely has three bars and two dots, with the possibility of one or two additional dots rather than fillers. The reading must be taken as 17 in order to connect 6 Pax of Date G with 3 Ceh for Date H. The latter must be restored with a coefficient of 3 rather than a possible 2 so that SS8 will lead on to 13 Pop in Date I. The complete Date H, as departure for SS8, is 3 Chicchan 3 Ceh. This removes any doubt that the day glyph of Date H is Chicchan, though it differs considerably from Thompson's 1950 examples of symbolic Chicchan. A peculiar feature of the Stela 3 Chicchan is that a scalloped line crosses the field of the sign as in Akbal. This variant feature appears more clearly in Date K (C19a) where Chicchan is again required by a fully legible portion of the text. Lines at the upper right of the Date H Chicchan seem to be remains of cross-hatching. Calculating back from Date H by the reconstructed but reliable SS7 gives 4 Lamat for Date G, eliminating doubt as to that.

The Chicchan signs are evidently not head-variant "personified" forms. Thompson (1950) features three examples of the symbolic form from Stela H and Temple 11 at Copan and Lintel 27 at Yaxchilan. In each case the very simple glyph consists of a pair of slanting ovals or "diagonal marks" such as may occur in the Yax affix. In his *Catalog* (1962) Thompson says that this simple sign is rare as a day sign in the inscriptions and in the codices. If Caracol Stela 3 was dedicated no later than 9.12.0.0.0, its two calendric uses of the more complex symbolic Chicchan sign apparently may predate the use of the simpler form at other sites, whether calendric or otherwise. However, so far as we know here, the Caracol version of this glyph may be a localism without much time depth. Even so, the scalloped transverse line in a day sign, considered in isolation, becomes a less positive indicator of Akbal than before.

Dates I-J, SS9

The uinal coefficient of the SS must be 4, as suggested by traces, in order to connect the two clear CR dates.

Dates J-K, SS10

By inspection the uinal coefficient of a two-term SS is probably high, and surely above 5; on ruling out 4 it must be 17 to connect the day coefficients of the two dates. The day of Date K must then be Chicchan, and the sign is similar to that proved to be such in Date H. It also follows that the damaged superfix of the month sign, above crossed bands as main sign, distinguishes it as Zip, not Uo.

Dates K-L, SS11

It is very unusual for a single continuous chronological text to begin on the back and end on the front of a stela. There is, however, no doubt about it here. Date K, with three of its elements clear by inspection, is the last date on the back. On the front, SS11 leads from it to Date L in the opening blocks of the panel where all signs and coefficients are clear by inspection.

Existence of Dates M-N-O, SS12, SS13, SS14

Beyond Date L we are dealing with a badly damaged area of the front. Nevertheless it is clear that in this area there were two groups of four glyphs each with five coefficients. The first two coefficients were prefixed and superfixed respectively to the same sign. In each case the last two coefficients may have been those of CR dates. This statement need be qualified only to the extent of noting that in the first group the coefficient of 1 at E6b is an unusually large dot. It is centered, without flanking fillers over what may be the remains of the uinal sign. That the second group includes an SS number is guaranteed by a still legible uinal sign as the first of the group.

Immediately after the second group is a third which shows two glyphs with three coefficients. The first two coefficients are prefixed and super-fixed above what may have been a uinal sign. The coefficient with the second sign, 19, is too high to be a day coefficient. The symbolic sign, by position, might be the tun-marker of an SS. No

date follows this unless there was possibly an SR date at E10b, upper half.

The mandatory conclusion seems to be that in this area we have remains of three more SS numbers, two of which lead to recorded terminal dates. The third SS leads to either a terminal date marked only by SR or to one that is suppressed.

Dates L-M, SS12

The direction of the count at this point is presumably forward, as before. By position the glyph at F6 should be a tun glyph. Although it is very badly eroded, certain lighting conditions suggest that it is a grotesque head. If it is such, it differs greatly from the head-variant tun sign in SS11, and from the later one in SS13. If this weakness in reading is passed over, the SS is taken to be 1.1.17. Inspection suggests that the kin coefficient might instead be 18 or 19 (with one or two dots rather than filler between the sure upper and lower ones). However, it must be 17 to connect the month coefficient 16 of Date L with a clear 8 for Date M. In full, the latter must be 1 Ahau 8 Kayab. In further confirmation of this CR, we have at E7a a possible day coefficient of 1, 2 or 3, with a degree of preference for one dot flanked by feather fillers. This is followed by traces of a month sign which may probably be taken as those of Kayab. An infixed circle may be restored as a Kan cross which is not at the upper or right margin as in Pop.

Dates M-N, SS13

A uinal coefficient of 7 is preferred by inspection, and is required to reach the clear day coefficient 8 of Date N from the reconstructed 1 of Date M. The month then must be Zec and the day Ahau. This is confirmed both by traces of the day sign within the preserved cartouche and by the asymmetrical outline of the postfix of the month glyph which is apparently limited in distribution to Pop, Kankin or Zec.

The extreme inspection limits for the day coefficient of Date L and for the uinals of the SS independently confirm that the count is in the forward direction. Backward counts of 4.7.0 or 4.8.0 from day coefficients 1 or 3 reach coefficients of 7, 9, 13 and 2 rather than the clear 8 of Date M.

It appears from this that there may well have been a Maya mistake in recording the month coefficient as 13 rather than the required 3. Although it cannot be claimed that this is a likely sort of error for a sculptor or calculator to make, there is precedent for it on Copan Stela N, east side, where the coefficient of Zip should certainly be three dots only, but one bar is added (Morley 1920:280).

Date N, a suppressed Date 0, SS14

The two glyphs and three legible coefficients of a probable SS follow immediately after Date N. The glyph with two coefficients has the "horseshoe" border completely covering top and sides as would be expected for a uinal sign. There is thus a strong presumption that an SS is recorded here, with no non-calendrical phrase recorded immediately after Date N. If a terminal date is recorded, it would be as an SR only, following SS14. This latter SS seems clearly to be 8.18 if there is no tun-term. The next glyph bears a coefficient of 19. Counting forward and backward from Date N by 8.18 reaches 4 Etznab and 9 Lamat respectively. A mistake might have occurred in carving three bars instead of no bar or in carving three bars instead of one bar. However, it seems inherently impossible that a number above 13 could have been carelessly recorded as a day coefficient because of the obvious error that it represents.

It is fairly clear that the sign with the coefficient 19 did not have the complete cartouche expected in day signs. Instead, it is fairly clear that it had a "horseshoe" border like the uinal sign. It may be said that the tun sign border does not normally reach the bottom of the glyph as it seems to here. But this effect is also approximated in one of Thompson's examples of the katun glyph and also characterizes four of the six fully legible symbolic tun signs on this same stela (SS1, SS2, SS3, SS7). Thus this detail tends to confirm the restoration of the tun sign. SS14 may then be confidently read as 19.8.18.

There are two basic alternatives for a suppressed Date 0 if we count 9.8.18 forward and backward from the reconstructed Date N:

I	Date 0	9.11. 3.15.18	6 Etznab 6 Chuen ??
II	Date 0	9. 9. 4.16. 2	10 Ik 0 Pop ?

The question marks allow for uncertainty as to the final direction of counting, and the necessary assumption of an unusual suppression of the terminal date without accompanying altar (although this latter may not have been true when the stela was originally erected). Alternative II is strongly favored of the two, since it ties back to the same LC and CR of Date F recorded earlier on the monument. As will be noted in pages 114-130, The Rulers of Caracol, 9.9.4.16.2 may have acquired importance as the accession date of a Caracol sovereign.

DEDICATORY DATE

According to the rules followed here the DD should fall at a tun end which is the latest date recorded, or less than a year earlier than an odd date which is the latest. Rarely it may have been suppressed and understood from the context. Assuming the latter situation here, we have an odd latest date. Judging by other Caracol monuments, the DD of Stela 3 was probably at the half-katun or katun end following one of the alternatives for Date 0 (or perhaps Date N). Allowing for the thin chance that the later alternative reading for the suppressed Date 0 may have been correct, two pairs of alternatives for the unwritten DD exist:

Ia	9.10.10.0.0	13 Ahau 18 Kankin	(Katun 12 Ahau current)
Ib	9.11. 0.0.0	12 Ahau 8 Ceh	(Katun 12 Ahau ended)
IIa	9.11.10.0.0	11 Ahau 18 Chen	(Katun 10 Ahau current)
IIb	9.12. 0.0.0	10 Ahau 8 Yaxkin	(Katun 10 Ahau ended)

Of these two sets, the earlier pair is definitely favored since it corresponds to counting SS14 back to 9.9.4.16.2, the prefered reading for Date 0. It introduces the possibility that Altar 7, with a giant 12 Ahau glyph, functioned originally with Stela 3 as an indicator of the current or ending katun in Short Count style. Altar 7 was evidently moved to its position of discovery from its original location. Evidence for this will be discussed in the section about Altar 7. The movement of the altar may have been associated with the breaking of Stela 3 into two portions, the movement of one or both and the re-setting of the top fragment.

In any interpretation, it appears that the DD was suppressed, since the only PE near the end of the text occurs at 9.10.0.0.0, 4.7.0 distant from the latest date recorded. This of course conflicts with the parameters just laid out for the selection of a DD. It seems apparent, if the earlier alternative for Date 0 is accepted and if Altar 7 was originally paired with Stela 3, that the DD of the stela could have been no later than 9.11.0.0.0. Therefore the DD may be justifiably interpreted to be 9.10.4.7.0—9.11.0.0.0.

STYLE DATING

There appears to be a conflict between epigraphically determined alternative DD's and Proskouriakoff's style-dating for the same monument. Before the large lower fragment was discovered, she obtained an ambivalent flat curve for the upper half of the monument which might crest in the area of 9.6.0.0.0. In regard to the lower portion, she states, ". . . the position of the feet, the sandals and the leg ornaments are all of Early Classic type." This, according to her area-wide scheme of stylistic time periods would place the monument before 9.5.0.0.0.

At Caracol it can be argued that the Early Classic monument style persisted through the period of Proskouriakoff's "hiatus" in her area-wide style-dating scheme. Both Stela 1 and Stela 3 at Caracol bear epigraphic dates that are somewhat more recent than the apparent style dates. By around 9.9.0.0.0, the style dates are much more in line with the chronological positions recorded on the monuments, as evidenced by Stelae 5 and 6 at Caracol.

Proskouriakoff suggests that Stela 3 represents the special case of an historical portrait of a non-contemporaneous person, shown in the style appropriate to his own time. It certainly appears that the figure on Stela 3 was copied from that on the earlier Stela 1. There is therefore the possibility that the same historical character was recorded on both monuments.

Note: The "Comment on the Inscription" originally carried a discussion by Satterthwaite of the appearance of the "up-ended frog" glyph on Stela 3, comparing it with some moon age dates and discussing the birth dates recorded. However, the passage did not attempt the full coverage of Caracol history that is necessary to develop the context of the Stela 3 inscription. Thus it misinterpreted some of the text. Because the material has been superseded by recent developments in the field of Maya history, and because a new section (V: The Rulers of Caracol) gives a more contemporary analysis, this portion has been deleted.

STELA 4

Location: In Plaza A3, slightly buried, not *in situ*
Associations: None evident
Dedicatory Date: 9.18.0.0.0???
Style Date: None calculated
Condition: Badly fragmented and incomplete
Photographs: Fig. 29c, d
Drawings: Fig. 5a, b
Other References: Satterthwaite 1951
                     Riese 1980:5
Carved Areas: Class 2: FB (M1)
Material: Slate
Shape: Unreconstructed
Dimensions: L: 3.28 m.?   HA: 2.60 m.?
                     W: 0.74 m.?   Th: ?
                     H above Floor: 2.72 m.?

GENERAL REMARKS

A. H. Anderson was first attracted to what is known of the slate Stela 4 when he noticed a small fragment of it projecting above the surface of the ground in 1950. This fragment was embedded in the roots of a small tree in an isolated position in Plaza A3. The flat surface of the Plaza here gave approximate control on the latest floor level, although the actual floor had disintegrated. Nearby, other fragments protruded slightly above the surface of the ground. Excavation done in 1950 showed the depth of the fragment-bearing deposit to reach a maximum depth of about 0.40 m. Figure 18c, showing the positions of various fragments *in situ,* is taken from the field sketch made at the time of excavation. It is not to scale, but distances were noted, including the 2.50 m. baseline that runs north-south.

Fragments which are hatched in the figure were of limestone, and were originally assigned the label of "Stone 8b." Numbered fragments were originally labeled "Stone 8a" but now bear the designation "Stela 4." In 1951 all the slate fragments were shipped to Philadelphia for attempts at fitting by Horace Willcox. The area represented in Fig. 18c and somewhat beyond had already been excavated without encountering any new large fragments and but a few small ones.

The original idea that the limestone fragments might represent another stela was abandoned for lack of real evidence, although the fragments of "Stone 8b" did not seem to be normal fill stones. These limestone blocks might have been building blocks used here as fill material. The slate fragments of Stela 4 might thus have served the same purpose in being deposited with them.

It is possible that further extension of the area excavated might reveal more of Stela 4, but there are no surface indications of this. Excavation showed that the monument was not originally erected here and then later subject to falling and breakage from natural causes. Several facts make this apparent. There were only four large long fragments at the locus, Fragments 1, 2a-b (these are evidently the result of breakage on the spot), 3 and 7. Fragment 7, whose front face was up, fits beside 2a-b which was found face down well to the south, between Fragments 1 and 3. Fragment 1 includes a central portion of the butt below a remnant of carving. Fragment 3 probably belongs beside Fragment 1 as a plain butt fragment reaching up the left or right side almost to the base of the carving. Unfortunately, severe flaking prevented a sure fit to Fragment 1. In any case, one side of the butt is absent. The small Fragment 9, along with 6, fits between 1 and the bottom and 2a-b and 7 on the top. The record is somewhat faulty, but the small unnumbered fragment of Fig. 18c was probably Fragment 5 which fits between Fragments 2a-b and 7. The pattern of dispersal of these fragments thus argues against mere disturbance by forest action.

A large portion of the stela, from the top to what is shown of the human figure in Fig. 5a, is entirely missing. There is but one sizable carved fragment from this locus which could not be fitted (Fragment 8, Fig. 27c), and this is certainly not large enough to aid greatly in reconstructing the original monument. There is no reason to suspect representation of more than one slate monument here.

It seems possible that Stela 4 became obsolete and was broken up at its original locus, with some of the fragments being used at the area of discovery as fill, or being buried with ceremonial overtones. It may not be chance that the four long fragments were placed more or less parallel to each other. The deposit reminds one of the surface to sub-floor positions of the fragments of Stelae 15 and 16 in Court A2. The breakup of Stela 4 is not necessarily dated to Classic times by subsequent placement of other whole monuments. There is the possibility that Stela 4 was the source of other groups of broken stone which seem to result from Postclassic activity.

Further speculation is possible. At one time it was thought that Fragment 3 was from the left side of the butt. This idea was based on an approximate but not actual fit to the left side of Fragment 1. But this reconstruction resulted in an estimate of 1.20 m. for the width of the complete stela. Better evidence makes the reconstructed width about 0.75 m. It may be that Fragment 3 is from the right side of the butt, the left side being missing at this locus but represented by the small *in situ* slate fragment of a butt labeled once as "Stela X," located behind the limestone Altar 3 in Court A1. This is a tenable hypothesis which leads to the identification of the locus of Altar 3 as the original one of Stela 4. The altar is Late Classic in style which indicates 9.18.0.0.0 rather than 9.5.0.0.0 as the approximate DD for stela and altar. The giant glyph 11 Ahau on the altar would then be referring to the current katun or to its end. The katun-naming hypothesis permits a similar dating for the giant glyph 11 Ahau of Altar 14 found nearby and apparently in an intentionally disturbed position.

A complicating factor in the assignment of "Stela X" to Stela 4 is that much of the butt of the Early Classic slate Stela 15, and all of the butt of the Late Classic slate Stela 21 are missing. However, Stela 21 carries the IS date 9.13.10.0.0 7 Ahau, when Katun 8 Ahau, not 11 Ahau, was current. It was determined that the supposed large butt fragment of Stela 15 did not fit the *in situ* "Stela X" fragment. On the whole it seems quite likely that Stela 4 was originally paired with Altar 3 when the current or lapsed katun was Katun 11 Ahau ending at 9.18.0.0.0.

RECONSTRUCTION OF DIMENSIONS AND PROPORTIONS

Nowhere do the fitted fragments which yield the solid line portions of Fig. 5a reach the sides of the design of the front. But the fractured right edge of Fragment 7, as seen from the front, curves inward and to the right to what seems to be definitely a remnant of the original right side, 2-3 cm. from the plane of the back. This edge is 0.37 m. from the axis of the human figure, measuring horizontally. Projecting the axis of the figure downward, we are clearly bisecting a design on a rectangular pedestal. There are many similar rectangular pedestals shown on monuments at the site, and they are always basically symmetrical and extend from one edge of the front surface to the other. We may conclude that the axis of the human figure is the axis of the stela, the figure being placed centrally. It follows that, if the remnant of right edge is correctly identified on Fragment 7, the width of the whole stela was about 0.74 m. In the plane of the front, where direct control is lacking, the total width may have been slightly more, rather than less, but failure to take this into account is not significant.

Clear indications of five glyph blocks in three columns and two rows appear at the base of Fragment 7. They are placed vertically with reference to the same reconstructed floor line depicted in the drawing of the front. Horizontally they are placed by measuring in from the supposed remnant of right edge, as is the vertical axis of the stone. Broken line indications of other now lost glyph blocks assume block heights of 0.13 m. and widths of 0.15 m.

According to the reconstruction of the front of Stela 4, the pedestal is almost as high as it is wide. A similar feature is seen on the slate Stela 21, of comparable width, at 9.13.10.0.0. The sandals of the figures on the fronts of the two monuments are also of a similar type. There seems to be no reason to question Stela 4 as being of the Late Classic. The guess date is based only on a possible original pairing with Altar 3 (11 Ahau 9.18.0.0.0?).

Because the top is missing altogether, the indicated height of carving represents only a surmise. On the back there must have been an uncertain number of rows above and below those indicated. Probably the sides were plain, but the supposed remnant of edge on Fragment 7 is not extensive enough to show this.

The maximum height of the plain butt, 0.56 m., is a firm figure. But, as noted, the suggested height of the carving (HA) is a mere supposition, perhaps an excessive one. It is supposed to allow for elements in the sky above the human figure, such as appear on the tall slender Stela 3, but which apparently do not appear on Stela 21 with its high "pedestal."

STONE GROUPS 46 AND 50 (FIG. 27)

Other slate stelae fragments came to light dur-ing exploration at Caracol. Many such pieces were discovered at the locus of Stelae 12 and 20 and labeled Stone Group 50. Another such set was located about 5.0 m. further south, again at the base of Platform A1 (Stone Group 46). After shipment to the University Museum, Willcox was able to piece together many of the fragments and thereby to find fits between Stone Groups 46 and 50. He attempted to fit the larger reconstructed pieces to Stela 4 or 15 without success. One of the fragments demonstrates that, as with Stela 4, the monument represented by the two fitted stone groups carried figural carving on the front and glyphic inscription on the back.

STELA 5

Location:	At front (west) base of Structure A13
Associations:	Stelae 6, 7 in line to south
Dedicatory Date:	9.9.0.0.0 3 Ahau 3 Zotz ??
Style Date:	9.9.0.0.0 ± 2 katuns (Proskouriakoff)
Condition:	Broken and split: front weathered but preserved; sides badly split and eroded
Photographs:	Fig. 31a, b
	Satterthwaite 1954:Figs. 2, 3, 5, 6, 7, 8, 21
	Willcox 1954:Figs. 56-62, 66, 67
	Beetz 1980:Fig. 10
Drawings:	Fig. 6a, b
Other References:	Satterthwaite 1954
	Willcox 1954
	Riese 1980:5-6
Carved Areas:	Class 3: FLR (M3)
Material:	Limestone
Shape:	Roughly parallel sides, rounded top
Dimensions:	L: 3.40 m. HA: 3.02 m.
	W: 1.22 m. Th: 0.39 m.
	H above Floor: 3.20 m.

GENERAL REMARKS

Stela 5 was discovered in front of Str. A13 at the northern end of a line of stelae that included Stelae 6 and 7. The three stones had been broken off near floor level by natural causes. All butts remained *in situ*. Stela 5 carried an incised inscription on the sides with the glyphs grouped inside frames carved in relief. There were five frames on each side. When the stela fell backward, large and small fragments split longitudinally as well as transversely. As a result, the five glyph frames on the left side and the upper four on the right split in half from top to bottom. Their inscriptions came to be partly on the sides of front and partly on the sides of back fragments. The tenth frame, on the butt, was not split and was therefore the only one not to lose entirely the glyphic contents by erosion.

The stela was discovered in 1950. In 1951 the front fragments and the carved portion of the butt were brought to Philadelphia and subsequently assembled in the University Museum. Since only the front and sides were carved, many of the back fragments were not transported to the Museum. A lower plain portion of the butt was also cut off to save weight. As assembled, the rear portions of the nine split frames are represented in plaster. The reconstruction has probably erred in making them higher than wide. The nearly complete tenth frame on the butt is flattened round in form. The interior diameters of this frame measure about 0.27 and 0.28 m. and the overall exterior diameter measures about 0.34 m.

STELA 5: GLYPH CLASSIFICATION AND CHRONOLOGICAL DECIPHERMENT

(Probable order of reading: left-right and downward across all four columns without
regard to ten frames containing the glyphs, reading from right side to left side.
Reconstructed number of blocks: $10 \times 20 = 200 + 20$ (front) = 220 total)

		Right Side	
		A1-D20	Presumably 80 blocks completely gone or illegible
		A21-B21	2 blocks completely eroded
		C21	Doubtful traces (divided block?)
		D21	Symbolic glyph, badly damaged (prefixed bar??)
		A22-C22a	Eroded
		C22b-D22	2-3 non-calendrical glyphs
		A23-B23	Eroded
X	(9. 9. 0. 0. 0)?	C23a-C23b	2-4, glyph lost (3 Ahau? reconstructed, 1 dot preserved); 3, damaged head-variant main sign of Zotz?
SS1?	− 18. 3.17/18	D23	17-18 (kins), 3 uinals, 18 tuns
???	(9. 8. 1.14. 3/2)	A24	Eroded
SS???	− 7. 3.15/14	B24-C24a	Eroded
Y	(9. 7.14.10. 8)	C24b-D24a	2-4 superfixed to oval main sign (3 Lamat, reconstructed); 16 over eroded main sign (Uo reconstructed)
		D24b	T740 "up-ended frog"
		A25-B25a	Eroded
SS2?	1. 5.11.12	B25b-C25b	Eroded except for 2-4 superfixed to destroyed main sign at C25b
Z	(9. 9. 0. 4. 0)	D25a-D25b	5 Ahau 3 Mol

		Left Side	
		E1-H25	Presumably 100 blocks completely gone or illegible

		Panel Z	
		I1-J2	4 glyph blocks, completely gone

		Panel Y	
		I3-N6	16 glyph blocks, completely gone

STELA 5: SUMMARY OF CHRONOLOGY

C23a-C23b	Date X		(9. 9. 0. 0. 0?) (3 Ahau) 3 Zotz
D23		SS1?	− 18. 3.17/18
(A24a-A24b)	???		(9. 8. 1.14.3/2)
(B24a-C24a)		SS???	(− 7. 3.15/14)
C24b-D24a	Date Y		(9. 7.14.10. 8) (3 Lamat) 16 (Uo)
(B25b-C25b)		SS2?	(1. 5.11.12)
D25a-D25b	Date Z		(9. 9. 0. 4. 0) 5 Ahau 3 Mol

COMMENT ON THE INSCRIPTION

SIZE OF TEXT AND ORDER OF READING

Only the frame on the right side of the butt fragment contains legible glyphs. All traces of carving have apparently been eroded away in the other frames. The preserved frame contained five rows and four columns of small glyphs, as indicated by surviving glyphs in the right one and one-half columns. Most but not all of these surviving blocks are divided into two glyphs. Some crowding of the carving is evidenced by the right column encroaching on the rising inner surface of the frame. It might be hazardous to assume such a high proportion of block division in the eroded frames as in this small sample (although this possibility is not excluded). A total of 200 blocks, twenty in each of ten frames, can be reasonably inferred for the text on the sides of the monument. With the addition of twenty glyph blocks from panels "Z" and "Y" on the front, this total of 220 suggests that an exceptionally long text has been almost completely lost through erosion. If true, this quantity of inscription would make the text of Stela 5 the longest at Caracol. The second longest text would then be on the companion Stela 6 which also carries its inscription in frames on the sides. The little that has been preserved of the Stela 5 inscription was protected by soil washed down from the structure immediately behind the butt. The glyphs on the sides are incised and thus even less resistant than the frames which were carved in low relief.

A continuous text beginning on the right side and running to the left side is postulated on the basis of comparison with Stela 6 nearby. It had earlier been thought that the text possibly ended on the right side and that the dates recorded in the last block on that side marked the terminal date of the inscription. This appears unlikely now, since the final few glyphs of the text should probably record name phrases or emblem glyphs rather than a CR.

Order of reading has been reconstructed as continuous across all four columns, partly on the basis of extrapolation from the similar but three-column Stela 6. Such a reconstruction is also necessary to allow sufficient space for the presentation of a name and EG following the T740 "upended frog" at D24b before SS2?. An order of reading across all columns is not at all unusual at Caracol. Besides Stela 6, this order of reading is also definitely used on Stela 15 (9.4.16.13.3) and Stela 21 (9.13.10.0.0). The alternative order would follow the more conventional Maya practice and read the Stela 5 text left-right and downward in double columns. This latter order would not only go against the obvious similarities between Stelae 5 and 6 but would strand the T740 "birth" marker without a name to refer to. It is therefore not considered to be a very likely alternative.

In the assignment of block designations, the assumed right-left (-front?) order of reading has been followed. Extrapolation from Frame X allows reconstruction of the two sides as each having four columns and twenty-five rows. The front panels offer more of a problem, since there is not enough remaining of the glyphs to visually determine the number of glyph blocks. In Frame X, the glyph blocks are about 8.0 cm. wide and 5.0 cm. high. Looking at Panel Z we can see that it can represent a single large glyph block 13 cm. wide and 14 cm. high or several smaller blocks of one-half, one-third or one-quarter the dimensions of the whole block (the possibility of even smaller glyph blocks is discounted). Quartering Panel Z (i.e. halving the dimensions), offers the best possibility in this case, yielding component glyph blocks approximately 6.5 cm. by 7.0 cm., which compares favorably to the size of the blocks in Frame X. Panel Y is assumed to have blocks of similar size to those of Panel Z, giving six columns across and six rows down.

POSITION OF DATE Z

Reconstruction of the chronology recorded by this badly damaged text is not simple. Several alternative readings can be made, no one of which is entirely satisfying. The broad limits for dates recorded on Stela 5 might be set by the range presented on the nearby and similar Stela 6. That monument marks dates from 9.5.19.1.2 to 9.8.10.0.0. Stela 5 might therefore be expected to have featured dates between perhaps 9.5.0.0.0 and 9.9.0.0.0.

The best preserved time record on Stela 5 is the CR 5 Ahau 3 Mol (Date Z) at D25a-D25b. Within the suggested time span this date must fall at 9.6.7.9.0 or 9.9.0.4.0. Any SS that may once have counted forward from the preceding Date Y is unfortunately lost. At this time there is no way to choose between the two alternative readings for Date Z.

RECONSTRUCTION OF DATE Y

Date Y is not so well preserved as Date Z, but does display a number of clues that help us to place it in time. The SR carries a dot on the right side of its superfix over a largely effaced cartouched main sign. The position of the dot allows reconstruction of the coefficient as 2, 3 or 4. A reading of 4 is perhaps the least likely, since the remaining dot is well in toward the centerline of the main sign. There is definitely no bar. The SR main sign is too ruined for speculation as to its original nature. A very clear superfixed coefficient of 16 shows with the VYr. Details of the main sign below have been eroded, but the outlines of the component members of the sign remain: a broad unbroken subfix and a similarly broad but not necessarily unbroken superfix. Month signs that fall into these parameters are Uo, Zip, Yaxkin (doubtful) or possibly Mac.

Without SS's that neatly connect forward to Date Z or back to Date X it appears impossible to reliably fix Date Y into the LC. However, immediately following the VYr is a T740 event glyph marking "birth." Two birth dates are known or postulated at Caracol (see pages 114-130):

9.6.12.14.6	5 Cib	14 Uo
9.7.14.10.8	3 Lamat	16 Uo

Of these, the first is immediately ruled out by the indisputable VYr coefficient of 16. The CR corresponding to Lord Storm-water Moon's birth date (3 Lamat 16 Uo) fits in all respects with the preserved evidence. The remains of the main sign of the SR agree as far as they are preserved with a possible reading of Lamat, and the

superfix of 2-4 is in accordance with the suggested reading of 3. For the VYr, a reading of Uo agrees nicely with the remaining outlines of the main sign, and the coefficient is of course a clearly preserved 16. It thus seems reasonable to place Date Y at 9.7.14.10.8, unless the birth date of a presently unknown character is being marked instead. This on the whole seems unlikely since this new character would not be mentioned on either Stelae 6 or 3.

RECONSTRUCTION OF DATE X

A fairly certain VYr position of 3 Zotz is about all that can be read of Date X. Curiously, this CR is not followed by an event glyph, as we might expect, but by an SS. It is reasonable to assume that this SS (D23) leads from Date X to Date Y. The remains show a clear 18 tuns and 3 uinals. The kin coefficient is probably 17 although there is a reasonable possibility that it is actually 18. Any coefficient would have been carved on the now lost left portion of the text. The SS as it stands reads ?.18.3.17-18. Reconstructing the katun coefficient as 0, 1, 2, 3 and 4 and subtracting and adding the total from the fairly secure position of Date Y at 9.7.14.10.8 yield the following results:

Count Back				Count Forward		
0.18.3.17-18	9.6.16.6.11-10	9-8	Zip	9. 8.12.14.5-6	3-4	Uo
1.18.3.17-18	9.5.16.6.11-10	9-8	Mol	9. 9.12.14.5-6	8-9	Muan
2.18.3.17-18	9.4.16.6.11-10	9-8	Mac	9.10.12.14.5-6	8-9	Yax
3.18.3.17-18	9.3.16.6.11-10	9-8	Cumku	9.11.12.14.5-6	8-9	Zec
4.18.3.17-18	9.2.16.6.11-10	4-3	Zec	9.12.12.14.5-6	13-14	Cumku

As can be seen, none of these arrives at a reading of 3 Zotz for the VYr. If SS1 was part of an SS "chain" that connected Date X to our reconstructed Date Y, then another date and another SS must have once existed between the preserved end of SS1 and Date Y.

Where then shall we place Date X? None of the Caracol monuments of similar age (Stelae 1, 3, 6, 13, 14, 15, 16) carries a date with a VYr position of 3 Zotz. The only hope of placing this date into the LC is derived from the possibility

that it marks a tun or katun end. This requirement is fulfilled for a katun end at 9.9.0.0.0 3 Ahau 3 Zotz. Other tun ends with a VYr of 3 Zotz occur at 9.5.7.0.0 and 9.12.13.0.0. The latter falls outside the range set for Stela 5 on the basis of comparison with Stela 6. A position of 9.5.7.0.0 is unappealing because it falls at an "odd" tun end without duplication on other monuments. The katun end at 9.9.0.0.0 might on the other hand reasonably be expected to be followed by a "hand scattering" glyph, which it is not.

Thus neither of the two tun-ending dates is very satisfactory.

If we select 9.9.0.0.0 as the position of Date X and assume that SS1 served in part to link Dates X and Y, then we might read SS1 as 18.3.17-18 counting back to the date 9.8.1.14.3. This would be followed by a postulated SS of 7.3.15-14 to lead to the fairly secure Date Y. Date Z might then be counted to by SS2, of which part is preserved at C25b. If the earlier option for Date Z is selected (9.5.7.9.0) we could have a pattern of dates and SS's counting steadily backwards from 9.9.0.0.0. If 9.9.0.4.0 is selected for Date Z, the pattern is one of counting steadily forward with a parenthetical backtrack to mention the birth date of an important person.

Outside of the reconstruction of Date Y, the placements of the temporal notations of this monument are not very satisfactory. Any attempt to assign a DD must remain tentative. Utilizing the assumption that Stelae 5, 6 and 7 formed some sort of set allows the suggestion that the three marked sequent katun or half-katun ends or perhaps even the same date. For Stela 6, 9.8.10.0.0 and 9.9.0.0.0 seem to be the most likely alternatives for DD's. A DD of or around 9.9.0.0.0 might be indicated for Stela 5 on the basis of one of the reconstructions for Date X of that monument. Stela 7 has lost all carving and can "float" in any reconstruction. Some alternatives for DD placement are presented below:

I		II		III	
Stela 6	9.8.10.0.0	Stela 6	9. 9. 0.0.0	Stela 6	9.9.0.0.0
Stela 5	9.9. 0.0.0	Stela 5	9. 9.10.0.0	Stela 5	9.9.0.0.0
Stela 7	9.9.10.0.0	Stela 7	9.10. 0.0.0	Stela 7	9.9.0.0.0

Alternative I has the advantage that it allows us to pair Altars 11 and 15 with Stelae 5 and 6 for the ongoing or elapsed Katun 3 Ahau, and to pair Altar 19 with Stela 7 for the Katun 1 Ahau.

ALTERNATIVE CHRONOLOGICAL DECIPHERMENT

As noted, many alternative readings of the chronology preserved on Stela 5 can be made. One such interpretation that received considerable attention read Date X as (9.9.0.0.0) 3 Ahua 3 Zotz, Date Y as 2 Akbal 16 Mac (9.7.2.0.3) and Date Z as (9.9.0.4.0) 5 Ahau 3 Mol. SS1 would then have counted forward 1.18.3.17 from Date Y (which it precedes) to Date Z, (which is separated from Date Y by a largely effaced SS2). SS2 would have served to count forward from Date X to Date Z without regard to the intervening SS1 and Date Y. As can be observed from the present description, this interpretation leads to a reading that is at best convoluted. Primarily for that reason, but also for consideration of the

birth marker at D24b, this earlier explanation of the text of Stela 5 has been abandoned.

ASSOCIATED ALTAR?

There were no altars found in front of Stelae 5, 6 or 7. Hints of a disturbed sub-altar cache were discovered before Stela 5 during excavation of that monument. Articles found in this supposed cache consist of a stone figurine, a thin strip of copper-gold alloy, and a tubular jade bead. These pieces were found only a short distance from the stela butt buried only slightly. The possibility that they represent a much later offering cannot be entirely ruled out.

Any altar that may have been associated with Stela 5 was probably of the Giant Glyph pattern. Under a preferred reading of the DD of the stela as 9.9.0.0.0, a Giant Glyph Altar should have borne a legend of 3 Ahau. This date occurs on a known fragment of Altar 15 (possibly also on Altar 11), which was reused as bedding or as part of a cache beneath Altar 14.

STELA 6

Location:	Centered at front (west) base of Structure A13
Associations:	In north-south line with Stela 5 (north), and Stela 7 (south)
Dedicatory Date:	9.8.10.0.0?
Style Date:	Front: 9.8. 0.0.0 ± 2 katuns
	Back: 9.9.10.0.0 ± 2 katuns
	Arrangement: 9.8.15.0.0 ± 1.25 katuns
Condition:	Broken, but found *in situ*; entire front and left side blurred by erosion; details well preserved on back and right side
Photographs:	Fig. 32a, b, c
	Satterthwaite 1954:Figs. 2, 9-11, 22
	Willcox 1954:Fig. 48
	Beetz 1980:Figs. 8a, b; 10
Drawings:	Figs. 7a, b; 8
Other References:	Satterthwaite 1954
	Willcox 1954
	Beetz 1980:8-9
	Riese 1980:6-7
Carved Areas:	Class 4: FLRB (M2)
Material:	Limestone
Shape:	Sides approximately straight and parallel; top flattened; cross section approximately rectangular with bulging sides
Dimensions:	L: 4.02 m. HA: 3.13 m. (front); 3.05 m. (back).
	W: 0.74 m. Th: 0.38 m.
	H above Floor: 3.28 m.

GENERAL REMARKS

This monument formed the center of a line of three stelae at the base of Structure A13. Stela 6 was broken off near floor level by natural agents. The butt remained *in situ*. The backwards fall broke the stela transversely and diagonally. Unlike that of other monuments at Caracol, this breakage did not significantly damage the carvings. Erosion, however, did obscure the front and obliterate the inscriptions on the left side. On the other hand, the back and the right side glyph panels are well preserved.

Stela 6 was discovered in 1950 and was shipped to Philadelphia in fragmentary form in 1951 and reconstructed in the Museum. Nearly all fragments were recovered, and the assembled stela is virtually complete.

STELA 6: GLYPH CLASSIFICATION AND CHRONOLOGICAL DECIPHERMENT

(Order of reading, left-right and downward in triple column without regard to
eight frames on each side containing the glyphs. Reconstructed number of blocks:
$16 \times 9 = 144 + 10$ (from Panels X, Y, Z) = 154 total)

Right Side

		A1	ISIG (eroded)
		B1-B2b	9 baktuns, 5 katuns, 19 tuns, 1 uinal, 2 kins (many elements reconstructed)
A	9. 5.19. 1. 2	C2-A3	9 Ik 5 Uo (SR eroded)
		B3	Event glyph? (possibly "seating" variant)
		C3-B4	Name phrase: 2 glyphs naming Lord Water (A4 is his characteristic "name" glyph) followed by the Caracol Glyph
		C4	1 non-calendrical glyph, eroded (reconstructed as a parent indicator)
		A5-B5	Name phrase: unidentified person followed by unidentified EG
		C5	SSIG
SS1	16.18	A6	18 (kins), 16 uinals
		B6-C6	2 non-calendrical glyphs
B	(9. 6. 0. 0. 0)	A7	9 Ahau
		B7a-B7b	2 non-calendrical glyphs
C	(9. 7. 0. 0. 0)	C7a-A8	7 Ahau 3 Kankin; End-haab (partly reconstructed)
		B8	1 non-calendrical glyph
D	(9. 8. 0. 0. 0)	C8a-A9	5 Ahau 3 Chen; End-haab (partly reconstructed)
		B9-C9	Name phrase for Lord Water followed by the Caracol Glyph
		A10	SSIG
SS2	5.16.12	B10-C10	12 (kins), 16 uinals, 5 tuns
		A11	Katun with lost coefficient, reconstructed as a part of SS2, marking 2 katuns and counting forward from Date B
		B11-C11	2 non-calendrical glyphs (possibly an event glyph and part of a name-title phrase)
		A12	Name of Lord Water
		B12-C13	4 non-calendrical glyphs
E	(9. 8. 5.16.12)	A14-B14	5 Eb 5 Xul
		C14-A15	2 non-calendrical glyphs
		B15-C15	Name phrase: Ahau-serpent followed by Caracol Glyph
		A16	SSIG
SS3	4. 1. 8	B16-C16	8 (kins), 1 uinal, 4 tuns
		A17-B17	2 non-calendrical glyphs
F	(9. 8.10. 0. 0)	C17-A18	4 Ahau 13 Xul
		B18	T710 "hand scattering" glyph
		C18	Half-period glyph (damaged)
		A19-C19	3 non-calendrical glyphs
		A20	Name of Ahau-serpent
		B20	1 non-calendrical glyph
		C20	3 katuns (interpreted to refer to third katun of life for Lord Water at B21)
		A21	1 non-calendrical glyph
		B21-A22	Name phrase for Lord Water concluding with the Caracol Glyph
		B22-C24	8 non-calendrical glyphs

Left Side

D1-F24   72 eroded glyphs

Panel X

xA1-xA5   5 lost glyphs

Panel Y

yA1-yA3   3 lost glyphs

Panel Z

zA1-zA2   2 non-calendrical glyphs

STELA 6: SUMMARY OF CHRONOLOGY

A1-A3	Date A	IS	9. 5.19. 1. 2	9 Ik 5 Uo
C5-A6		SS1	16.18	
A7	Date B		(9. 6. 0. 0. 0)	9 Ahau (3 Uayeb)
C7a-A8	Date C		(9. 7. 0. 0. 0)	7 Ahau 3 Kankin; End-haab
C8a-A9	Date D		(9. 8. 0. 0. 0)	5 Ahau 3 Chen; End-haab
A10-C10		SS2	5.16.12	
A14-B14	Date E		(9. 8. 5.16.12)	5 Eb 5 Xul
A16-C16		SS3	4. 1. 8	
C17-A18	Date F		(9. 8.10. 0. 0)	4 Ahau 13 Xul
B18-C18				T710 "hand scattering" half-period

COMMENT ON THE INSCRIPTION

DESCRIPTION OF CARVING

This stela, like the nearby Stela 5, has incised glyphs placed in flattened round frames on the sides. Unfortunately there are only occasional traces of glyphs surviving in the eight frames on the left side of Stela 6. Enough is preserved to indicate the same arrangement as on the right side which is preserved except for the upper frame. It is clear that the text is read left-right and downward across all three columns. Column letters and row numbers are assigned without reference to the frames as on Stela 5.

ORDER OF READING THE SIDES; BLOCK DESIGNATIONS

The IS in the first frame on the right side had not yet been noticed when Stela 6 was first assigned column designations. For this reason the original lettering of the columns was carried out under the assumptions that: a) a single continuous text passed from one side to the other; and that, b) the beginning was on the left side. Because of the ignorance of the IS and because of the resulting misapplication of these two assumptions the original block labels were incorrect. The present work rectifies that error.

The order of reading used in this work was first noticed by Thompson (Satterthwaite correspondence). Careful scrutiny of the left side cannot conclusively rule out the possibility that a second IS existed there (and hence the possibility of two independent texts on the two sides).

Although it is fairly certain that the inscription opens on the right side with an IS, comparison with Stela 3 opens the possibility that a continuous text may have terminated on the front or back rather than on the left side. The three panels on the front and back of Stela 6 are much smaller than the front panel of Stela 3 and seem to be inserted so as not to disturb the human figures. Given the information available, it seems best to consider the text as beginning on the right side and terminating on the left with one, two or three independent texts being displayed on the front and back.

DATES A AND B; SS1

The opening frame of the inscription is heavily weathered, and the ISIG all but effaced. The period glyphs and their coefficients are all heavily damaged, but in many cases distinguishable. Although any single glyph might be disputable, the whole forms a convincing pattern as a manifestation of an IS number.

With acceptance of this, by position the uinal and kin terms are in a single divided block (B2).

Since the kin coefficient is surely 2, the day name of the CR may be restored as Ik. Visual inspection then suggests that the day coefficient is 9. Confirmation of this comes from a calculation of SS1 back from the clear 9 Ahau of Date B. There is no evidence of either an LS or 819 day cycle clause after the IS. Therefore the month position should be recorded immediately after the 9 Ik. Inspection leaves little doubt that 5 Uo was recorded at that point with the required prefix being somewhat larger than normal and overlapping the main sign. If this identification is questioned, the traces of crossed bands in the main sign make 5 Zip the only alternative. Alternatives for the IS date substituting Zip for Uo within Baktun 9 are presented below:

9 Ik 5 Uo	9 Ik 5 Zip
9.0.13.11.2	9.2. 6. 2.0
9.3. 6. 6.2	9.4.18.15.0
9.5.19. 1.2	9.7.11.10.2

Only the third position of 9 Ik 5 Uo meets the requirement that there be four dots in the tun coefficient and only it shows a uinal coefficient of 1 which is preferred by inspection. The tun coefficient of 19 rather than 14 or 9 is also preferred by inspection. On the basis of these agreements, it is justifiable to restore the lost katun coefficient as 5 and the baktun coefficient as 9 rather than the inspectionally possible 8.

Counting SS1 forward from 9 Ik 5 Uo reaches the CR of 9 Ahau 3 Uayeb. The month sign and its coefficient might be expected to appear immediately after the day sign. The sign in this position (B7a) has a coefficient of 3 but is not similar to any known form of Uayeb or indeed any other month as listed in Thompson's examples (1950). Evidently the month position of Date B, at a katun end, was suppressed and its position taken by a non-calendrical glyph with a coefficient of 3. The theoretical alternative would be a radically new form for Uayeb.

DATES C AND D

Date C appears in the divided Block C7. There are two oval signs with coefficients of 7 and 3 if one dot is restored in each case for symmetry. Ahau may be safely taken to be the name of the day, since the CR is followed by the end-haab glyph. It is not linked to Date A by SS, but it may nevertheless be confidently placed at a tun end.

This is supported by the similar presentation of Date D as a CR followed by an end-haab glyph. Date D then can be tied to the known Date F at 9.8.10.0.0 through SS2 and SS3. Its reading falls at 9.8.0.0.0. Presumably the end-haab glyph after Date C was understood in the same manner, so the month name can be restored as 3 Kankin at 9.7.0.0.0.

SS2 AND DATE E, SS3 AND DATE F

SS2 is preserved at B10-C10 as 5.16.12 followed by a katun sign in the next block, A11. There is space in a scaled-off area to the left of the katun for a numerical or other prefix. The katun was originally thought to represent an "isolated" katun or perhaps a katun with coefficient of zero, since the SS as preserved connects from Date D to Date E. It seems a more likely possibility that the katun actually served to enlarge the SS so that it would count forward from the previous SS rather than from the previous date. In this case, the preceding SS1 brought the count forward to 9.6.0.0.0 (Date B) before two CR's without SS's marked succeeding katun ends. A coefficient of 2 for the katun at A11 would serve to bring the count forward from Date B while accounting for the presence of the katun glyph at this location.

The CR of Date E is a very clear 5 Eb 5 Xul (A14-B14). Although the glyphs are not at all unusual, their positions are. Rather than following immediately after the SS, the CR is separated by eight glyph blocks. It appears that a double clause or sub-clause arrangement is set up for this date by the splitting of the chronological statement. SS3 counts neatly forward to Date F at 9.8.10.0.0, where the CR is once again separate from the SS. In this case only two glyph blocks intervene. The CR of Date F is an unobscured 4 Ahau 13 Xul (C17-A18). The day sign and coefficient of both Dates E and F (as well as the block that precedes Date F at B17) are prefixed by a "caterpillar" over a ring of dots (T53). This same prefix is found attached to the day sign of the Stela 1 IS which records 9.8.0.0.0 5 Ahau.

DEDICATORY DATE

The latest surviving date, at 9.8.10.0.0, is the last stated on the right side. In 1954 it was listed as the probable DD with a single question mark.

It was thought at the time to be the last date recorded in the whole text, with a beginning on the completely eroded left side. With the reading of the IS, it now is most likely that the last half of the long text is the part that has actually been lost and that 9.8.10.0.0 could be regarded only as an early limit for the DD. Since the first half of the text shows only forward counting, the left side possibly carried the chronological count forward from 9.18.10.0.0 to a later katun end or perhaps half-katun end as the DD. With this assumption and with Stela 5 apparently at 9.9.0.0.0, some guesses for the DD of Stela 6 might be 9.9.10.0.0 or 9.10.0.0.0. Either avoids going beyond Proskouriakoff's late style date limit of 9.10.0.0.0 after averaging for the figures on front and back. Both agree with but do not depend on a theory that the Giant Glyph Altar 19 once served Stela 6 and named the current or lapsed katun in Short Count style. The question of the DD would be complicated if the two sides were to be read as separate texts, as the case with some Quirigua monuments.

Evidence from the study of non-calendric glyphs at Caracol suggests that Stela 6 was dedicated to a ruler who did not retain power past 9.9.4.16.2 (see pages 114-130). If the DD of this monument was to be within the lifetime of this ruler, it could not have been as late as 9.9.10.0.0 or 9.10.0.0.0. Rather, 9.8.10.0.0 or 9.9.0.0.0 becomes the likely choice for a DD. It is not unlikely that 9.8.10.0.0 was the DD for Stela 6 as the "hand scattering" sign suggests. The left side text could then have carried the count forward only a small amount in a largely non-calendric statement (or there may have existed an independent chronology on the left side if it was an independent text). Alternatively, Stela 6 might have marked the same DD as is presumed for Stela 5, 9.9.0.0.0. Following the assumption that the three stelae erected before Structure A13 (Stelae 5, 6, 7) formed a pattern with their DD's, three alternatives have been outlined (see also discussion of Stela 5):

	I	II	III
Stela 6	9.8.10.0.0	9. 9. 0.0.0	9.9.0.0.0
Stela 5	9.9. 0.0.0	9. 9.10.0.0	9.9.0.0.0
Stela 7	9.9.10.0.0	9.10. 0.0.0	9.9.0.0.0

It should be noted that Stela 7 has lost all trace of carving and thus may be manipulated freely in time. To avoid multiple marking of the same DD, alternatives I or II might be favored. Alternative I would allow us to assign Giant Glyph Altars 11 and 15 to Stelae 5 and 6 and Giant Glyph Altar 19 to Stela 7. Under the third alternative, the three stelae could have formed a contemporaneous set. However, the set would, on the basis of present evidence, be short a Giant Glyph Altar if they were all originally accompanied by such.

STELA 7

Location:	At front (west) base of Structure A13, butt *in situ*
Associations:	Stelae 5 and 6 in line to north
Dedicatory Date:	9.9.10.0.0???
Style Date:	Indiscernible
Condition:	Broken into twenty-five pieces by natural causes; all carving almost entirely eroded
Photographs:	Fig. 33a Satterthwaite 1954:Fig. 4
Drawings:	None
Other References:	Satterthwaite 1954 Willcox 1954 Riese 1980:7
Carved Areas:	Class 3: FLR (M3) ?
Material:	Limestone
Shape:	Sides straight and parallel, top rounded
Dimensions:	L: ? HA: ? W: 0.65 m. Th: 0.42 m. H above Floor: ?

GENERAL REMARKS

Stela 7 was discovered in 1950 at the same time that Stelae 5 and 6 were exposed. It stands at the south end of the monument group formed by Stelae 5, 6 and 7 in line at the west base of Structure A13. All three stelae broke near ground level and fell backwards (toward Structure A13). All breakage and falling of Stela 7 appear to have been due to natural causes. The butt remained *in situ* and the upper parts of the stela fractured transversely and longitudinally.

At the time of discovery, Stela 7 had decomposed into four large and twenty-one smaller fragments. These were very heavily eroded and only five pieces showed traces of carving. Due to the poor condition of the monument, the number of carved surfaces was not precisely determined. Examination of the larger pieces indicated that the back probably was plain. The condition and poverty of preserved sculpture on this monument led to its being left at the site after work was completed.

The assumption used in this report, that Stelae 5, 6 and 7 formed a set marking a pattern of LC positions, provides the only possibility for even guessing at a DD and at a classification of carved areas. Difficulties of assigning a DD have been covered during the discussions of Stelae 5 and 6. In those places it was concluded that a likely hypothetical date for Stela 7 is 9.9.0.0.0, 9.9.10.0.0 or 9.10.0.0.0, with 9.9.10.0.0 being somewhat favored.

Though erosion and breakage of all surfaces lead to equally hypothetical conclusions in regard to the question of carved surfaces, it could be assumed from the fact that both Stela 5 and Stela 6 have relief frames enclosing glyph blocks on the sides that Stela 7 also showed this fairly unusual feature. It is this possibility that is noted with a question mark on the synopsis, although it seems that evidence of frames in relief on the sides should have been preserved if they did indeed exist. In this regard, Stela 5, despite weathering of the side inscriptions, still plainly shows the frames that enclosed them.

STELA 8

Location:	In south part of Court A1, facing southeast
Associations:	Near but not with Altar 14 (and Altar 15 fragment below Altar 14)
Dedicatory Date:	9.19.0.0.0?
Style Date:	Undetermined
Condition:	Broken and badly eroded except for a fragment of the upper left corner
Photographs:	Fig. 33b, c Satterthwaite 1954:Fig. 18 (a cast)
Drawings:	Fig. 9
Other References:	Satterthwaite 1954 Willcox 1954 Riese 1980:7
Carved Areas:	Class 1; F (M7)
Material:	Limestone
Shape:	Very uncertain. Slightly bulging sides, top rounded
Dimensions:	L: ? HA: 2.55 m.? W: 1.18 m.? Th: 0.52 m. H above Floor: ?

GENERAL REMARKS

Stela 8 was located in 1951 in Court A1 just to the west of Altar 14. The butt of the stela was leaning back 60-70° from the perpendicular. The upper part of the stela had broken off. Both the upper and lower portions had lost major fragments from their edges, some of which were never recovered. Although the stela is generally heavily eroded, it is still apparent that the sides and back were uncarved. Erosion has almost totally worn away the bulk of the carving on the front. When discovered, the butt was turned so that the front faced well south of the east-west axis of Court A1. Whether it was placed in this position or was twisted by the action of natural or human agencies could not be determined. Following excavation and photography in 1953, the stela was left at the site.

STELA 8: GLYPH CLASSIFICATION AND CHRONOLOGICAL DECIPHERMENT

(Order of reading in Panel W: downward in single column.
Number of glyph blocks: 3 + 2(3?) + 2(?) + 6 = 13(14?))

Panel W

A	9.19.(0. 0. 0)?	wA1-wA3	ISIG (Mol variable?), 9 baktuns, 19 katuns (reconstructed as 9.19.0.0.0 9 Ahau 18 Mol)
		Panel X	2(3?) illegible glyph blocks
		Panel Y	2 illegible glyph blocks
		Panel Z	6 illegible glyph blocks

COMMENT ON THE INSCRIPTION

SILHOUETTE OF THE MONUMENT;
ARRANGEMENT OF GLYPH PANELS

The drawing of Stela 8 is a composite formed of fitted sketches of separate photographs of each fragment. A fitting of the pieces at the site demonstrated that a sure fit was not possible due to the amount of material lost from between the recovered fragments. The photograph in Fig. 33b shows a provisional fitting of the upper fragments which was certainly wrong in placing Panel W too low. As shown in the drawing, the fragment carrying Panel W may be a bit too high and turned too much. But its placement relative to Panel X is substantially correct. Panel X was on a separate fragment that was articulated with the upper fragment of the stela immediately to its right.

It is tempting to piece together Panels W and X as a continuous glyphic statement. However, clear space (represented by stipple in the drawing) to the right of blocks wA2 and wA3 demonstrates that Panel W probably consisted of a single column of three blocks. Conceivably, but improbably, it might have been an inverted L-shaped panel with a missing fourth block "wB1." Panel X is apparently not spatially closely related to Panel W.

Examination of field photographs raises the possibility that there may have been another glyph block above xB1. In this case, a reconstruction could be made of Panels W and X as parallel and distinct columns of three glyph blocks each. Such a possibility would allow the IS to continue in Panel X, which panel would then display the tun, uinal and kin glyphs and their coefficients. It is also possible that the IS continued through Panel X into Panel Y, since the existing glyphic traces in Panel X do not prohibit tun and uinal signs.

DEDICATORY DATE

Below, Caracol Stela 8 is compared to three texts in which there is evidence that an IS was "truncated" by suppression of zero kin, uinal or tun positions and even of the CR:

ISIG/Mol?	9.19.(0. 0. 0	9 Ahau	18	Mol)				Caracol Stela 8
ISIG/ ?	?. ?. 0.(0. 0	?	?	?	?)			Xutilha Stela 6
ISIG/Yax	9.(0. 0. 0. 0	8 Ahau	13	Ceh)				Tikal Burial 160
ISIG/ ?	10. 3.(0. 0. 0)	1 Ahau	3	Yaxkin				Jimbal Stela 2

The many question marks given for the Xutilha example represent illegibility due to erosion. The form of the Xutilha ISIG is fairly clear; the three supposed period glyphs all may have been bird heads and there are positive indications of this for baktun and tun positions. The baktun and katun coefficients are taken to be illegible head-variants and the outline of a symbolic zero is visible in the tun place. The four glyphs form the left leg of an inverted L-shaped panel. Despite erosion, it seems clear that the kins and uinals of the IS and the terminal date were not recorded among the smaller glyphs of the panel nor in others on the stone. Proskouriakoff's style date estimate for the Xutilha stela suggests that the complete IS was probably 9.18.0.0.0, 9.19.0.0.0 or 10.0.0.0.0. The Xutilha stela differs from Caracol Stela 8 in that the former cuts off after the tun term rather than before, even though that term is at zero.

This seems to be a mere difference in the style of saying the same thing at two widely separated sites, possibly at precisely the same katun end. The Tikal Burial 160 text demonstrates the possibility of truncation before the katun term if it is interpreted correctly. Two glyphs only were painted on the tomb wall with no room for additional columns (Haviland n.d.).

Stela 8 at Caracol presents a fairly legible check on the IS interpretation. The variable of the ISIG almost surely indicates the correct patron for the reconstructed month position of the terminal date, Mol. At Tikal, the ISIG variable seems clearly to be that for Yax, while Ceh is required. In view of the probably correct variable at Caracol, it seems safe to invoke a Maya mistake in this particular in the Tikal text.

With the Xutilha, Jimbal and Tikal parallels for comparison we may safely consider the truncated IS interpretation for Caracol Stela 8 as reasonable.

INTERPRETATION OF THE GLYPHS
OF THE INITIAL SERIES

At wA1, the main sign of the ISIG is a clear tun with room for a "pedestal" subfix. There is a tall superfix. Part of the left comb element can be seen next to a central element that includes an arch resting on the main sign. A trefoil superfix above this is not preserved but cannot be said not to have existed. Details within the "arch" of the superfix are lost. Among Thompson's examples of month patron signs, closest correspondence to this variable is seen in his Fig. 22, *38* and *39* for Mol (1950). Both show the arch form rising from the main sign, which is seen elsewhere only in symbolic variants for the Ceh month patron. The identification of the patron as that for Mol by inspection is not absolute, but seems preferable.

The sign in the katun position (wA3) has a preserved tun main sign with a superfix that is unclear but not at odds with an interpretation as a katun superfix. The coefficient for the katun is a clear 19.

In the baktun position (wA2) between the ISIG and the katun sign appears a glyph with a clear coefficient of 9. This sign does not appear to be a head-variant period glyph, nor does it appear to be the paired cauac signs that form the conventional symbolic baktun glyph. Rather, the space is divided vertically into what appears to be a main sign and superfix. Photographs show that the "prefix" of this sign may have been the normal double cauac symbolic baktun sign. There appear to be hints of two ovoid signs of equal size side by side.

A three-quarter border covers the sides and top of the lower portion of the unusual presumed baktun sign. There are also two parallel lines defining a vertical band at the center of the enclosed field.

A similar baktun glyph variant appears at the same LC position at the site of Hatzcap Ceel a few miles away. (Thompson 1931:264-266). Thompson feels that the eroded Altar 2 at that site recorded an IS of 9.19.0.0.0. Of this he says that the baktun position is filled by, ". . . a very worn glyph, the upper part of which might be the cycle (baktun) sign." The photograph of that monument (Plate 29) shows overlapping ovoid signs of equal size of which the left one retains the border of a cauac sign. This photograph further shows that the main sign had definite remains of a centered vertical band extending across the field from top to bottom just as in the Caracol example. It definitely does not show any remains of a tun sign as drawn below double cauac in Thompson's collection of symbolic baktun signs (1950:Fig. 26, *22*). Caracol Stela 8 and Hatzcap Ceel Altar 2 between them seem to establish a variant baktun sign.

STELA 9/ALTAR 4

	Stela 9	Altar 4
Location:	In center of Court A1. Butt of Stela 9 apparently *in situ*. Stela faces altar to east on east-west axis of Court A1	
Associations:	Altar 4 near but not of primary association	Stela 9 near but not of primary association
Dedicatory Date:	9.18.0.0.0-10.0.0.0 0??	9.3.0.0.0 2 Ahau 18 Muan?
Style Date:	Undetermined	
Condition:	Badly shattered and eroded	Broken and weathered around edges. Top lightly eroded
Photographs:	Fig. 34a	Fig. 40d
		Satterthwaite 1951:Pl. XIV
Drawings:	Fig. 10	Fig. 20d
Other References:	Satterthwaite 1954	Satterthwaite 1951, 1954
	Riese 1980:7-81	Beetz 1980:7
		Riese 1980:15-16
Carved Areas:	Class 1: F(M7)	Altar Class 1: T
Material:	Limestone	Limestone
Shape:	Roughly parallel sides; flattened top beveled from front to back.	Irregular round

Dimensions:

Stela 9		Altar 4	
L: 3.25 m.?	HA: (back) 1.96 m.?	Max. W: 1.77 m.	Th: 0.30 m.?
W: 1.25 m.	(front) 1.81 m.?	Min. W: 1.65 m.	
	Th: 0.36 m.		
H above Floor:	(back) 2.45 m.?		
	(front) 2.30 m.?		

GENERAL REMARKS

These two monuments were located by Satterthwaite and Anderson in 1950. The altar was probably discovered earlier, since it was just to the side of a logging road. Stela 9, unfortunately, proved to have been lying underneath the road and had suffered heavy damage from the trucks. Both monuments were left at the site upon the completion of fieldwork.

When excavated, the altar and stela butt appeared to be *in situ*. The upper part of Stela 9 had fallen backward, apparently through the action of natural agencies. Stela 9 and Altar 4 rested in the approximate center of Court A1, facing Platform A10. They were oriented a little south of west, exactly in line with the east-west axis of Court A1. They also lie on a line drawn from the top of Platform A10 to the top of Structure A2.

Altar 4 was not badly damaged as found. Fragments broken from the upper right represent the only sizeable breakage. This monument was not entirely excavated, but was undercut to determine the thickness and the nature of the lower surface.

Both the butt and the fallen upper portion of Stela 9 were severely broken and weathered. The stela lay face up a little below the surface of the ground. This position led to considerable erosion of the front, which was the only carved surface. Despite the fact that the stela is badly fractured and that much of the carving is missing, the remaining portions were found articulated in the proper spatial orientations. Thus the possibility of intentional breakage seems to be ruled out. Fracturing seems reasonably explained as resulting from the wheels of mahogany trucks, while the missing pieces were probably crushed to rubble by the same agent. An interesting feature of Stela 9 is the probable beveling of the top. The upper left fragment of the stela retained a portion of the sloping section, while the position of the back fragments indicates that the beveling continued along the entire width of the monument.

ALTAR 4: SUMMARY OF CHRONOLOGY
A1   Date A   CR (9. 3. 0. 0. 0) 2 Ahau (18 Muan)

COMMENT ON THE INSCRIPTION

The inscription on Stela 9 was restricted to four panels on the front. The minimum number of glyph blocks represented was: Panel W, 9; Panel X, 2; Panel Y, 3; Panel Z, 3. This yields a minimum total of seventeen glyph blocks for the stela. Panel Z was badly damaged and may have contained four blocks.

There is little doubt that the glyphs were incised rather than in relief. Careful inspection could reveal no trace of carving in the glyph areas despite the fact that relief glyphs would have left deep channels between blocks. Uneven erosion could have obscured such channels. However, examination showed erosion to have been uniform and not excessively deep.

Altar 4 bears the only readable inscription of this pair since the glyphs of Stela 9 are thoroughly eroded. It was originally thought that the giant glyph 2 Ahau carved on the altar could be used to date both monuments, in as much as the two were thought to have been found *in situ* at the original site of erection. Under this hypothesis, the date on Altar 4 could apply to either 9.3.0.0.0 or 9.16.0.0.0, following the assumption that the Giant Glyph Altars marked current or recently lapsed katun names. The "notched" Ahau represented on the altar leads to the selection of the earlier date, 9.3.0.0.0, as that more likely to be commemorated by this monument since this form of Ahau is a generally "early" trait.

In contradiction to the selection of an early date for the altar, the layout of the figure on Stela 9 is most similar to the two spatially proximal monuments found in Court A1, Stelae 8 and 11. Stelae 8, 9 and 11 all display a large central figure with diagonal serpent bar and a subsidiary figure in the lower left corner. The inscriptions on these stelae are on the fronts in discrete panels of glyphs. The monuments that Stela 9 would be closest to temporally if it did indeed date to around 9.3.0.0.0 (Stelae 13, 14, 15, 16), show none of these features. Stelae 13, 14 and 16 have main figures holding horizontal serpent bars. Stelae 13 and 16 carry no inscriptions on the front. Stelae 14 and 15 do possess front inscriptions, but in large single blocks of text rather than in discrete dispersed panels. None of these four early stelae show any evidence of a secondary figure.

Stela 9 and Altar 4 are therefore apparently not an original stela/altar pair. With stylistic disjunction between the stela and the altar and the only partial job of excavation done around the monuments, the idea that the two were found associated *in situ* can probably be safely disregarded. In support of this, it can be noted that Stelae 8 and 11 nearby were also discovered with secondarily placed altars of much earlier date in front of them.

The most likely DD for Altar 4 remains in the katun ending at 9.3.0.0.0. At the present time, there is no known Caracol stela of similar age which can be hypothesized to form a pair with this altar. Its original locus of erection is therefore also entirely unknown.

A possible DD for Stela 9 can be known only generally by comparison with the apparent DD's of Stelae 8 and 11. These two monuments carry dates of 9.19.0.0.0 and 9.18.10.0.0?? respectively. After this, Stela 19 marked 9.19.10.0.0 and Stela 17 marked 10.1.0.0.0. If the possibility of two stelae commemorating the same katun end were excluded, then Stela 9 might be considered to have borne a DD of either 10.0.0.0.0 or 9.18.0.0.0 (possibly marked by Stela "X"/4 and Altar 3). It seems safest to mark its DD as a range falling between 9.18.0.0.0 and 10.0.0.0.0??.

STELA 10

Location: In Court A1, facing 15 degrees south of west. Butt apparently *in situ*
Associations: None
Dedicatory Date: 10.3.0.0.0??
Style Date: Undetermined
Condition: Incomplete. Broken and badly eroded
Photographs: Fig. 34b, c
Drawings: Fig. 11
Other References: Satterthwaite 1954
Riese 1980:8
Carved Areas: Class 1: F (M5)
Material: Limestone
Shape: Parallel sides, rounded top
Dimensions: L: ?   HA: ca. 2.00 m.
W: 1.04 m.   Th: 0.28 m.
H above Floor: ca. 2.05 m.

GENERAL REMARKS

Stela 10 was found lying face up in Court A1. The butt was still standing with the long axis oriented 15° east of north. This would have caused the monument to face a little further south than would be the case if it were aligned with the tilted east-west axes of the court. Two large fragments with carving were present along with several small unfitted ones. The monument was left at the site when fieldwork concluded.

STELA 10: GLYPH CLASSIFICATION AND CHRONOLOGICAL DECIPHERMENT

(Order of reading: reconstructed as left-right and downward in two columns. Number of blocks: 14 total)

		Front Side	
		A1a	11 Ik, *ti* prefixed
		A1b	11, main sign eroded
		B1a-A5b	6 divided blocks, eroded but apparently non-calendrical
		B5a	? Imix, *ti* prefixed (coefficient lost)
		B5b-A6b	1½ eroded blocks
		B6a	11 Caban, *ti* prefixed
		B6b	10?, main sign lost (possibly month sign?)
		A7a-B7a	1½ eroded blocks, apparently non-calendrical
A	(10.0.0.0.0??)	B7b	1-3 Ahau (1 Ahau preferred), *ti* prefixed

COMMENT ON THE INSCRIPTION

Stela 10 shows several bar-and-dot numerals and at least four calendrical glyphs. At A1a there is a fairly clear 11 Ik with a *ti* prefix. A possible coefficient of 11 follows at A1b. However, 11 is not an appropriate coefficient for correspondence with the day sign Ik. Thus if the divided opening block of the text carries a CR date, it is a confused one.

At B5a is an Imix with *ti* prefix and obliterated coefficient. An 11 Caban at B6a also carries a *ti*

prefix. Again, at the end of the text, block B7b is an Ahau with a *ti* prefix. Of these, the 11 Caban at B6a is the only one that might be followed by a month sign and coefficient of 10 at B6b. Since no SS's are discernible, all four day signs are floating dates.

The Ahau at B7b offers the only possibility for chronological placement, since the assumption can be followed that this day marked a katun end. Examination of the area where the coefficient should be for the Ahau reveals an oblong element with a short decorative curl carved in. This element is located above the Ahau and to the left. To the right of it, the rest of the coefficient is destroyed. By postulating a symmetrical arrangement, the coefficient can be reconstructed as a single central dot flanked by two decorative elements. A DD of 1 Ahau is therefore preferred, although 2 or 3 Ahau is also possible.

Alternative LC positions at the different readings of the Ahau coefficient are (assuming a katun or half-katun end to be marked):

1 Ahau	2 Ahau	3 Ahau
9. 3.10.0.0	9. 3. 0.0.0	9. 2.10.0.0
9.10. 0.0.0	9. 9.10.0.0	9. 9. 0.0.0
9.16.10.0.0	9.16. 0.0.0	9.15.10.0.0
10. 3. 0.0.0	10. 2.10.0.0	10. 2. 0.0.0

The crudeness of the stela and its entirely glyphic carving demonstrate its dissimilarity to any other known Caracol monument. Perhaps Stela 17 with its bulky glyphs provides the closest comparison that can be made to Stela 10. A CR on Stela 17 dates that stone to 10.1.0.0.0, which would seem to suggest that Stela 10 might be similarly placed into Baktun 10. The fact that Stela 10 is all glyphic and carved only on the front places it with other monuments of Baktun 10 (Uaxactun Stela 10 at 10.0.0.0.0, Stela 12 at 10.3.0.0.0; Jimbal Stela 2 at 10.3.0.0.0). If Caracol Stela 10 can be considered reliably placed in Baktun 10, the preferred reading of 1 Ahau for the day of the DD suggests that the monument can be placed at 10.3.0.0.0.

STELA 11/ALTAR 19

Location:	In northern part of Court A1. Butt of stela *in situ*. Altar is east of stela, misoriented	
	Stela 11	**Altar 19**
Associations:	Near but not with Altar 19	Near but not with Stela 11
Dedicatory Date:	9.18.10.0.0??	9.10.0.0.0?
Style Date:	9.16.0.0.0 ± 2 katuns	
Condition:	Fallen backward and broken into three large pieces and the butt. Upper tip missing. Surface well weathered	Heavily weathered, but carving well preserved
Photographs:	Fig. 35a, b	Fig. 43c
Drawings:	Fig. 12	Fig. 26b
		Satterthwaite 1954:Fig. 35
Other References:	Satterthwaite 1954	Satterthwaite 1954
	Riese 1980:8-9	Riese 1980:22
Carved Areas:	Class 1: F(M7)	Altar Class 1: T
Material:	Limestone	Limestone
Shape:	Roughly parallel sides; round pointed top	Flattened round
Dimensions:	L: ? HA: ca. 3.25 m.	W max: 1.81 m. Th: ca. 0.30 m.
	W: 1.15 m. Th: ca. 0.28-0.35 m.	W min.: 1.78 m.
	H above Floor: ca. 3.48 m.	

GENERAL REMARKS

Altar 19 was discovered at the end of the 1953 field season at Caracol. Exploration in the area of the newly found altar revealed a fallen stela resting supine beneath the roots of a tree. This monument, Stela 11, had broken from its butt (found *in situ*) and fallen backwards. It separated into three large pieces when it fell. Both stela and altar were in fairly good condition despite having their upper surfaces exposed to weathering. They were essentially complete, the only notable loss being that of the extreme tip of Stela 11. A 30 cm. deep excavation as wide as the stela failed to locate the missing fragment within 1.50 m. of the broken edge. Since the three fallen portions of Stela 11 were closely articulated at the time of discovery, it would be reasonable to assume that the tip should have been found close by its point of articulation if it was indeed part of the monument at this locus. The fact that it was not found raises a question about possible secondary erection of the stela at this locus. Despite this small doubt, it seems likely that Stela 11 was discovered at its point of primary erection and that the tip had been lost during carving or transport to that place.

As a stela-altar pair, Stela 11 and Altar 19 line up properly on a line parallel to the slightly northward tilted east-west axis of Court A1. However, the altar was rotated approximately 5° counterclockwise away from the axis and its general orientation was the reverse of what it should have been. That is, the bottom of the design of the altar was on the side closest to the stela. To an observer standing before the pair, the altar would have been viewed upside down.

Limited time and the circumstance of the stela being located under a tree prevented a thorough excavation of the monuments. They were dug only around the edges in an attempt to ascertain whether the reverse faces were carved. This examination indicated that neither stela nor altar was so inscribed. Time pressures also prevented excavation of the stela butt. At the completion of fieldwork, Stela 11 and Altar 19 were left *in situ* at Caracol.

STELA 11: GLYPH CLASSIFICATION AND CHRONOLOGICAL DECIPHERMENT

(Order of reading: Panel X, Main panel and Panel Y; left-right and downward
in double column; Panel Z, downward. Number of blocks: 6 + 12 + 8 + 2 = 28)

Panel X

xA1	ISIG (reconstructed)
xB1	9 baktuns (reconstructed)
xA2	17 or 19 katuns (main sign partially reconstructed; possibly an error in the coefficient—should be 18 to agree with CR at A1-B1)
xB2	0? tuns (main sign partially reconstructed; possibly an error in the coefficient—should be 10 to agree with CR at A1-B1)
xA3	0 uinals (partially reconstructed; main sign carries superfix)
xB3	0 kins (reconstructed)

Main Panel

A   9.18.10. 0. 0??

A1-B1	10 Ahau 8 Zac (main signs partially reconstructed; coefficients secure)
A2-A4	5 eroded glyph blocks; apparently non-calendrical
B4	Half-period glyph
A5	1 non-calendrical glyph, eroded
B5	T760? female parent indicator, eroded
A6-B6	Name phrase: unidentified female character followed by Caracol Glyph

Panel Y

yA1-yB3	6 eroded glyph blocks; no sure evidence of calendrical notation (may carry name phrase of a Caracol monarch)
yA4	Caracol Glyph
yB4	T502.25:502 *bacab* title (Schele n.d.)

Panel Z

zA1-zA2	2 eroded blocks, non-calendrical

STELA 11: SUMMARY OF CHRONOLOGY

xA1-B1	Date A	IS? 9.18.10.0. 0?? 10 Ahau 8 Zac
B4		Half-period glyph

ALTAR 19: SUMMARY OF CHRONOLOGY

A1	Date A	CR (9.10. 0. 0. 0) 1 Ahau 8 Kayab

STELA 11/ALTAR 19: COMMENT ON THE INSCRIPTION

DESCRIPTION OF THE CARVING; ARRANGEMENT OF GLYPH BLOCKS

A left-facing standing figure is depicted on the stela front holding a decorated bar at a diagonal running upward from right to left. There is a second very small figure in the lower left corner facing the main figure. Both figures stand on a block of decoration, probably a mask that fills the lower 65 cm. of the scene. These can be seen in both the drawing and the photograph. The figures, the basal decoration, and the four areas of glyphic text are all enclosed in a deeply cut frame. All the carving except one glyph panel is cut in shallow relief and set off from the background by very deep relief around the edges of the figures and glyph panels. A fourth glyph panel (Panel Z) is incised into the background.

To the left of the main figure above the smaller figure is located the main glyph panel. Panel X is above and to the left of the main figure, Panel Y at the lower right of the main figure, and the incised Panel Z is between the small figure and the legs of the main figure.

The drawing (Fig. 12) shows the minimum number of glyph blocks. There was another row of glyphs above the top of Panel X which have broken away and eroded. Taking this into account, the number of glyph blocks has been reconstructed as:

Panel X	6
Main panel	12
Panel Y	8
Panel Z	2
Total	28

DEDICATORY DATE

Inspection of the inscription of Stela 11 reveals an apparent CR date at A1-B1. At A1, a bar-dot coefficient of 10 is prefixed to a cartouche-enclosed main sign with three-part subfix. At B1, a main sign with three-quarter cartouche carries two superfixes, a subfix and a coefficient of 8. Block A1 can quite likely be identified as Ahau while the three-quarter frame of A1 indicates that it is either Chen, Yax, Zac or Ceh. Of these four month signs, only Chen and Zac bear double superfixes. Visual inspection indicates that the upper superfix almost certainly bears a circular element to the left. This would indicate Zac to be the most probable reading. In the attempt to place this CR into the LC, the assumption can be made that it marked a katun, half-katun or quarter-katun end. With this assumption, the only two LC dates between 8.4.0.0.0 and 10.4.0.0.0 fulfilling all the conditions are:

9.15. 5.0.0   10 Ahau 8 Chen
9.18.10.0.0   10 Ahau 8 Zac

Of these, the second is favored by visual inspection. The earlier date agrees slightly better with a style date of 9.16.0.0.0 2 katuns (Proskouriakoff, correspondence with Satterthwaite) although the style graph is broad enough to not rule heavily against a 9.18.0.0.0 date.

THE INITIAL SERIES

In Panel X are two destroyed glyph blocks followed by a glyph with a coefficient of 19 or possibly 17, succeeded by three partially effaced blocks. Blocks xA1 and xB1 would represent the positions of an ISIG and a baktun glyph if the text was opened with an IS date. At xA2 the subsequent glyph block is of a form that could have been a katun sign with large superfix and multi-part subfix. Although the upper part of the main sign at xB2 is destroyed, the lower part shows a three-part subfix which would agree with the possibility of a tun sign. The coefficient at xB2 appears from photographs to be a zero. Glyph blocks xA3 and xB3 also probably bear coefficients of zero. The main sign at xA3 has a three-quarter frame and three-part subfix, both of which agree with its reading as a uinal sign. However, the sign carries a superfix, which is uncommon for a uinal sign. The glyph at xB3 is too broken to read, but certainly shows nothing to contradict its reading as a kin sign.

If Panel X did record an IS of 9.19.0.0.0, then the CR following should be 9 Ahau 18 Mol. However, as discussed above, the CR following at A1-B1 bears the coefficients 10 and 8 for the day and month signs respectively, with the reading 10 Ahau 8 Zac favored. If the reading of 9.19.0.0.0 were to be accepted, this would present us with the highly unusual circumstances of an IS without a CR that is immediately followed by a CR of a date one-half katun earlier.

Unfortunately, after the CR at A1-B1 the text does not show further dates connected by SS's that might allow backtracking for confirmation of the IS reading. One final piece of evidence comes from block B4 which carries a half-period glyph. This might be interpreted as support for the reading of the date of this monument as 9.18.10.0.0. From this, it appears that there may well have been a Maya mistake in carving the IS.

DEDICATORY DATE OF ALTAR 19

Altar 19 is carved with a giant 1 Ahau glyph showing side-notching. By the katun-naming hypothesis, this monument could be expected to commemorate a date in a current or expiring Katun 1 Ahau. Possible katuns are 9.10.0.0.0 and 10.3.0.0.0, with the notched form of the Ahau strongly favoring the earlier date. By this, it appears that Altar 19 commemorates a katun that had ended over eight katuns prior to the DD of Stela 11. In combination with the misalignment of the altar in relation to the stela this leads to the conclusion that the altar at least was almost certainly moved here from its original locus of placement. Following a theory that the Giant Glyph Altars originally all paired with stelae, it can be suggested that Altar 19 originally was placed with Stela 7 in front of Structure A13.

STELA 12

Location:	In Court A1, in front of Platform A1. Butt *in situ*; body of stela fallen to level of court. Butt incorporated into Platform A1a
Associations:	Stela 20, 1.5 m. to the north
Dedicatory Date:	None
Style Date:	None
Condition:	Broken up and heavily eroded
Photographs:	None
Drawings:	None
Other References:	Satterthwaite 1954 Riese 1980:9
Carved Areas:	Plain
Material:	Limestone
Shape:	Uncertain
Dimensions:	L: ca. 2.50 m.　　HA: ? W: ca. 1.00 m.　　Th: ? H above Floor: ca. 1.90 m.

GENERAL REMARKS

Stela 12 was discovered lying on the Court A1 floor in front of Platform A1a. In this position it rested about 1.5 m. south of the fallen Stela 20. Work carried out by the University Museum and by A. H. Anderson in 1951, 1953 and 1954 revealed a pair of north-south oriented superimposed vaulted tombs (Burials 2, 3) lying within and beneath Platform A1a. Burial 3 was entirely below the level of the plaster floor of Court A1, while the chamber of Burial 2 extended from 0.63 m. below to 0.64 m. above that same level.

Excavation of Platform A1a turned up a vertically oriented fragment of the butt of Stela 12 about 35 cm. below the level of the Court A1 floor. The erection of Stela 12 thus in all probability preceded the construction of Platform A1a and the erection of Stela 20 upon that platform. Since the location of the fragment of the butt of Stela 12 was within the boundary of Platform A1a, the stela was apparently submerged for about 1.00 m. of its above-floor height within the platform. This would have left exposed only about 90 cm., less than half the face of Stela 12. The sequence of building and placement at this locus allows a theory that Stela 12 was erected before the time that the two apparently contemporaneous burials were deposited. Stela 20 was erected as Platform A1a was built with the burials within it, with the possible purpose of commemorating them.

Stela 12 is described in field notes as being entirely plain and devoid of carving. Erosion may have obliterated any carving that originally existed, since this stela was well worn on all surfaces. The appearance was in fact so unremarkable to the observers that the stela had not been photographed upon completion of fieldwork.

There are no monuments at Caracol that can be reliably identified as originally uncarved. Neither Stela 7 nor 12 presently shows any carving, but both are so damaged that any inscription could have been lost. Altars 8 and 9 are described as "plain." However, it now appears that neither stone actually represents a monument.

STELA 13

Location:	In front of Structure A4 on Platform A1, not axial. Facing south and a little west. Butt *in situ*
Associations:	Near Stela 14/Altar 7 and buried fragments of Stelae 15 and 16
Dedicatory Date:	9.4.0.0.0
Style Date:	Undetermined
Condition:	Broken into two main fragments; small area at upper left missing or not recognized; carved surfaces in poor to bad condition
Photographs:	Fig. 36a, b
Drawings:	Fig. 13a, b
Other References:	Satterthwaite 1954 Beetz 1980:8 Riese 1980:9
Carved Areas:	Class 2: FB (M1)
Material:	Limestone
Shape:	Basically parallel sides, rounded top. Front is flat with rounded edges; back rounded without edges
Dimensions:	L: ? HA: 1.95 m. W: 0.82 m. Th: 0.35 m. H above Floor: 2.15 m.

GENERAL REMARKS

The grouping of monuments on Platform A1 that includes Stelae 13, 14, 15, 16 and Altar 7 was discovered and excavated in 1950. The butts of Stelae 13 and 14 were found apparently *in situ,* while the other two stelae were found broken and somewhat scattered below Altar 7. Excavation around the monuments revealed at least two floors as well as evidence of two superimposed caches. The sequence of deposition at this spot seems to have begun with the laying of a cache on the limestone bedrock surface that rises in a bulge below Platform A1. The cache contained pottery that was typologically Early Classic by comparison with the Uaxactun ceramic sequence (Smith 1955). A floor, now largely broken up, immediately overlay this cache. The butts of Stelae 13 and 14 were set into this floor or possibly were abutted by it. A second floor abutting the two monuments may then have been laid.

A second cache of Late or possibly Terminal Classic date was then set in immediately over the earlier cache. Around this time, Stelae 15 and 16 were broken up, since fragments of them, along with the upper cache, were directly covered by Altar 7. Following the setting of Altar 7 in front of Stela 14, another floor was laid that abutted Altar 7 and Stelae 13 and 14. By the time of discovery, Altar 7 had sunk through this later floor so that only an edge of it projected above the floor level. Stela 14 had apparently leaned forward and then snapped off. The body of the stela lay face down while the butt was tilted forward about 45°. The tilting of the monument crushed the floors in front and thereby obscured the stratigraphic relationships.

Excavation data covered above indicate that Stela 14 and Altar 7, although in association, probably did not originally form a stela-altar pair. This conclusion is supported by a discrepancy in the DD's of the two monuments. The breakup of Stelae 15 and 16 at this site is sure evidence of monument removal and movement. The lower cache found in front of Stela 14 and underneath the same floor that is presumably contemporaneous with that monument suggests that an altar was originally placed before the stela to pair with it. The cache is not a likely commemorative for Stela 14 by itself, since otherwise sub-stela caches are unknown at Caracol. It seems a likely hypothesis that Stela 14, and by extension Stelae 13, 15 and 16, were originally paired at this locus by Giant Glyph Altars that were subsequently moved to new locations in antiquity.

The top half of Stela 13 broke off and fell

backward, face up. Despite the fact that the incised glyphs of the back were protected from erosion after the fall, they are quite worn. It therefore seems that the stela had stood exposed to the elements for some time before collapsing. The butt remained in position, nearly erect. Excavation failed to reveal traces of flooring immediately next to the stela butt. Thus stratigraphic correlation remains far from positive, although the height of the carving in relation to the elevation of the various floors can be used as a rough guide. A possibility yet exists that all four stelae were removed from dispersed loci of primary placement and assembled here by reason of their coherently sequent katun-marking dates. However, the assumption that the four monuments were originally erected in an east-west line will be followed throughout this text.

STELA 13: GLYPH CLASSIFICATION AND CHRONOLOGICAL DECIPHERMENT

(Order of reading: left-right and downward in double column.
Number of blocks: 64 (back, none identified on front))

Back Text

		A1-B2	ISIG (partly reconstructed)
		A3	5-10 baktuns (reconstructed as 9)
		B3	4 katuns (coefficient sure, sign reconstructed)
		A4-B4	0 tuns, 0 uinals (coefficients certain)
		A5	? kins (reconstructed as 0)
A	9. 4. 0. 0. 0	B5	13 (main sign eroded, reconstructed as Ahau)
		A6-B6	G9, F (reconstructed by position and partial remains)
		A7	MA 10-14?? (by position)
		B7	MN (by position and surviving traces; coefficient, if any, prefixed and now lost)
		A8	Glyph X (by position)
		B8	MT 10 (very clear)
		A9	16 or 18 ? (oval main sign with oval superfix; reconstructed as 18 Yax)
		B9	1 non-calendrical
SS1?		A10-A11	3 blocks (A10 completely lost, others nearly so)
B?		B11-A12	Badly eroded (month position at A12 shows possible coefficient of two damaged bars and some dots; oval main sign with oval superfix and subfix)
		B12-A13	2 badly eroded blocks
		B13-A16	6 non-calendrical (badly eroded)
		B16-D1	3 eroded blocks, coefficients possible
		C2	1 non-calendrical with prefixed and superfixed single bars (traces of main sign not right for a uinal sign)
		D2-C13	20 eroded blocks; probably all are non-calendrical. Traces allow the possibility of coefficients, but usually not in sequent blocks
SS2?		D13-D14	3 blocks, eroded (possible traces of an SS)
C		C15	10 Cib (damaged; Cib marking survives in part)
		D15	1 block, eroded (month, by position)
		C16-D16	2 non-calendrical, eroded

STELA 13: SUMMARY OF CHRONOLOGY

A1-A9	Date A	IS	9.4.0.0.0	13 Ahau, G9, F, MA?, MN?, MT 30, 18 Yax
A10-A11		SS1?		
B11-A12	Date B?		(?.?.?.?.?)	? ? 10-14? ?
D13-D14		SS2?		
C15-D15	Date C		(?.?.?.?.?)	10 Cib ? ?

COMMENT ON THE INSCRIPTION

RECONSTRUCTION OF THE INITIAL SERIES

By inspection, extreme limits for the baktun coefficient can be set at 5-10, since a single prefixed bar survives. Coefficients for the next three positions are clear, although the main signs are not. The katun coefficient is 4, and the tun and uinal coefficients are zero. The kin coefficient is totally lost. A position of 13 is marked by the SR and the day sign itself has a three-part suffix and complete cartouche. Using the preserved portions of the date gives us eight alternative positions for the IS:

Preserved portions

| 5-10. | 4.0.0. | ? | 13 | ? | ? | ? |

Reconstructed alternatives

5.	4.0.0. 9	13 Muluc	17 Chen	G9
6.	4.0.0.10	13 Oc	3 Pop	G1
7.	4.0.0.11	13 Chuen	14 Yax	G2
8.	4.0.0.12	13 Eb	0 Uo	G3
9.	4.0.0. 0	13 Ahau	18 Yax	G9
9.	4.0.0.13	13 Ben	11 Zac	G4
10.	4.0.0. 1	13 Imix	4 Uo	G1
10.	4.0.0.14	13 Ix	17 Uo	G5

The choice is between a katun end date at 9.4.0.0.0 and seven "odd" date alternatives. A VYr date at A9 is badly eroded but clearly bears a coefficient of 16 or higher. The single dot that survives is neatly centered. Symmetry thus requires that any dots reconstructed must be in flanking pairs. The VYr coefficient must either be 16 or 18 by this reasoning. This then favors the reading of 9.4.0.0.0 for the IS. At this same position, Glyphs G9 and F are needed. Traces in agreement with these are found in the proper positions at A6-B6.

LUNAR SERIES

Following the certain Glyph F at B6 are four blocks of a Lunar Series. The arbitrary moon age for the LC position 9.4.0.0.0 is 11.93 (using a base of 13.26), so the pattern of lunar notation should be D-C-X-A. Almost nothing survives in the Glyph D position at A7, although the coefficient of the postulated glyph should be about 12. Under some lightings of the monument, there do appear to be traces of two bars with perhaps some dots. At B7, existing remnants of the main sign agree with a reconstruction of Glyph C, and

there is space for a lost numerical prefix. The space for Glyph X at A8 is again nearly obliterated. Block B8 however preserves a clear Glyph A with coefficient of 10.

SECONDARY SERIES DATES B(?) AND C

There appears to be a coefficient of 10 or greater prefixed to what may be a symbolic month sign at A12. If this is indeed the case, then the SR of this postulated Date B has been lost from the preceding block B11. Similarly, there are no signs of an SS preceding the hypothetical date. Blocks A10 and B10 are thoroughly eroded and A11 bears no numerical prefix.

Block C2 bears a damaged main sign with single bars prefixed and superfixed. The sign does not appear to have been that of a uinal, which seems to rule out the possibility of its representing an SS.

At C15, the sign that seems to be the SR of Date C is a clear Cib with a coefficient of 10-13. Block D15, which presumably carried the VYr, is entirely lost. The three blocks D13-D14 seem to have marked an SS. D13 partly preserves a bar or bars in a prefix position. It may have recorded the uinals and kins of the SS, but all traces of the main sign are lost. C14 has a clear coefficient of 5 or higher and a main sign of a form compatible with a reading of a tun. D14 then shows the outline of a sign that agrees with a reading of katun. The coefficient, if any once existed, has been lost.

STYLISTIC DETAILS

An accurate style date using the Proskouriakoff system is not possible because of the bad condition of the carving. What few details are preserved indicate that the design was similar to that of Stela 16 which has a satisfactory style date of 9.4.0.0.0 ± 12 katuns.

On Stela 13, the figure stands on some sort of non-glyphic lower panel, presumably a mask. The legs are in left profile, separated slightly below knee level with the feet overlapping rather than being tandem as on Stela 16. Vertical parallel lines both in front of and behind the figure of Stela 13 are comparable to similar features on Stela 16. As on Stela 16, the torso on Stela 13 must be in front view with the arms cradling a horizontal ceremonial bar. Bits of the lower lines of the character's arms as well as the left-side serpent head of the bar attest to this reconstruction. The face and headdress on Stela 13 are in left profile like Stela 16, with the same characteristics in the grotesque faces on the headdresses.

In shape, Stela 13 is somewhat irregular, and Stela 16 is much more so. Both monuments were fashioned from blanks without removing natural depressions. Also, the two stelae both place the text on the back. Although Stelae 13 and 16 are found to share quite a number of features, Stelae 14 and 15 are quite different in layout and carving, although located at the time of discovery in close proximity to the others.

STELA 14/ALTAR 7

Location:	In Court A2 on Platform A1. Butt of stela *in situ*	
	Stela 14	**Altar 7**
Associations:	Near Stela 13, Altar 7, and buried fragments of Stelae 15 and 16	Near Stelae 13 and 14 and buried fragments of Stelae 15 and 16
Dedicatory Date:	9.6.0.0.0	9.11.0.0.0
Style Date:	Undetermined	
Condition:	Broken into two pieces. Weathered nearly smooth.	Well preserved
Photographs:	Fig. 35c Willcox 1954:Fig. 53	Fig. 41c Satterthwaite 1951:Pl. XV Satterthwaite 1954:Fig. 4 Willcox 1954:Figs. 52-55
Drawings:	Fig. 14a	Fig. 21c
Other References:	Satterthwaite 1951, 1954 Willcox 1954 Riese 1980:10	Satterthwaite 1951, 1954 Willcox 1954 Riese 1980:17
Carved Areas:	Class 1: F (M7)	Altar Class 1: T
Material:	Limestone	Limestone
Shape:	Roughly parallel sides tapering from top to bottom. Top rounded square; bottom rounded point.	Round; rectangular cross section
Dimensions:	L: 3.45 m. HA: 2.45 m. W: 0.80 m. Th: 0.27 m. H above Floor: 2.55 m.	Max. W: 1.38 m. Th: 0.28 m. Min. W: 1.28 m.

GENERAL REMARKS

Stela 14 and Altar 7 were discovered in 1950 in close spatial association with Stelae 13, 15 and 16, as is discussed in the "General Remarks" section of Stela 13. The top half of Stela 14 lay face down on the ground while the butt remained *in situ* tilted forward (south) at a 45° angle. Excavation revealed Altar 7 beneath and a little to the east of the fallen upper section of Stela 14. As earlier noted there exists a sequence of floors and caches that suggests that Altar 7 was moved to the locus of discovery from its original site of placement. A disturbed lower cache below Altar 7 apparently represents the remains of a sub-altar cache for a now removed altar that originally paired with Stela 14. Remains from this lower cache are typologically Early Classic, which is in general agreement with the DD of the stela. Immediately below Altar 7 another cache bearing Late Classic ceramic material was found. This upper cache apparently dedicated the placement of Altar 7 in a secondary setting before Stela 14.

Stela 14 was so weathered that it was originally thought to be uncarved. Night photography revealed that it was actually carved with fine incision. Careful highlighting and latex casts of the carvings then allowed drawings to be made. Altar 7 was, on the other hand, well preserved and was shipped to Philadelphia while the stela was left at Caracol.

STELA 14: GLYPH CLASSIFICATION AND CHRONOLOGICAL DECIPHERMENT

(Order of reading: left-right and downward in three double columns.
Number of blocks: 48)

Main Text

		A1-B2	ISIG with month indicator Chen
		B3-A5	9 baktuns, 6 katuns, 0 tuns, 0 uinals, 0 kins; all clear head-variants of period glyphs
A	9. 6. 0. 0. 0	B5	7-9 Ahau (9 reconstructed from IS)
		A6-B6	Partially eroded glyphs (MA and MN of an LS?)
		A7	Coefficient of 3 attached to an unusual glyph read as Uayeb
		B7-D7	13 non-calendrical glyphs
		C8	Name of Lord Water
		D8-C9	2 non-calendrical glyphs
SS1	−16.18	D9-E1	10-19 kins (shell or animal head variant of kin sign with *ak* postfix; two bars with effaced dots by inspection—third bar reconstructed by calculation), clear 16 uinals at E1
B	(9. 5.19. 1. 2)	F1-E2	9 Ik 5 Uo or Chen (Ik reconstructed; VYr reconstructed as 5 Uo)
		F2-F7	9-11 non-calendrical glyphs
		E8	Name of Lord Water
		F8-F9	3 non-calendrical glyphs

Panel Z

xA1-zA3	3 non-calendrical glyphs

STELA 14: SUMMARY OF CHRONOLOGY

A1-A7	Date A	IS	9. 6. 0. 0. 0	9 Ahau 3 Uayeb
D9-E1		SS1	−16.18	
F1-E2	Date B		(9. 5.19. 1. 2)	9 Ik 5 Uo

ALTAR 7: SUMMARY OF CHRONOLOGY

A1	Date A	CR	(9.11. 0. 0. 0)	12 Ahau (8 Ceh)

COMMENT ON THE INSCRIPTION

STELA 14: DEPARTURES FROM SYMMETRY; GLYPH BLOCK COUNT

In reconstructing the appearance of Stela 14, ground level was arbitrarily set at 0.10 m. below the bases of blocks B9 and D9 to make this irregular row of glyphs as horizontal as possible. As a result, the long axis leans noticeably to the right of vertical at least as far up as the level of the face of the principal figure. The major character is thus well to the right of the true central position. Various lines of carving deviate from the horizontal according to this orientation. For example, the small T-shaped panel and glyph block rows 1-3 diverge from the horizontal in different directions. The layout of blocks for the text is so irregular as to raise some doubt whether D7-E7 ever existed. It is possible that those blocks were squeezed out and blocks D6-E6 were made somewhat taller. The T-shaped panel inserted into the top of the glyph-bearing portion of carving reduces the number of glyph blocks from an expected fifty-four to forty-eight. Three glyph blocks in the lesser panel then raise the total number of glyph blocks to fifty-one. The number of glyphs as opposed to glyph blocks is reduced to forty-eight by the oversize ISIG.

STELA 14: PARTIAL RECONSTRUCTION OF DATES A AND B

The baktun coefficient of Date A displays a bar and a single preserved dot at the upper extreme of the block. Symmetry suggests that the number can be reconstructed as either 7 or 9. The katun coefficient is a clear 6, and the tun, uinal and kin coefficients are all zero. Details of the main sign of the SR are lost, but it should be

Ahau for a katun end. The coefficient of the reconstructed Ahau is partly lost, but may be read as 7, 8 or 9. Taking into account the well preserved katun coefficient and the possibilities for the baktun coefficient, two alternatives offer themselves:

7.6.0.0.0   11 Ahau 8 Cumku
9.6.0.0.0   9 Ahau 3 Uayeb

Neither of these agrees with an ISIG variable of Chen. A check of all katuns ending on 7, 8 or 9 Ahau between 7.0.0.0.0 and 9.19.0.0.0 reveals that there are no katun ends in that span that fall in the month Chen. It seems to be far simpler to suggest a Maya mistake in carving the month variable than to suggest that they erred in the carving of one or more coefficients. On this basis, the reading of 9.6.0.0.0 9 Ahau is preferred.

Clear confirmation of the LC reading might be expected to result from a search for the VYr record. Following immediately after the SR are a pair of glyphs that might (though it is dubious) record Glyphs D and C of the LS (A6-B6). Glyphs X, B and A are often suppressed in early texts. Since the VYr date of an IS regularly follows an LS, it might be suspected that the clear coefficient 3 in A7 is that belonging to the re-

quired month Uayeb. A serious objection is that the complex glyph is not a previously known head-variant for Uayeb, but a symbolic form differing radically from known ones. However, it is reasonable to suggest that newly discovered dates in Uayeb might show nonstandardization since Uayeb is not an ordinary month. It should be mentioned that this same date 9 Ahau 3 Uayeb at 9.6.0.0.0 is undoubtably mentioned later on Stela 6. There also the 9 Ahau is followed by a glyph with coefficient 3, but the symbolic glyph is different from that found on Stela 14. Indeed, it seems likely that the glyph on Stela 6 is something other than a month sign.

Other endorsement of the IS reading might be derived from an SS number leading to another date. Bar-and-dot numbers appear appended to glyphs at C6 and D7. However, neither of these occurences seems to be that of calendrical glyphs. Another set of coefficients is found with blocks D9-E1. The main sign of a unial term is clear at E1 with a coefficient of 16. Preceding that is a partly damaged glyph with two bars prefixed. The SS is clearly of two terms only and is followed by a CR date at E2-F1. A coefficient of 9 is borne by the SR and the VYr is either 5 Uo or 5 Chen. There are thus only four possibilities to consider, if we remember that the SS must be less than a tun:

	5 Uo				**5 Chen**		
Ia	9.5.19. 1. 2	9 Ik	5 Uo	IIa	9.5.19. 8. 2	6 Ik	5 Chen
	16.18				9.18		
IS	9.6. 0. 0. 0	9 Ahau	3 Uayeb	IS	9.6. 0. 0. 0	9 Ahau	3 Uayeb
	1. 7				8. 7		
Ib	9.6. 0. 1. 7	10 Manik	5 Uo	IIb	9.6. 0. 8. 7	7 Manik	5 Chen

Alternative Ia is the clear preference, because only this requires the clear 16 uinals of the SS and reaches the clear day coefficient 9. The only difficulty is with the kins of the SS at D9. By inspection, one would read 10-14 kins, with two bars and space for dots, rather than the desired 15-19 with three bars. The condition of the stone is such that erosion may have removed sure evidence of a third bar on the right, partly overlapped by the special kin sign. If it was a second Maya mistake, it is a relatively easy error involving units.

The kin sign is somewhat irregular in outline and has lost all interior details. It has the *ak*

postfix which is found with the shell and animal head kin sign variants. There is no reason to doubt that this occurrence was one or the other.

STELA 14: POSSIBLE LUNAR SERIES

Caracol Stela 16 carries a reduced LS of the pattern D-C-A. Stela 14 has no Glyph A but may show D and C at A6-B6. The glyph at A6 seems to be a grotesque head with lost prefix and cannot be identified as a known form of Glyph D. The next glyph, at B6, is a more likely Glyph C. The expected hand sign is clear. However, at upper right, the remains do not seem to be those of the required moon sign. B6 might actually be best read as an end-haab glyph. Further down, at B7, is a clear record of what would be Glyph D without coefficient had it appeared before a recognizable form of Glyph C.

STELA 14: STYLISTIC DETAILS

The principal figure sits on a belly-down victim who in turn rests on a grotesque face-on mask. The latter is partly hidden behind a small-scale centrally placed seated figure and flanked by profile figures on either side. The main character holds a ceremonial bar in horizontal position. These features had already appeared with and below a standing figure on Stela 16 at 9.5.0.0.0. 9.6.0.0.0 is thus not too early for them to appear on Stela 14. It is possible to question whether or not the zero signs of Stela 14 lacked the protruding ends of crossed bands. They are absent on Stela 16 at 9.5.0.0.0, present on Stela 1 at 9.8.0.0.0 and on Stela 3 considerably later. Therefore one might expect to find either at the 9.6.0.0.0 of Stela 14.

ALTAR 7: DEDICATORY DATE

For Stela 14, 9.6.0.0.0 may be taken as a sure IS and, by normal rules, as the DD. On the theory that the Giant Glyph Altars name the current or ending katun, the accompanying Altar 7 should read 9 Ahau if it was indeed intended to pair with the stela. The altar was originally read as 7 Ahau, but 12 Ahau is certainly the correct reading (Satterthwaite 1951:37; 1954:32). The altar presumably refers to the katun of 9.11.0.0.0 12 Ahau, 5 katuns later than the DD for Stela 14.

It must be concluded (given the supposed function of the Giant Glyph Altars) that either the stela or the altar has been moved from its original location. The presence of two caches on different levels below the altar seems to be good evidence that it was the altar which was moved. Confirming evidence that the stela was not moved is its position beside Stela 13 with the DD of 9.4.0.0.0, both apparently undisturbed except by natural causes.

STELA 15

Location:	In Court A2 on Platform A1; in fragments under Altar 7
Associations:	Stelae 13, 14, 16 and Altar 7
Dedicatory Date:	9.7.0.0.0??
Style Date:	Undetermined
Condition:	Incomplete; badly broken and fragmented; surface preservation is good where carving was not destroyed by breakage
Photographs:	Fig. 36c Satterthwaite 1951:Pl. XIV Satterthwaite 1954:Figs. 2-3
Drawings:	Fig. 14b
Other References:	Satterthwaite 1951, 1954 Willcox 1954 Riese 1980:10-11
Carved Areas:	Class 1: F (M7)
Material:	Slate
Shape:	Sides parallel; top probably rounded; cross section, where preserved, shows bulging front and flat back
Dimensions:	L: ca. 3.10 m. HA: 1.85 m. W. 0.62 m. Th: 0.18 m. H above Floor: ?

GENERAL REMARKS

The fragments of this slate stela form one of the units of a grouping of monuments which also includes the limestone Stelae 13, 14, 16 and the secondarily positioned Altar 7. Stela 15 differs from the others in other ways but shares with Stela 16 the historical fact that it was broken up in ancient times. This destruction occurred at or before the time of placement of Altar 7 at its locus of discovery. The slate of Stela 15 is friable, and the breaking-up process reduced the monument (though not the limestone Stela 16) to many large to medium-sized fragments, and uncounted numbers of small to tiny ones. It can thus be concluded that the original functioning grouping of monuments consisted of Stelae 13, 14, 15 and 16, perhaps in a row and possibly each with an accompanying Giant Glyph Altar (see Stela 13, "General Remarks"). The postulated altars were removed and Stelae 15 and 16 broken up sometime before the placement of Altar 7. Fragments of those two stelae were found beneath the altar.

Many fragments of stone were fitted together to allow the reconstruction shown in the drawing of Stela 15. The exact number of glyph rows could not be determined. Our drawing follows the assumption that the lowest certain row was the original last row. Possibly there was another row or two with correspondingly increased height. The question could not be settled by the fitting of a large fragment that was presumably part of the plain butt.

After fitting all the fragments possible, there remained a residue of fifteen unfitted carved flakes, four of which were definitely glyphic. These fragments have not been illustrated, since nothing of importance can be identified, except that one shows part of a *u*-bracket and a double-lined glyph border.

Yet another of the unfitted carved fragments seems to depict the spotted tail of a jaguar. Presumably it comes from the scene above the inscription. There is the theoretical possibility that the fragment came to the locus by chance, and represents another example of presumably very late scattering of carved slate fragments at the site.

STELA 15: GLYPH CLASSIFICATION AND CHRONOLOGICAL DECIPHERMENT

(Order of reading main text: left-right and downward by rows across all six columns.
Reconstructed minimum number of blocks: 84+4=88)

Main Text

		A1	ISIG, variable unreadable
		B1	9 baktuns (partially reconstructed)
		C1	2, 3 or 4 katuns (4 katuns reconstructed)
		D1	6 or 16 tuns (6 reconstructed; main sign partly reconstructed)
		E1	7, 8, 12 or 13 main sign lost (13 uinals reconstructed)
		F1	3 kins (main sign damaged and reconstructed)
A	9. 4.16.13. 3	A2	4 Akbal (coefficient reconstructed by symmetry; main sign partially effaced but reconstruction certain)
		B2-A3a	Lunar Series; G2, MA 8, MN 1, X2, B?, MT? (all these glyph blocks are damaged by flaking and erosion)
		A3b	6 or 16 (coefficient is partly lost; the main sign is clear)
		B3-F4	11 blocks completely lost or damaged; no surviving evidence of calendrical glyphs
SS1??		A5-C5	3 blocks completely lost (SS postulated by position)
B?	(?. ?. ?. ?. ?)	D5a	Day sign cartouche with numerical superfix
		D5b	Completely lost (month sign position reconstructed)
		E5-C10	29 blocks completely lost or damaged; no surviving evidence of calendrical glyphs
SS2		D10	9 (kins), 7-8 uinals
		E10-B11a	3½ blocks, completely lost
C?	(?. ?. ?. ?. ?)	B11b	3-4 superfixed to day sign cartouche
		C11a	Month position reconstructed; complete cartouche without pedestal
		C11b	Oval sign with subfix and a probable numerical superfix above 15
		D11a-B13	11 blocks completely lost or damaged; no surviving evidence of calendrical glyphs
		C13	Tikal EG
		D13-F14	9 blocks completely lost or damaged; no surviving evidence of calendrical glyphs

Panel Z

zA1-zA4	4 blocks, completely lost

STELA 15: SUMMARY OF CHRONOLOGY

A1-A3b	Date A	IS	9. 4.16.13. 3	4 Akbal G2, MA 8, MN 1, X2, B?, MT?, 16 Pop
A5-C5		SS1??		
D5a	Date B?			
D10		SS2	7-8. 9	
B11b-C11a	Date C?			

COMMENT ON THE INSCRIPTION

THE INITIAL AND LUNAR SERIES

The key to understanding the chronology of Stela 15 is the order of reading across all six columns. This is the order used on Stela 21 (four columns), Stela 6 (three columns) and probably Stela 5 (four columns?). Reading across rows is thus not at all unusual at Caracol.

Although there is too much damage to read the IS date purely by inspection, its existence is guaranteed by the definite ISIG at the beginning of the text. An opening LS is similarly evidenced by the appearance of Glyphs D and C in the expected positions (C2, D2). The variable element of the ISIG is largely effaced but may be the jaguar head as the patron of the month Pop.

At B1, the left half of a coefficient 9 is clear,

above a clear cauac sign. The latter is overlapped by an oval sign on the right which bears traces of a curving line of dots on the interior, as is expected for a second cauac sign. The left margin of the third dot of the coefficient is also visible. A reconstruction of a double cauac below a coefficient of 9 is considered certain.

The space of the expected katun sign at C1 is badly eroded. Remains of a damaged large lower dot of a prefixed coefficient are practically certain, with no room for a bar. Only the outline of the main sign survives, but it is correct for a symbolic katun. The block may be safely read as 2, 3 or 4 katuns.

A sure single dot flanked by fillers above a bar or bars is included in the superfixed coefficient of D1. Two parallel incised lines seem to define three bars. However, these lines do not reach the right end and appear to have been joined by a short vertical line. This coefficient might be reconstructed as 16 (three bars) or 6 (one decorated bar). The outline of the glyph is clearly that of a tun sign by comparison with the tun element of the ISIG.

At E1, the presumed uinal position includes a prefixed coefficient with upper and lower dots. The area between them suggests a scaled-off third dot, although a lost filler is possible. There is a bar in relief, with traces of an incised dividing line. Because one of these traces is at the top, the preferred reading is of two bars. It is possible that this upper trace is accidental, so the reading of the coefficient is 7, 8, 12 or 13. The interior of the main sign itself is lost, and no evidence for or against a reading as uinals can be found.

A clear 3 is the coefficient of the kin position (F1). The glyph itself is badly damaged, but does preserve a complete cartouche. Both the day sign and coefficient follow at A2 and are relatively clear. Two preserved upper dots are placed so that two lower ones must be restored for symmetry. The day sign has the appropriate cartouche and carries definite traces of interior Akbal markings. These include part of the horizontal scalloped dividing line and attached curved lines above.

Glyph G of the LS may be reconstructed at B2 by position between the SR and Glyph D. The block is in very bad condition, but evidently has no coefficient. This excludes G1, G4 and G5. G2 and G3 are favored because they may include a curved line of dots such as is preserved in the upper left corner of our Glyph G. The outline of what appears to be an unusual form of Glyph D (comparable to one on Copan Stela A) accompanies a coefficient that may be reconstructed as 8 at C3. Outlines of the component glyphs of block D3 confirm that the sign was Glyph C. No clear coefficient survives, although the possible remains of a bar exist at the left. The whole may be safely read as 1C or 5C. Position and traces of what may be the serpent head of X2 indicate that E3 marked Glyph X. Glyph X2 may appear with 1C, and its identification seems firm. Position after Glyph X leads us to expect Glyph B at F2. Details are hard to make out, but there seems to be no correspondence to the usual depictions of Glyph B. Presumably it is a rare variant. Glyph A is then expected at A3a by position after Glyph X and B and before the certain VYr. However the left half of the block is thoroughly destroyed and can give no evidence either way.

The main sign at A3b is certainly that of Pop. The mat element is clear beside a circular element to the right which is doubtless a Kan cross. The superfixed coefficient appears to consist of three bars and one, two or three dots. Since the SR day is surely Akbal, this coefficient must have a central dot with flanking fillers. The ends of the bars are eroded, so the alternative possibilities of 6 and 16 must be allowed for on the chance that there is actually a single large decorated bar.

Alternatives for five of the fourteen elements of the IS-LS have been allowed. To narrow down the possible readings, all Baktun 9 LC positions for the two CR positions have been tabulated:

Possible Initial Series Positions

	Katun 2,3,4	Tun 6,16	Uinal 7,8,12,13	Glyph G2,G3	Arbitrary Moon Age and Deviation
I: 4 Akbal 16 Pop					
1 9. 2. 4. 0. 3	*	0	0	0	
2 9. 4.16.13. 3	*	*	*	*(G2)	10.69 (2.69)
3 9. 7. 9. 8. 3	0	0	*	0	
4 9.10. 2. 3. 3	0	0	0	0	
5 9.12.14.16. 3	0	0	0	0	
6 9.15. 7.11. 3	0	0	0	0	
7 9.18. 0. 6. 3	0	0	0	0	
II: 4 Akbal 6 Pop					
1 9. 0. 1. 7. 3	0	0	*	0	
2 9. 2.14. 2. 3	*	0	0	0	
3 9. 5. 6.15. 3	0	*	0	0	18.43 (10.53)
4 9. 7.19.10. 0	0	0	0	0	
5 9.10.12. 5. 3	0	0	0	0	
6 9.13. 5. 0. 3	0	0	0	*(G3)	23.45 (15.45)
7 9.15.17.13. 3	0	0	*	*(G2)	15.25 (7.56)
8 9.18.10. 8. 3	0	0	*	0	

Key: (*) and (0) indicate that the element in question is respectively within or outside of the limits specified. Moon age deviations above 4.00 are outside Teeple's limits

The distribution of agreement and non-agreement symbols shows at a glance that only Alternative I-2 at 9.4.16.13.3 can be correct. This is confirmed by selected arbitrary moon ages and deviations added at the right. At Alternative I-2 with tun coefficient 16 we are within Teeple's limits, but far outside them at Alternative II-3. The apparent panel decoration of a single bar must be attributed to freak damage or, conceivably, to a Maya mistake. The moon evidence also rules out Alternatives II-6 and II-7, within the Glyph G limits.

The 9.4.16.13.3 reading agrees with all five sets of within limits controls. On the other hand, only one of the other theoretical possibilities agrees with as many as two of these controls. Thus it is evident that no question mark is required for the I-2 reading (other than single ones for the last two glyphs of the LS).

LUNAR SERIES PATTERN

The pattern of the LS as reconstructed may be compared with those of the two others in the Plaza A2 monuments grouping which seem clear and firmly dated:

Stela 13: E/D - C - X? - - - - - - - A   (DD 9.4.0.0.0)
Stela 16: E/D - C - - - - - - - - - - A   (DD 9.5.0.0.0)
Stela 15: E/D - C - X - - - - - B - A?

If the assumption that Stela 15 dates to 9.7.0.0.0 is correct, then the stela gives one of the earliest appearances of Glyph B. There is only one other supposed appearance before 9.8.0.0.0. This occurs at 9.7.0.0.0 on Stela 0 of Pusilha (Satterthwaite 1958:130). This situation could also be interpreted in two other ways: 1) Glyphs B and A were not in fact recorded on Caracol Stela 15, which would give the unexpected pattern E/D - C - X; or, 2) the DD of Stela 15 was actually considerably later than the IS date.

SECONDARY SERIES DATES

It has been inferred that Stelae 13, 14, 15 and 16 stood together as an original grouping of monuments. Stela 15 is set apart from the other three stelae by a number of characteristics, despite the fact that its IS falls between those of Stelae 13 (9.4.0.0.0) and 16 (9.5.0.0.0). The quantity of differences suggests that Stelae 15 was carved and erected later than the other three stelae of the set.

Stela 15 is a slate monument. The other slate stelae at Caracol were noticeably larger and fell into Late Classic times (manifested by an IS of 9.13.10.0.0 on Stela 21 and by out-turned feet on a fragment of Stela 4). Three stelae of the grouping of monuments in Court A2 open with an IS/LS, but only on Stela 15 is it possible that

Glyph B was recorded. This is another feature not expected in Early Classic times. Only on this one of the three IS/LS bearing monuments is the ISIG in a single block. The order of reading by complete rows is a striking difference in monument style that ties it with the later Stelae 5, 6 and 21. Finally, the IS is an "odd" date, unlike the other three stelae. This fact indicates that the DD was probably not earlier than the IS and probably was at a later tun end LC position. The full list of differences causes one to suspect that the DD may have been a katun or more after the 9.6.0.0.0 of Stela 14.

SS leading forward from the IS to a later and dedicatory tun end date would agree with the apparent pattern locally represented on the right side of Stela 6. This pattern cannot be excluded from a monument with as much missing text as Stela 15. On the other hand, there are positive surviving hints that Stela 15 was not a one-date monument. The left half of D5 is occupied by a glyph with complete cartouche, "pedestal" suffix and a superfix which may be the remains of numerical dots or of a damaged bar. This suggests an SR day sign. The missing right half of the glyph block may have given the month position of a complete CR. An SS could have preceded in the three completely eroded blocks A5-C5. Allowing for block division, it could have contained a katun term and an SSIG, though no coefficients are visible.

At D10 an oval sign is probably the uinal sign of an SS, since it has a clear coefficient 9 in the prefix position, and a fairly clear coefficient of 7 or 8 as superfix. The SSIG may be lost or absent from the preceding block C10. The SS number may have lost tun and katun terms in the lost right portion of Row 10. At B11b there seems to be the right portion of a day sign cartouche with "pedestal" and superfixed coefficient 3 or 4. The month position may have appeared next, at C11a, where a complete cartouche lacks a suffix. There is considerable lost space above, which might have contained a high coefficient, or a superfix below a low coefficient. Under this interpretation one is puzzled by the next block, where the outline might be that of a month sign, and the superfix seems to have involved bars, with room for lost dots.

These probable remains of chronological glyphs are so distributed that each date was followed by substantial numbers of non-calendrical hieroglyphs. Both the left and right portions of the last known row are lost, so a fourth date at or near the close is not excluded.

DEDICATORY DATE

Reasons have been given for guessing that Stela 15 had a DD later than its IS and probably later than the dedicatory 9.6.0.0.0 of Stela 14. The latter may be taken as an early limit. The actual DD probably was later than 9.6.0.0.0 since it is unlikely that such different monuments as Stelae 14 and 15 would be erected in the same group at the same time.

There are three imprecise approaches to guessing at a late limit for the DD of Stela 15. First, stratigraphy shows that this stela was broken up by the time of placement of Altar 7, for which the DD was probably 9.11.0.0.0. Second, the pose of the surviving feet and legs of the small human figure is similar to those of Stelae 13 and 16, with profile feet pointed in one direction. The most specific correspondence is to Stela 13, at 9.4.0.0.0. On Stela 13 the feet are overlapping and not in tandem as on Stela 16 at 9.5.0.0.0. These are Early Classic traits, belonging in the pre-hiatus Early Classic period of Prouskouriakoff's 1950 analysis. The overlapping profile feet might have persisted locally into her area-wide hiatus period continuing to 9.8.0.0.0, but probably not beyond it. Third, on multi-date monuments, of which Stela 15 is surely an example, the total spread of dates may be very great, but generally within about three katuns. Applying such a yardstick here drops the late limit for the DD to 9.7.0.0.0 if katun-marking is favored. Glyph style might seem to contradict this early a date. However, loss of most incised detail in the predominantly relief glyphs and the exclusively glyphic use of incision on various dated stelae make direct local comparisons difficult.

The DD of Stela 15 may well have been recorded, but if so it cannot be reconstructed on the basis of surviving epigraphy. This is unfortunate in view of its various unusual epigraphic features. However, we may guess with assurance that a tun end DD, recorded or implied, fell between 9.6.0.0.0 and 9.10.0.0.0 as extreme and probably excessive limits. The late limit is especially dubious since it presupposes the break-up of the stela less than a katun after it was erected, at which time the theory of obsolescence could hardly be invoked.

Within these extreme limits for Stela 15, Katuns 9.5.0.0.0, 9.6.0.0.0, 9.8.0.0.0 and 9.9.0.0.0 were marked by Stelae 16, 14, 1 and 5. This leaves 9.7.0.0.0 as a gap in the katun-marking pattern as known. Such a gap may have been filled by Stela 15, with four katuns as a minimum period of use before it became obsolete and was leveled to make way for the re-positioned Altar 7. The four stelae of the original Court A2 grouping would also mark sequent katuns. It appears that this local pattern offers the best possibility for guessing at a DD, although it is certainly far from proven.

STELA 16

Location:	In Court A2 on Platform A1
Associations:	Stelae 13, 14, 15 and Altar 7
Dedicatory Date:	9.5.0.0.0
Style Date:	9.4.0.0.0
Condition:	Broken and somewhat eroded; preservation of carving varies from good to excellent; butt is missing
Photographs:	Fig. 37a, b Satterthwaite 1954:Figs. 2, 12, 13, 14, 17 Beetz 1980:Figs. 6, 10
Drawings:	Fig. 15a, b Satterthwaite 1954:Fig. 16 Riese 1980:Fig. 1
Other References:	Satterthwaite 1954 Beetz 1980:8 Riese 1980:11
Carved Areas:	Class 2: FB (M1)
Material:	Limestone
Shape:	Irregular; tapers almost to a point at the top, and tapers somewhat toward the bottom
Dimensions:	L: ? HA: 2.10 m. W: ca. 0.74 m. Th: 0.30 m. H above Floor: ca. 2.20 m.

GENERAL REMARKS

Stela 16, now located in the University Museum in Philadelphia, was discovered during excavation supervised by A. H. Anderson in 1951. Survey by Anderson and Satterthwaite at this locus in 1950 had missed Stela 16 while finding Stelae 13, 14, 15 and Altar 7. Excavation revealed that Stela 16 was broken into two large fragments which lay amongst the fragments of Stela 15 below the plaster floor upon which Altar 7 rested (see Stela 13, "General Remarks"). This circumstance suggests that Stela 16 was toppled, quite probably by intentional human action, during the preparation of the locus for the installation of the secondarily placed Altar 7. Excavation failed to locate the butt of the stela.

The piece of stone used for Stela 16 is very irregular in outline. Although smooth-surfaced, the back face is also irregular in profile. Minimal preparation of the stone after quarrying is suggested by the nature of the back and sides. In contrast, the front face presents a straight profile and cross section with a smooth surface. The text on the back is entirely inscribed, an unusual technique for so early a monument. Two small areas of incised glyphic inscription also appear on the front. On both faces the carving has held up very well against the action of erosion, although the short hieroglyphic inscriptions on the front have virtually disappeared.

STELA 16: GLYPH CLASSIFICATION AND CHRONOLOGICAL DECIPHERMENT

(Order of reading: Main text [back], left-right and downward in double column for six blocks after ISIG, broadening to left-right and downward in two double columns. Number of blocks: 76 + 3 + 3 = 82)

Main Text

A1-B1	ISIG, variable element unclear but not contradictory to a head variant for month Zec
A2	9 baktuns (head-variant period glyph partially reconstructed by position)

	B2	5 katuns (head-variant period glyph partially reconstructed by position)
	A3	0 tuns (head-variant period glyph partially reconstructed by position)
	B3	0 uinals (head-variant period glyph very clear)
	A4	0 kins (head-variant period glyph clear)
	B4	1 non-calendrical glyph
A 9. 5. 0. 0. 0.	A5	11 Ahau (cartouche of main sign preserved, interior detail lost)
	B5-B7	G9, F, MA 7, MN 5, MT 9 (all main signs clear; all coefficients clear except for the 9 of Glyph A, which can be reconstructed by symmetry from the preserved left portion)
	A8	18 Zec? (reconstructed by position; the block is almost entirely lost)
	B8-A17	18 non-calendrical glyphs
	B17	Name of Lord Jaguar
	A18	1 non-calendrical glyph
	B18	T670 female parent indicator
	A19-D19	32 non-calendrical glyphs (many blocks lost through breakage and erosion)

Panel Y

yA1-yA2	3 blocks, largely eroded

Panel Z

zA1-zA4	3 blocks, completely lost

STELA 16: SUMMARY OF CHRONOLOGY

A1-A8	Date A	IS	9.5.0.0.0	11 Ahau G9, F, MA 7, MN 5, MT 9, 18 Zec

COMMENT ON THE INSCRIPTION

DEDICATORY DATE

Stela 16 opens with a clear IS and LS. Very few elements are lost or too severely damaged to reconstruct. The IS at A2-A4 records the date 9.5.0.0.0 using head-variants of the period glyphs with bar-dot coefficients. At A5, a "notched" sign within a cartouche bears the coefficient 11. This may be safely assumed to be 11 Ahau, part of the CR position accompanying the IS. The second part of the CR (the VYr) is largely missing, but is probably represented at A8 by the bottom left corner of a glyph.

An LS appears between the two halves of the CR. Glyphs G9 and F at B5-A6 are normal in appearance and position. At B6-A7, moon age 7 and moon number 5 are recorded. The moon age of 7 is well within Teeple's limits, showing a variance of +.53259. The moon number 5 is within the uniformity system. Glyph A is largely preserved at B7 along with the left end of its subfixed coefficient. Enough of a remnant is preserved to show a dot over the extreme end of a bar, suggesting that the coefficient of Glyph A was 9 in this instance.

Nothing to suggest an alternative DD is shown in the rest of the preserved text on Stela 16. Bar-dot coefficients appear at B9?, A10, B11, B13, B15 and C10, but none in a context allowing reconstruction of an SS or CR. The major difficulty in checking the possibility of other dates is the total lack of CR notation other than that accompanying the IS. Curiously, a "completion of haab" glyph (Thompson 1950:Fig. 32) appears at B16. Its association with neighboring glyphs is problematical. Similarly, its association with the tun end of the IS is questionable since it is seventeen blocks distant.

STELA 17/ALTAR 10

Location: To the southeast of Group B in an area of unmapped low mounds.
Associations: Stela 17 facing Altar 10 at E 15°N, 1.70 m. distant.

	Stela 17	**Altar 10**
Dedicatory Date:	10.1.0.0.0	10.1.0.0.0?
Style Date:	Undetermined	
Condition:	Broken and incomplete. The inscription is lightly eroded but largely preserved. The scene below is more heavily eroded	Broken and badly eroded except in certain restricted areas
Photographs:	Fig. 38a Satterthwaite 1954:Figs. 1, 19	Fig. 41d Satterthwaite 1954:Figs. 1, 14
Drawings:	Fig. 16a Riese 1980:Fig. 2.	Fig. 22
Other References:	Satterthwaite 1954 Willcox 1954 Riese 1980:11-12	Satterthwaite 1954 Willcox 1954 Riese 1980:18
Carved Areas:	Class 3: FLR (M3)	Altar Class 1: T (Scene)
Material:	Limestone	Limestone
Shape:	Roughly parallel sides; round-pointed top; flat front and convex back.	Irregular oval
Dimensions:	L: ? HA: 2.34 m. W: 0.85 m. Th: 0.32 m. H above Floor: ca. 2.21 m.	Max. W: 1.15 m. Max. Th: 0.12 m. Min. W: 0.90 m.

GENERAL REMARKS

In 1951, Stela 17 and Altar 10 were found lying *in situ* in an unmapped area of low mounds some 350 m. to the southeast of Group B. After excavation, both monuments were shipped to Philadelphia. The stela had broken and fallen, leaving a piece of its butt in the earth. Altar 10 was similarly broken, but its fragments remained in position relative to each other after fragmentation. As originally erected, Stela 17 faced Altar 10 on a bearing of approximately E 15° N. Stela 17 fell forward over the altar thus causing its pieces to be scattered over and past the altar. The surface condition of the two monuments varied greatly from fragment to fragment. Upper fragments of Stela 17 lay face down and had remained fairly intact. Their inscriptions are well preserved. On the other hand, the lower part of the stela and the bulk of the carved surface of the altar had flaked and eroded badly. Little trace of carving was recognizable in many places. Surviving inscription on the altar seems to have been preserved by being shielded from erosion by a large fragment of the stela that lay upon it.

Originally there was also carving on the sides of Stela 17. Remains of four large cartouches can be made out on the right side and two on the upper left. The lower part of the left side is destroyed, leading to the conclusion that there were originally four large cartouches on this side also. Each cartouche apparently carried a single large glyph with affixes. Little more can be observed about these glyph blocks since they have been largely eroded.

It cannot merely be assumed that an altar found before a stela belonged with it from the beginning. But there is no reason to doubt such association in the case of Stela 17/Altar 10. The altar consisted of four large fragments in position with reference to each other. Possibly the altar broke when the upper part of the stela fell on it. The butt of the stela was still in place and more or less erect. Between stela and altar is a gap of only 0.70 m. A field sketch of the outlines of the butt and altar fragments shows that the altar was normally oriented so as to be viewed by an observer standing before the pair.

The designs on the two monuments are themselves compatible. Stela 17 displays two facing seated human figures and the altar shows two figures facing a central one. All five figures wear similar turban headdresses. Enough survives to show that glyph carving was similarly clumsy and crude on both. Each monument has minor glyph panels as well as a main text with chronology.

STELA 17/ALTAR 10
GLYPH CLASSIFICATION AND CHRONOLOGICAL DECIPHERMENT

STELA 17

(Order of reading: reconstructed as beginning at B1 and proceeding left-right and downward in double column to C5b; thence read to A4 and A5.
Number of blocks: 12 + 2 + 2 + 5 + 4 + 4 = 29)

		Main Text	
A	(10. 0.19. 6.14)	B1-C1	13 Ix 17 Zec (month coefficient apparently records 18)
		B2-B3	3 non-calendrical blocks
		C3	3 haab anniversary?
SS1	11. 6	B4	6 (kins), 11 uinals (coefficients corrected or interpreted)
		C4a	1 non-calendrical glyph or prefix
		C4b	Posterior date indicator
B	(10. 1. 0. 0. 0)	B5a-B5b	5 Ahau 3 Kayab (certain by inspection)
		C5a	T710 "hand scattering" glyph
		C5b	1 non-calendrical glyph
		A4a-A4b	2 non-calendrical glyphs (probably names or titles for Lord Storm-water Maize at A5a)
		A5a-A5b	Name phrase for Lord Storm-water Maize followed by the T502.25:502 *bacab* title
		Right side	
		vA1-vA4	4 glyph blocks, eroded
		Left side	
		wA1-wA4	4 glyph blocks, eroded
		Panel X	
		xA1a-xA1b	2 non-calendrical glyphs
		Panel Y	
		yA1-yA2	2 non-calendrical glyphs
		Panel Z	
		zA1-zA3	5 non-calendrical glyphs

ALTAR 10

(Order of reading: main [oval] panel, clockwise starting at Block 1.
Number of blocks: 12 or 24 + 8 + 2 = 22 or 34)

		Main Panel	
A	(?. ?. ?. ?. ?)	1-2	CR date (glyphs illegible; SR coefficient 11-13, VYr coefficient 11-13 or 16-18)
SS1	?. 7	3	7-8 (kins), 11 uinals
B	(?. ?. ?. ?. ?)		Date is inferred from presence of SS1; 9 or 21 blocks follow (completely lost except for traces of 2)
		Panel Y	
		yA1-yB4	8 non-calendrical glyphs
		Panel Z	
		zA1	Name of Lord Storm-water Maize
		zA2	Unidentified EG variant?

STELA 17/ALTAR 10: SUMMARY OF CHRONOLOGY

Stela 17

B1-C1	Date A	IS	(10. 0.19. 6.14)	13 Ix 17 Zec
B4		SS1	11. 6	
B5a-B5b	Date B	CR	(10. 1. 0. 0. 0)	5 Ahau 3 Kayab

Altar 10

1-2	Date A	CR	(?. ?. ?. ?. ?)
3		SS1	?. 7
	Date B		(?. ?. ?. ?. ?)

COMMENT ON THE INSCRIPTION

STELA 17: ORDER OF READING

An irregularly arranged panel of glyphs above two seated human figures represents the main text of Stela 17. Columns B and C of this text each has five rows. Column A actually contains only two rows but is numbered as if it had five. This irregularity raises uncertainty as to where the reading should begin. The eye is drawn most naturally to the uppermost glyphs, those at B1-C1. These two blocks record a CR date and verify that the two columns are to be read together in a normal left-right and downward fashion. If columns B and C are to be read together, then placement of the two blocks of row A becomes a problem. Presumably it could have preceded the CR notation at C1-D1. However, the presence of the "imix-comb-imix" title at A5b leads us to expect a name in blocks A4a-A5a. The known structure of Maya clauses (see page 115) indicates that such a name should follow, rather than precede, a chronological statement. If Blocks A4 and A5 are postulated to follow C5b, then the putative name does occur shortly after a CR marking a period end (5 Ahau 3 Kayab at B5a-B5b).

ALTAR 10: ORDER OF READING

A flattened oval band of glyphs which frames the center scene represents the main text of Altar 10. Only three blocks of the main oval band are even partially legible. These are simply numbered 1-3. They are not standardized as to widths but as a group they are placed more or less symmetrically with reference to the vertical axis of the scene. Presumably the reading began with the SR portion of a CR date at 1. This is labeled Date A of the altar. The presence of SS1 at Block 3 then implies a now lost Date B.

There is room in the complete band as restored for about eighteen more blocks. Traces indicate that there were three blocks covering about the same space as 1-3, placed more or less symmetrically with reference to the horizontal axis on the right. The condition of the band elsewhere between and on both sides of these two groups allows that there may have been plain areas. This is very uncertain, however. If there were, one would reconstruct three-block groups at the bottom and left also, for a total of four groups of three blocks each. This notion is perhaps more plausible in view of the later three-block groups on the periphery of the four-lobed band of Altar 13. Allowing for the possibility, we may say there were at least twelve blocks in the band. If, as seems more likely, the entire band around the scene was filled with a continuous text, the total number of glyphs would be twenty-four on the basis of the size of the known glyph blocks.

In addition to the main text, there are at least two lesser panels set into the background of the central scene. Below and to the left of the right human figure of the scene, there seems to have been a rectangular feature, which was conceivably a third background glyphic panel.

STELA 17: DEDICATORY DATE;
RECONSTRUCTION OF DATES A, B AND SS1

Two CR dates appear in the preserved main panel of the Stela 17 text. The first such date occurs at the start of the text (B1-C1) and apparently reads 11-13 Ix 16-18 Zec. A little further along, at B4, an SS of 5 (kins) 11-13 uinals precedes another CR, separated by only a posterior date indicator (C4). The second CR records a clear 5 Ahau 3 Kayab. This CR, Date B, is followed immediately by a "hand scattering" glyph which usually occurs in such a position at period ending dates. Taking Date B to mark a

PE, the only real possibility is for it to mark the LC position 10.1.0.0.0. This late date is in general agreement with the apparent crudity of carving of the monument.

Looking back to the opening CR of Date A, the apparent reading is of 13 Ix 18 Zec. This particular combination is impossible under either the Classic Maya or the Postclassic Maya calendric systems. The dots of the coefficients of the day and month signs are somewhat worn, which prevents the identification of any as merely decorative fillers.

Before resolving the above difficulty, let us turn to the SS and the final CR. We have identified Date B as marking 10.1.0.0.0. The SS intervening between the two CR dates can be presumed to connect them. Visual inspection indicates that the flanking dots of the uinal coefficient of the SS both are decorated with lines whereas the center is not. Since the clearly numerical dots in the Kayab coefficient show no such decoration, it can be assumed that these two dots are not numerical elements. By subtracting the apparent SS of 11.5 from (10.1.0.0.0) 5 Ahau 3 Kayab, a date of (10.0.19.6.15) 1 Men 18 Zec would be reached, disagreeing with the obvious Ix at B1. However, by proceeding back one more kin, a CR of 13 Ix 17 Zec is reached. This latter CR is in agreement with the remains of Date A if the center dot of the VYr coefficient at C1 is considered to have been originally decorative rather than functional. The sum of conclusions reached through visual inspection and calculation suggests that the coefficient at C1 was 17, and that the kin coefficient at B4 lacks a dot. This latter interpretation demands hypothesis of a Maya mistake, since there is no place at B4 where a dot could have been eroded.

STELA 18

Location:	In Plaza B1, approximately 11.00 m. west of Str. B28
Associations:	Stone 33G to the north at the same locus
Dedicatory Date:	Undetermined
Style Date:	Undetermined
Condition:	Broken and heavily eroded; the carvings are very faint; the back shows deep "channels." The butt is missing and the top has fragmented off
Photographs:	Fig. 38b
Drawings:	Fig. 16b
	Satterthwaite 1954:Fig. 25
Other References:	Satterthwaite 1954
	Riese 1980:12
Carved Areas:	Class 1: F
Material:	Limestone
Shape:	Uncertain
Dimensions:	L: ? HA: ?
	W: ca. 0.75 m. Th: ca. 0.31 m.
	H above Floor: ca. 2.50 m.

GENERAL REMARKS

Exploration in Plaza B1 in 1951 revealed a set of four limestone fragments in close proximity to each other some 11 m. west of Structure B28. They lay in an approximate north-south line. The southernmost three pieces proved to be part of a single monument, Stela 18. The fourth fragment was of somewhat irregular shape and bore no carving; its width was too great to comfortably be considered part of the stela and it also lacked the peculiar "channels" noted on the underside of the stela. Thus it has been concluded that this fragment, presently numbered Stone 33G, was independent of the monument.

Local excavation failed to find the butt of Stela 18. However, the limited extent of the work failed to rule out the possibility that a butt was indeed present at this locus. Excavation revealed two plaster floors beneath the fragments, sagging somewhat where they actually passed beneath the stones. The first floor, which lay 0.17 m. below the ground surface, dropped 0.08 m. at the edge of the monument. The second floor, 0.20-0.25 m. down, also dropped 0.08 m. This had the effect of leaving Stela 18 (which tilted down from west to east) and Stone 33G 0.08-0.12 m. off the uppermost floor. Such a displacement could be explained by the stela falling after site abandonment or by secondary disturbance. Stela 18 was left at Caracol when work concluded.

COMMENT ON THE INSCRIPTION

Carving on Stela 18 displays little in the way of intelligible glyphic inscription. Most of the carved face is taken up by a large serpent head with open mouth. A band of glyphs (Panel Y) is apparently infixed to its lower jaw. This inscription is only five or at most six blocks in length. Below the lower jaw of the serpent head is a glyph panel of two blocks in conventional orientation (Panel Z). Details of the glyphs are almost all confusing. The opening block at yA1 is entirely lost. Blocks yB1-yC1 carry numerical coefficients which might seem to be indicative of the presence of a CR date except that they both apparently have coefficients of 16 or greater. The rest of the inscription in Panel Y is a muddle of eroded glyphs. Interpretation is complicated by the fact that the line of glyph blocks is not oriented along a single axis. Curving of the line of blocks causes portions of each glyph to be compressed or elongated in turn to fit the available space. The final two glyph blocks at zA1-zB1 are clearer and decipherable. Block zA1 is a possible Caracol Glyph and block zB1 a clear T502.25:502 *bacab* title. This suggests that a sovereign's name had occurred in the now illegible Panel Y. Such unusual decoration and glyphic style suggest either a very late (i.e. post 10.0.0.0.0) or a very early (pre 9.4.0.0.0) date. The former seems more likely, given the crudity of the glyphs.

STELA 19

Location:	In Plaza B1, before Structure B5, apparently on or not far from the front-rear axis of the latter. The axis of the stela faced about S4°E magnetic
Associations:	Altar 12 and Altar 13 nearby
Dedicatory Date:	9.19.10.0.0 8 Ahau 8 Xul
Style Date:	Undetermined
Condition:	Broken into many fragments; most carved surfaces are badly weathered and not completely recorded
Photographs:	Fig. 39a, b Satterthwaite 1954:Fig. 23
Drawings:	Figs. 17a, b; 18a
Other References:	Satterthwaite 1954 Riese 1980:12-13
Carved Areas:	Class 3: FLR (M3)
Material:	Limestone
Shape:	Top slightly and asymmetrically rounded; sides are parallel so far as they are known, but might possibly converge toward the bottom; cross section rectangular with slightly bulging sides
Dimensions:	L: ? HA: ? W: ca. 1.10 m. Th: ca. 0.50 m. H above Floor: ca. 3.70 m.

GENERAL REMARKS

Systematic survey of Plaza B1 in 1951 revealed Stela 19. Superficial excavation showed the butt to be *in situ*. A row of stones about 0.10 m. high behind the butt might be interpreted as the remains of a "stela platform." The upper portion of the stela broke off about 0.30 m. above the postulated platform top and fell back and somewhat to the stela's right. When found, the upper part of Stela 19 was broken into at least nineteen fragments which lay in approximate position relative to each other. Apparently breakage was inflicted by natural causes only.

As reconstructed, this was the tallest stela known for the site. It is comparable in this respect with approximately contemporaneous stelae at Xutilha and Ixkun. The height (and considerable width) of Stela 19 contrasts to the dimensions of Stela 17, probably erected only 30 tuns later.

STELA 19: GLYPH CLASSIFICATION AND CHRONOLOGICAL DECIPHERMENT

(Order of reading: left-right and downward in double column in Frame-panels Z and
presumably also in Panels X and Y. Minimum number of
glyph blocks including reconstructions: 16+4+24=44)

Frame-panels Z

Left Side

A?	(?. ?. ?. ?. ?)	zA1	Traces of possible coefficient 3 prefixed to main sign
		zB1	Lost through erosion
		zA2-zB4	6 non-calendrical glyphs, damaged
		zA5-zB6	4 reconstructed blocks (entirely lost)

Right Side

		zC1-zD1	2 non-calendrical glyphs, damaged
B	(9.19.10. 0. 0)	zC2-zD2	8 Ahau 8 Xul ("eyes" of symbolic Ahau glyph lost; otherwise sure by inspection)
		zC3-zD6	8 non-calendrical or lost blocks

Panel X

		xA1-xH1	14 blocks, badly damaged
C	(?. ?. ?. ?. ?)	xG2-xH2	CR date? (possible traces of a day sign with coefficient of 8; coefficient of 8 with lost month sign)

Panel Y

		yA1-yB2	Name phrase?: 4 non-calendrical blocks naming PCZ; block at yB2 carries T74.184 prefix

COMMENT ON THE INSCRIPTION

RECONSTRUCTION OF STELA HEIGHT; PLACEMENT OF FRAMES

Measurement of the better-preserved right-side fragments of Stela 19 allows reconstruction of its above-floor height as about 3.70 m. Fragments themselves do not fit perfectly and some adjustment is necessary. The figure of 3.70 m. includes an addition of 0.10 m. to bring the glyph frames on the right side into an even spacing.

Since there are three frames on the right side, it can be postulated by symmetry that there were three on the left also. A fragment or fragments bearing the lowermost glyph frame on the left side might well have been left below the surface after the rapid investigation of the locus. The reconstruction assumed for both sides places the centers of the middle frames at about 1.50 m. above floor level. This height was probably not far from eye level for Maya readers. It may be speculated that the three frames as a group were spaced and positioned to keep them all within range of easy reading, resulting in the asymmetrical long expanses of plain sides above the upper frames. In any case, the visual effect is quite different from that of Stelae 5 and 6, where the available height is less, and a larger number of frames is necessary to accommodate the long inscriptions.

ORGANIZATION OF THE FRONT DESIGN

Time pressures diverted the attentions of researchers at Caracol until it was really too late to thoroughly record Stela 19. For this reason, the photographic record of the monument is partially unsatisfactory. There seem to be the remains of a bit of a human calf carved just above the top of Panel Y. If the top of Panel Y represents the base of the main figure-carving, a considerable stretch of stone is left below to be filled by either another figure or perhaps a block of glyphs. The size and shape of the blocks of Panel Y suggest it was part of a larger block of text rather than being a sudsidiary panel worked into the background of the design. It seems unlikely that a grotesque basal mask could appear below a panel of text separating it from the feet of the main figure, but this may be considered as a possibility. If the entire lower portion of the front were filled with text, this would be similar to the basic plan of Caracol Stela 21 and similar to the late Stela 1 at Ixkun. It is also very possible that there was a "two-level" design on the front of Stela 19. This sort of design would conform to that of Stela 6 at Xutilha and the equally late Stela 4 at Ixkun.

RECONSTRUCTION OF CHRONOLOGY

The fact that preservation of carving is extremely poor on Stela 19 makes any sort of decipherment confusing. It is difficult to suggest where the text started. The upper glyph frame on the right side opens with a pair of non-calendrical glyphs (zC1-zD1). For this reason, we can probably eliminate this side as the starting point for a text. On the left side at zA1 appear the remnants of a sign with complete cartouche on a three-element "pedestal" subfix. To the left are bits of a coefficient which, under certain lightings, appear to be a large central dot with damaged crescentic fillers. This block could well represent the SR portion of a CR date and might well serve as the beginning of a text, possibly independent of that on the front.

No identifiable SS follows the damaged Date A at zA1-zB1. It is possible that such an SS, leading forward to Date B on the right side, once existed in the lost lowermost glyph frame on the left side. At zC2 is found a sign that bears all the elements of Ahau save the eyes, which have been eroded. The coefficient is clearly 8. The VYr position following at zD2 is equally certain as 8 Xul.

The texts on the front of Stela 19 offer little of chronological use. The preserved bit of Panel X ends at the lower right with a pair of glyphs that appear from what remains to have been a CR.

Block xG1 has an apparent prefix of 8 attached to a sign with a complete cartouche. Following this is a block with a coefficient of 8 but a lost main sign. Lower down, the glyphs of Panel Y appear to be all non-calendrical.

Thus Date B at zC2-zD2 is the only preserved date we have to work with. Since all the readable glyph blocks between Date B and the end of the text are non-calendrical, the possibility that this might represent the DD is enhanced. The text ends with four unseen glyph blocks which could contain an SS and terminal CR, but space would be rather cramped for that. A date of 8 Ahau 8 Xul almost certainly marks the LC position 9.19.10.0.0 since this is the only tun-ending position for over two baktuns. It is possible that the CR of Date C also marked 9.19.10.0.0 since it bears the form of 8 ? 8 ?. Some support for this date as DD is offered by the style of presentation and carving of the glyph frames on the sides. On Stela 19 the frames are in relief and enclose glyphs which are also carved in relief. Similar glyph-enclosing frames are known for Stela 6 at 9.8.10.0.0 and Stela 5 at 9.9.0.0.0?? but with incised glyphs. Stela 17 shows the technique at 10.1.0.0.0 with a single glyph enclosed in each frame carved in relief as Stela 19. Stela 20 also carries relief glyphs carved in frames (on the front of the stone rather than on the sides) but does not display a known date at the present.

STELA 20

Location:	Butt found semi-erect on the west face of Platform A1a facing Court A1
Associations:	Stela 12 nearby, 1.50 m. to the south
Dedicatory Date:	Undetermined
Style Date:	Undetermined
Condition:	Broken into two large fragments; moderate to heavy erosion of carved surfaces; glyphic inscriptions largely effaced
Photographs:	Fig. 39c
Drawings:	Fig. 18b
	Satterthwaite 1954:Fig. 26
Other References:	Satterthwaite 1954
	Riese 1980:13
Carved Areas:	Class 1: F (M7)
Material:	Limestone
Shape:	Irregular sides tapering toward butt; rounded(?) top; both front and back bulge in cross section
Dimensions:	L: ca. 2.20 m. HA: ?
	W. 0.75 m. Th: 0.45 m.
	H above Floor: ?

GENERAL REMARKS

Investigation of Court A1 in 1950 revealed the upper portion of Stela 20 lying face down on the eastern edge of the court. Excavation showed the butt of the stela to be *in situ,* semi-erect and set into the front of the small platform A1a. This same small platform incorporated Stela 12 about 1.50 m. to the south of Stela 20. Excavation of Platform A1a revealed two apparently contemporaneous superimposed vaulted tombs within (Burials 2, 3). The locations of the stelae butts suggest that Stela 12 may have predated construction of the tombs, and that Stela 20 was set into Platform A1a during their building (see Stela 12, "General Remarks").

Both Stela 20 and Stela 12 broke from their bases and fell into Court A1. Despite the fact that Stela 20 lay face down, the carving suffered heavily from erosion. The front was apparently divided into two levels of design including three glyph-bearing panels. Beneath this were four glyph-enclosing frames. On the uppermost "de-sign level," the outline of a serpent's mouth appears to the left, facing a column of glyph blocks to the right (Panel T). Only the lower two and a half glyph blocks are left intact since the upper part of the monument is missing. These lower two blocks carry coefficients of 12 or 13 and 12 respectively. If this was a CR date, it was not a tun ending. The second "design level" has a seated figure filling the left side of the space facing a much smaller seated figure in the lower right corner, with two narrow presumably glyphic columns between (Panels U, V). If these two columns did indeed carry glyphs, they were certainly incised and have been totally eroded.

Margins of the upper two glyph frames (Panels W, X) on the third "design level" are entirely intact, while only parts of the upper portions of the glyph frames (Panels Y, Z) are preserved. Only Panel X shows any trace of glyphic inscription. In this frame, the glyphs are carved in shallow relief in three rows of four columns. Glyph block xA2 carries a fairly clear coefficient of 11, 12 or 13, but the main sign is unreadable.

STELA 20: GLYPH CLASSIFICATION AND CHRONOLOGICAL DECIPHERMENT

(Order of reading: downward in single column in the presumably opening Panel T;
downward in single column in Panels U and V; presumably left-right and downward
in two double columns in each of the four glyph Panels W, X, Y and Z.
Reconstructed total of glyph blocks: 4?+3?+3?+12+12+12+12=58)

		Panel T	
		tA1-tA2	2 lost or eroded glyph blocks
A?	(?. ?. ?. ?. ?)	tA3	Coefficient of 12 or 13 superfixed to eroded main sign (SR of a non-tun-ending CR?)
		tA4	Coefficient of 12 superfixed to eroded main sign (VYr of CR?)
		Panel U	
		uA1-uA3	3 or possibly 4 eroded incised glyphs (reconstructed)
		Panel V	
		vA1-vA3	3 or possibly 4 eroded incised glyphs (reconstructed)
		Panel W	
		wA1-wD3	12 eroded incised glyph blocks
		Panel X	
		xA1-xB1	2 eroded incised glyph blocks
B?	(?. ?. ?. ?. ?)	xA2	Coefficient of 11-13 attached to eroded main sign (part of lost CR?)
		xB2-xD3	9 eroded incised glyph blocks
		Panel Y	
		yA1-yD3	12 eroded or lost incised glyph blocks
		Panel Z	
		zA1-zD3	12 eroded or lost incised glyph blocks

STELA 21

Location:	On the floor of Court A1 in front of the north end of Platform A1
Associations:	None recognized
Dedicatory Date:	9.13.10.0.0
Style Date:	9.14.0.0.0 as the midpoint of smooth curve
Condition:	The butt and a large fragment of the top missing; portions of two glyph blocks have flaked off; damage from erosion minimal and preservation excellent
Photographs:	Fig. 39d
Drawings:	Fig. 19
Other References:	Riese 1980:13-14
Carved Areas:	Class 1: F (M7)
Material:	Slate
Shape:	Parallel sides; cross section rectangular with bulging faces
Dimensions:	L: ? HA: ca. 2.10 m.
	W: 0.85 m. Th: 0.28 m.
	H above Floor: ?

GENERAL REMARKS

Well after the University Museum ceased field work at Caracol, A. H. Anderson unearthed the center portion of the slate Stela 21. This monument was found in 1958 lying buried on the floor of Court A1 at the base of the northern end of Platform A1. Its butt and missing upper portion were not searched for beyond local excavation. They may well have been located at a hypothetical locus of erection on Platform A1 or possibly (in the case of the top) somewhere near where the stela fragment was found. The monument was hidden by Anderson to protect it from theft when he left the site. It was unearthed later for Satterthwaite to photograph and record. In the spring of 1978 the Commissioner of Archaeology for Belize, Elizabeth Graham, organized the removal of Stela 21 by helicopter to Belmopan where it awaits display.

Anderson considered it possible that the stela may have been hurled down from Platform A1 intentionally. However it seems equally possible that it could have broken and slid from a locus of erection near the edge of Platform A1 and come to rest at the bottom of the rubble tailings of that construction. Indeed, so little do we know about the circumstances of discovery of the stone, that it may well have had a butt fragment in place not too far from where it was found.

STELA 21: GLYPH CLASSIFICATION AND CHRONOLOGICAL DECIPHERMENT

(Order of reading: Main text, left-right and downward by rows across all four columns,
Panel Z, presumably downward in single column. Minimum reconstructed
number of blocks: 16 + 3 = 19)

Main Text

		A1	ISIG (variable is an animal head with large eye as in the Cumku patron)	
		B1-C1	9 baktuns, 13 katuns (well preserved head-variants)	
		D1a-D1b	10 tuns, 0 uinals (damaged period glyphs are head-variants; the super-fixed coefficients are damaged but clear)	
A	9.13.10. 0. 0	A2a	One-half block completely lost (reconstructed to include 7 Ahau and possibly also 0 kins)	
		A2b	2-3 Cumku (restoring one or two dots to right for symmetry; coefficient 3 reconstructed)	
		B2	1 block completely lost except for upper left (possibly Glyphs G9 and F)	
		C2a-A3a	Glyphs of Lunar Series; MA 19, MN 1?, X2, B, MT ? (many of these blocks are damaged, but all are sure readings)	
		A3b-B3b	3 non-calendrical glyphs (event?, name? and title? glyphs by position)	
		C3a	SSIG?	
SS1	?.19.12. 4	C3b-D3	4 (kins), 12 uinals, 19 tuns (symbolic uinal, head-variant tun sign; all coefficients clear)	
B	(?. ?. ?. ?. ?)	A4-C4	3 blocks completely lost (presumably including Date B)	
		D4a-D4b	1 block damaged (traces of 2 non-calendrical glyphs)	
		Panel Z		
		zA1-zA3	3 non-calendrical glyphs	

STELA 21: SUMMARY OF CHRONOLOGY

A1-A3a	Date A	IS	9.13.10. 0. 0	7 Ahau 3 Cumku G9?, F?, MA 19, MN 1?, X2, B, MT ?
C3b-D3		SS1	?.19.12. **4**	
A4-?	Date B		(?. ?. ?. ?. ?)	

COMMENT ON THE INSCRIPTION

ORDER OF READING

The key to this text, as for those of Stelae 5, 6 and 15, is the order of reading by rows across four columns with considerable division of blocks into left and right halves. A "by rows" reading is established by legible baktun and katun terms of the IS at B1-C1 and by the clear Glyphs B and A of the LS at D2-A3. Other readable chronological glyphs fit the pattern except for the location of the VYr position of the IS at D2a preceding the LS rather than following it.

RECONSTRUCTION OF THE INITIAL SERIES

If we suppose that a complete IS was originally recorded, then we can postulate the loss of both the kin term and the SR day 7 Ahau from the half-block A2a. In this case, A2a would have been divided into upper and lower halves, a device not used elsewhere in the text. However, in the long text of Stela 3 there are two divided blocks in which the left or the right half contains only upper and lower non-calendrical glyphs (Stela 3, C20 and D20). Possibly the same technique was employed on Stela 21. Alternatively, the kin term might have been suppressed to save space with the understanding that its coefficient was zero.

RECONSTRUCTION OF THE LUNAR SERIES

There is a seeming irregularity in the position of the VYr date 3 Cumku of the IS. Since the VYr is not postponed to position after Glyph A, it is expected to be followed immediately by Glyph D. Instead the largely destroyed Block B2 intervenes. A surviving remnant at the upper left of B2 might be part of the superfix of Glyph G9, with Glyph F completely lost from the right half.

The moon age recorded by Glyph D at C2a is very clearly 19. Following this is a damaged glyph that can be reliably recognized as Glyph C. Above the Glyph C elements is what seems to be a single bar suggesting the reading 5C. Such a reading would make it a non-Uniformity Period moon number. This is not an impossibility, but is very rare. It would also disagree with Glyph X2 in the next block (D2a) which calls for 1C (*no* coefficient) or 2C. The superfixed bar at C2b does not fully cover the main sign as might be expected for a numerical bar. A damaged superfix of moderate height extends clear across the end of the shortened bar. All these factors lead to the conclusion that there probably is a non-numerical superfix of which the bar was an element.

Block D2a clearly shows the upturned head and upper jaw of the celestial monster element of Glyph X2. At D2b the expected animal head of Glyph B is uncertain by inspection but a diagnostic "one arm" sky sign below a bracket superfix is clear. The main sign of Glyph A is preserved at A3a, but the numerical subfix is lost.

A moon age of 19 for Stela 21 yields an arbitrary deviation of 0.08 which is well within the allowable range. With the reading of 1C for Stela 21, it is also in agreement with the Uniformity moon numbering system.

THE DEDICATORY DATE

Part or the whole of an SS is shown at C3b-D3. The now lost blocks A4-C4 presumably carried the terminal Date B and possibly a katun term to complete the SS which is preserved as 19.12.4. If blocks B4-C4 were divided into halves there is scarcely room for another SS and CR to be included. Thus Dates A and B were apparently the only two recorded. Since Date A is the only one of the two to mark a PE (hotun end in this case) it must be taken as the DD.

III: THE ALTARS

ALTAR 1

See "Stela 1/Altar 1" for a discussion of this monument

ALTAR 2

Location:	In Plaza A3
Associations:	None apparent
Dedicatory Date:	9.17.0.0.0 13 Ahau ?
Style Date:	Undetermined
Condition:	Broken into two large fragments; erosion has effaced much carved details, but preservation generally fair
Photographs:	Fig. 40b Satterthwaite 1954:Fig. 32
Drawings:	Fig. 20b
Other References:	Satterthwaite 1951;1954
	Riese 1980:15
Carved Areas:	Altar Class 1: T
Material:	Limestone
Shape:	Square with rounded corners
Dimensions:	Max. W: 1.17 m. Th: 0.30 m.
	Min. W: 1.12 m.

GENERAL REMARKS

As discovered, Altar 2 was lying partly buried in humus with its upper surface exposed. It was located in Plaza A3 approximately 40 m. east of the edge of Platform A1 and about 40 m. west of Structure A23. It rested above but not necessarily on an eroded plaster floor. The location of this monument in Plaza A3 in company with its uncertain relationship to the floor suggests that this was a secondary placement.

Erosion has damaged the surface of Altar 2 although the broad outlines of carving are still visible. The coefficient of the large Ahau is partially effaced and the details of the inset spot glyphs are largely destroyed. None of the large raised spots around the perimeter of the upper surface appear to have ever carried any carving.

77

ALTAR 2: GLYPH CLASSIFICATION AND CHRONOLOGICAL DECIPHERMENT

(Order of reading: unknown. Number of glyph blocks: 12 + 1 = 13)

	Panel Y		
	y1-y12		12 badly eroded glyph blocks
	Panel Z		
A	(9.17. 0. 0. 0)	zA1	12-13 Ahau (13 Ahau reconstructed)

ALTAR 2: SUMMARY OF CHRONOLOGY

zA1	Date A	(9.17. 0. 0. 0)	13 Ahau (18 Cumku)

COMMENT ON THE INSCRIPTION

DESIGN CHARACTERISTICS; COMPARISON WITH ALTAR 17

Altar 2 displays a number of features shared only by Altar 17 at Caracol. These two monuments are termed "spot-complex" altars since they each carry "spot glyphs" countersunk in circular depressions as well as circular raised "spots" of approximately equal size but with smooth tops. With reconstructions for symmetry, there were twelve spots as well as twelve spot glyphs on each stone. Graham reports a similar occurence of an unspecified number of illegible spot glyphs on the 5 Ahau Stela 2 at Altar de Sacrificios (Graham 1972:13-15; Fig. 9). The distinguishing characteristics of Altars 2 and 17 are tabulated below for comparison:

Altar 2	Altar 17
Square	Rectangular
12 spot glyphs in frame	12 spot glyphs in border
12 spots attached to frame	12 spots on sides, not attached
Head-variant Ahau(?)	Full-figure Ahau(?)
Coefficient superfixed	Coefficient prefixed
Simple Ahau cartouche with double lining	Simple Ahau cartouche without double lining
Diagonal placements of four spot glyphs and spots on top	No diagonal placements of spot glyphs or spots

DEDICATORY DATE

Unfortunately, the twelve spot glyphs of Altar 2 are in poor condition or missing. It is possible that they contributed to the chronology of the monument originally by specifying the LC position of the large central Ahau date. The coefficient of the Ahau on Altar 2, though damaged, can be seen by inspection to have two bars and a dot at the extreme right. Another dot can be reconstructed by symmetry at the far left of the bars, and a third dot or a filler can be postulated to fill the gap between. The coefficient is thus read as either 12 or 13 with no preference by inspection.

It is assumed that the large central glyphs with coefficients on Altars 2 and 17 were Ahau glyphs which functioned as did the dates on the Giant Glyph Altars to mark dates in a "Short Count" manner. Briefly stated, the Short Count hypothesis postulates that the large Ahau dates of these monuments served to commemorate a given katun by naming its final day. The actual date with which a "Giant Ahau" monument might be associated could fall either at the same ending day marked or possibly at some point in the ongoing current katun.

Turning to the question of possible LC positions permitted by the katun-naming hypothesis for Altar 2, there are several possible positions for Katuns 12 Ahau and 13 Ahau:

9. 4.0.0.0	13 Ahau
9.11.0.0.0	12 Ahau (marked by Altar 7)
9.17.0.0.0	13 Ahau
10. 4.0.0.0	12 Ahau

It should be noted that it is considered quite possible that this monument may have marked the half-katun ten tuns earlier than the actual katun-ending day. This seems to exclude the 9.11.0.0.0 date as a possibility since it is already marked by Altar 7, a monument very different from Altar 2. The date 10.4.0.0.0 can also be excluded from consideration since it is close to the extreme late limit for monument carving in the Maya area as a whole, three katuns later than the firmly dated Caracol Stela 17 and one katun later than the tentatively dated Stela 10.

These two methods of elimination, if valid, require reading Altar 2 as 13 Ahau at an early or late position. Similar reasoning allows us to narrow the placement of Altar 17 to 9.16.0.0.0 2 Ahau (see Altar 17, "Comment on the Inscription"). Stylistic similarity of the two spot-complex altars indicates that they probably marked temporally proximal positions. A choice of the late alternative LC position for Altar 2 places it only one katun later than Altar 17, at 9.17.0.0.0.

Placing Altars 2 and 17 at 9.17.0.0.0 and 9.16.0.0.0 respectively leaves them without any known stelae pairs. This in no way contradicts our assumption that Giant Glyph Altars were originally paired to stelae, because the two altars in question are very different from other such monuments. Since Altars 2 and 17 apparently carried an inscription other than that of the giant glyph, it is entirely possible that they were meant to stand independent of any other monument association. It is indeed conceivable that they were erected on edge as stelae rather than flat as altars.

ALTAR 3

Location:	In front of Structure A1, possibly *in situ*
Associations:	Butt fragment of Stela "X" (Stela 4??)
Dedicatory Date:	9.18.0.0.0 11 Ahau
Style Date:	Undetermined
Condition:	Well preserved; only slight damage from erosion and chipping
Photographs:	Fig. 40c Satterthwaite 1951:PL. XV
Drawings:	Fig. 20c Satterthwaite 1954:Fig. 39
Other References:	Satterthwaite 1951; 1954 Riese 1980:15
Carved Areas:	Altar Class 1: T
Material:	Limestone
Shape:	Irregular round
Dimensions:	Max. W: 1.78 m. Th: 0.35 m. Min. W: 1.77 m.

GENERAL REMARKS

Altar 3 was noted in 1950, resting near the surface of the ground. Excavation that same year revealed that the monument sat on three cylindrical limestone "legs." The bottom of the altar lay on a mass of crushed limestone fragments, which might indicate that a floor once existed flush with the altar and enclosing the legs. No other evidence of floors was found in the local digging around the stone. From a field drawing it appears possible that the lower ends of the legs may have rested on limestone bedrock. One of the legs was on the northern axis, one on the western axis and the third to the southeast. Each leg was about 0.30 m. in height and about 0.28 m. in maximum diameter. They bulged near the top and tapered toward the bottom. Altar 3 was only lightly eroded, and the carving of a giant 11 Ahau showed very clearly. To the south of the altar, 0.40 m. distant, was the fragment of slate stela butt labeled stela "X." This latter monument most probably represents a portion of the butt of Stela 4. The stela and altar are approximately on the center line of Structure A1, the stairway of which begins about 1.60 m. south of Stela "X." Excavation failed to discover any trace of a sub-altar cache.

ALTAR 3: SUMMARY OF CHRONOLOGY

A1	Date A	CR	(9.18.0.0.0)	11 Ahau (18 Mac)

COMMENT ON THE INSCRIPTION

DEDICATORY DATES OF THE TWO 11 AHAU GIANT GLYPH ALTARS (ALTARS 3 AND 14)

Following the katun-naming hypothesis, an 11 Ahau Giant Glyph Altar should mark either the LC position 9.5.0.0.0 or 9.18.0.0.0 (or perhaps 9.4.10.0.0 or 9.17.10.0.0). Since both Altars 3 and 14 at Caracol mark 11 Ahau, it is reasonable to speculate that one marked the earlier and the other marked the later LC position. However, it is not easy to choose specific LC positions for each altar on the basis of stylistic likenesses and differences. In the following table, a comparative list of stylistic traits appears:

	Altar 3	Altar 14
Similar large size?	Yes	Yes
Same shape?	Yes	Yes
Legs?	Yes	No
Cartouche:		
Notched?	No	?
Double lining?	No	Yes
Relatively wide?	No	Yes
Notched pedestal element?	Yes	No (glyphic?)
Scalloped frame?	Yes	Yes
Fillers?	Feather(?)	Crescent

These categories show differences between the two altars, but in themselves do not seem to indicate relative "earlyness" or "lateness." The double lining and the relatively wide cartouche of Altar 14 do not occur on Altar 3, but they do occur on other Giant Glyph Altars of "early" date (Altars 2, 6, 7) and also on the very late Altar 16. The characteristic of legs, as below Altar 3, appears also with the "early" Altar 11 in a placement which was probably secondary, and therefore possibly late. The sum of these features suggests that Altar 3 was later than Altar 14.

Three similarities between Altars 3 and 14 appear as traits of early Giant Glyph Altars but not on the late Altar 16. These traits are similar large size, irregular round shape and presence of scalloped frame. This might suggest earlyness rather than lateness for both 11 Ahau altars. However, there is no compelling evidence against their survival down to 9.18.0.0.0. A modified glyphic scalloped frame is dated no earlier than 9.19.10.0.0 by the scenic Altars 12 and 13. Three Alternative Sets are presented below, based on the assumption that generally only a single Giant Glyph Altar would be carved for a given katun end:

I	9. 4.10.0.0	Stela "X" (Stela 4?)	/Altar 3
	9. 5. 0.0.0	Stela 16	/Altar 14
II	9.17.10.0.0	Stela "X" (Stela 4?)	/Altar 3
	9.18. 0.0.0	?	/Altar 14
III	9. 5. 0.0.0	Stela 16	/Altar 14
	9.18. 0.0.0	Stela "X" (Stela 4?)	/Altar 3

For Sets I and III it would be assumed that Altar 14 originally served the broken-up Stela 16 and was shifted to a secondary position. Movement of some sort is required because the altar was placed over the fragment of Altar 15 which has been assigned with confidence to 9.9.0.0.0. The re-setting of the monument is believable because Altar 14 was placed askew with reference to the axes of the court, and also displays no relation to any particular architectural feature nor to the nearby Stela 8. Set II given above does not require postulation of secondary placement since it dates Altar 14 later than the 9.9.0.0.0 of Altar 15, although it does allow it. With the late solution outlined by Set II, Altar 14 does not presently pair with any known stela.

If an assumption is followed that the Giant Glyph Altars were made to accompany stelae, Sets I and III would have to be endorsed, since under Set II, Stela 16 and Altar 14 both presently remain unpaired. Following this assumption and taking into account the evidence for "lateness" of Altar 3, Alternative Set III is favored.

ALTAR 4

See "Stela 9/Altar 4" for a discussion of this monument

ALTAR 5

Location:	Before Structure A3, west of Altar 6
Associations:	None apparent
Dedicatory Date:	9.6.0.0.0 9 Ahau??
Style Date:	Undetermined
Condition:	Broken and badly eroded; most of the right half missing
Photographs:	Fig. 41a
Drawings:	Fig. 21a
Other References:	Satterthwaite 1951; 1954 Riese 1980:16
Carved Areas:	Altar Class 1: T
Material:	Limestone
Shape:	Irregular oval
Dimensions:	Max. W: 1.93 m. Th: 0.40 m.
	Min. W: 1.40 m.

GENERAL REMARKS

Altar 5 lay on the surface about 2 m. south of the west part of Structure A3. Only a large fragment of the left portion of the monument was found, and this bit was much worn by erosion. Excavation was carried out to check for legs or caches, but nothing was found. The altar apparently lay above rather than on the uppermost level of eroded flooring found in the area.

ALTAR 5: SUMMARY OF CHRONOLOGY

A1	Date A	CR	(9.6.0.0.0)	9 Ahau (3 Uayeb)

COMMENT ON THE INSCRIPTION

Carved details of Altar 5 are badly preserved. What little of the coefficient remains shows a bar with a dot placed towards its left end. Symmetrical reconstruction allows 7, 8 or 9 as the coefficient if we discount the unlikely possibility of a lost dividing line and two narrow bars. The design of Altar 5 apparently differs from that of other Giant Glyph Altars at Caracol. The glyph is not centered vertically and is bordered by an area marked off into rectangles which may be the remains of two rows of completely eroded glyphs. If so, there is less reason to suspect original association with a stela since the DD may have been indicated on the altar itself.

The maximum diameter of Altar 5, 1.93 m., is exceeded only by those of two others of sure measurement: Altar 1 and the nearby Altar 6. This fact indicates that the DD of Altar 5 should probably be close to those for Altars 1 and 6. A table of katun ends with Ahau coefficients 7, 8 or 9 in Baktun 9 outlines possible positions for Altar 5, bearing in mind that the actual LC position of the monument could fall anywhere within the ongoing katun:

9. 0.0.0.0	8 Ahau (too early?)
9. 6.0.0.0	9 Ahau
9. 7.0.0.0	7 Ahau (Altar 6)
9.13.0.0.0	8 Ahau
9.19.0.0.0	9 Ahau
10. 0.0.0.0	7 Ahau (Altar 16)

The early 8 Ahau position given in this list requires a dubious backward stretch of the known local carving period of some three katuns in length. The two 7 Ahau positions are satisfactorily marked by other Giant Glyph Altars. If we eliminate these three possibilities, only the two 9 Ahau positions and the late 8 Ahau position remain for consideration.

There is very little evidence besides the large size of Altar 5 that can be used to assist in its chronological placement. But unless very large size as a feature of Giant Glyph Altars appeared sporadically through many katuns, the selection of LC positions is limited to 9.6.0.0.0 9 Ahau by similarity to Altars 1 and 6. This is by no means a certain assignment, although it appears to be the best guess. In combination with LC positions of other Giant Glyph Altars, some of which are equally tentative, this placement provides marking by these monuments for nine sequent katuns with but a single break:

9. 3.0.0.0	2 Ahau	Altar 4	
9. 4.0.0.0	13 Ahau		Stela 13
9. 5.0.0.0	11 Ahau	Altar 14	Stela 16
9. 6.0.0.0	9 Ahau	Altar 5	Stela 14
9. 7.0.0.0	7 Ahau	Altar 6	Stela 15
9. 8.0.0.0	5 Ahau	Altar 1	Stela 1
9. 9.0.0.0	3 Ahau	Altars 15 and 11	Stelae 5 and 6
9.10.0.0.0	1 Ahau	Altar 19	Stela 7
9.11.0.0.0	12 Ahau	Altar 7	Stela 3

It should be noted that this table includes many reconstructions of DD's for both stelae and altars.

The organization presented in the above table places Altars 5, 6, 1 and 15, the largest ovoid altars known at the site, at sequent katuns. It also allows hypothetical reconstructions of original stela/altar pairings. Altar 14 and Stela 16 were both discovered in disturbed positions. Stela 16 was broken and buried before 9.11.0.0.0, and Altar 14 was moved from its original site of erection to a secondary position at the southern end of Court A1. However, the identical DD's presented on the two stones suggest that they were originally paired. Stela 14 and Altar 5 similarly mark the same Katun (9.6.0.0.0) 9 Ahau under this reconstruction and might have originally formed a pair.

An attempt to find an association between Altar 6 at 9.7.0.0.0 7 Ahau and a stela is frustrated initially. However, Stela 15 with its long unreadable text following the IS of 9.4.16.13.3 may actually have had a DD much later than that single preserved date. Indeed, bits of two SS's can be observed on Stela 15. If we hypothesize

that Stela 15 and Altar 6 did originally mark the same Katun (9.7.0.0.0) 7 Ahau, then only Stela 13 (9.4.0.0.0) of the four stelae found together in Court A2 remains without any potential Giant Glyph Altar pair. This hypothesis is, of course, only reasoned speculation, and can be only tentatively accepted until tested by further research.

Support for the pairing of Altars 14, 5 and 6 with Stelae 16, 14 and 15 might be derived from the evidence for removal of an altar from in front of Stela 14 (see Stela 13, "General Remarks"). If these monuments were paired when first erected, then it appears that the altars were all stripped away for placement or disposal in Court A1 where they were found. This is an economical hypothesis, since it allows for all the monument disturbance in Court A2, both altar movement and stela destruction, to have occurred as a single event. The altars were all displaced to the same area (Court A1) which in turn allows us to speculate that an altar pair for Stela 13 might eventually also be found in the same court.

ALTAR 6

Location:	At north end of north-south axial line of Court A1
Associations:	None apparent
Dedicatory Date:	9.7.0.0.0 7 Ahau
Style Date:	Undetermined
Condition:	Broken into three large fragments; carving worn but still easily readable
Photographs:	Fig. 41b
	Willcox 1954:Fig. 49
Drawings:	Fig. 21b
	Satterthwaite 1954:Fig. 37
Other References:	Satterthwaite 1951;1954
	Willcox 1954
	Riese 1980:16
Carved Areas:	Altar Class 1: T
Material:	Limestone
Shape:	Irregular oval
Dimensions:	Max. W: 2.25 m. Th: 0.46 m.
	Min. W: 1.93 m.

GENERAL REMARKS

Altar 6 was in many fragments but substantially complete when discovered. The carving on the surface was largely intact despite damage from splitting and erosion. Below it were three cylindrical limestone legs approximately 0.25 m. in diameter and 0.30 m. in height, on which it apparently had been balanced before falling and slipping southward.

Excavation suggested that the three legs may have rested on a plaster floor with possibly a still earlier floor below that. No cache was found below the altar.

ALTAR 6: SUMMARY OF CHRONOLOGY

A1	Date A	CR	(9.7.0.0.0)	7 Ahau (3 Kankin)

COMMENT ON THE INSCRIPTION

Altar 6 displays a clear SR date of 7 Ahau as does Altar 16. Altar 6 shows the apparently earlier traits of a notched pedestal element and a scalloped border. Altar 6 is the largest altar at Caracol and Altar 16 is the smallest, which also suggests a temporal priority for Altar 6 since there appears to be a trend for altar size generally to decrease with time. Altar 16 was found in Group B which contains the late Stelae 18 and 19 and the late Scene Altars 12 and 13. Altar 6 was found in Court A1 near both early and late monuments. Differences between the two altars are felt to reflect an actual difference in date. Accordingly, in line with the Short Count hypothesis, Altar 6 is assigned to 9.7.0.0.0 7 Ahau and Altar 16 to 10.0.0.0.0 7 Ahau, 260 tuns later. Both of these dates are within the local carving period as presently established.

Excavation at the location where Altar 6 was found produced no sign of erection of an accompanying stela. The altar was thus either unaccompanied by a stela or originally sited elsewhere as a companion to a stela with a DD marking 7 Ahau. In the latter instance, the altar would have been moved to its present position by some later human activity. This hypothesis is favored as has been discussed (Altar 5, "Comment on the Inscription"). Accordingly, we have tentatively suggested that Stela 15 might once have paired with Altar 6 in Court A2 atop Platform A1.

ALTAR 7

See "Stela 14/Altar 7" for a discussion of this monument

ALTAR 8

Location:	In Plaza A3
Associations:	None apparent
Dedicatory Date:	None (plain altar)
Style Date:	None
Condition:	Eroded
Photographs:	None
Drawings:	None
Other References:	Satterthwaite 1954
	Riese 1980:17
Carved Areas:	None
Material:	Limestone
Shape:	Rectangular
Dimensions:	Max. W: 0.60 m. Th: ca. 0.21 m.
	Min. W: 0.56 m.

GENERAL REMARKS

The plain stone called Altar 8 was located in the northern part of Plaza A3, evidently unassociated with any structure or monument. It was first thought to be a building stone but was catalogued as a monument because of its fairly large size. This block is no longer felt to actually be an altar. However, its description is included in this report for the sake of continuity in numbering.

ALTAR 9

Location:	In Plaza A3
Associations:	None apparent
Dedicatory Date:	None (plain altar)
Style Date:	None
Condition:	Eroded
Photographs:	None
Drawings:	None
Other References:	Satterthwaite 1954
	Riese 1980:17
Carved Areas:	None
Material:	Limestone
Shape:	Oblong
Dimensions:	Max. W: 1.20 m. Th: 0.20 m.
	Min. W: 0.93 m.

GENERAL REMARKS

Altar 9 is a plain block of limestone found resting in Plaza A3. It may have been located on a north-south centerline of the plaza along with Altar 2 about 15.2 m. to the south, although this association is tenuous. Description of this stone is here included for the sake of continuity in altar numbering despite the fact that it is no longer felt to actually represent a monument.

ALTAR 10

See "Stela 17/Altar 10" for a discussion of this monument

ALTAR 11

Location:	At the northern base (stairway?) of Structure B2
Associations:	None apparent
Dedicatory Date:	9.9.0.0.0 3 Ahau ??
Style Date:	Undetermined
Condition:	Flaked around edges but otherwise intact; badly eroded
Photographs:	None
Drawings:	Fig. 21d
Other References:	Satterthwaite 1954
	Riese 1980:18
Carved Areas:	Altar Class 1: T
Material:	Limestone
Shape:	Irregular oval
Dimensions:	Max. W: 1.68 m. Th: 0.28 m.
	Min. W: 1.35 m.

GENERAL REMARKS

Altar 11 rested on square cut-limestone blocks on the north edge of Structure B2. The supports appear to have been fragments of structural debris used secondarily as altar supports. In this regard, they contrast with the cylindrical legs used as supports for Altars 3 and 6. The surface of the altar is much worn and almost smooth. By daylight it appeared to be devoid of carving; night lighting brought out a few details of the frame, cartouche and coefficient. Altar 11 seemed to be placed on the centerline of Structure B2 and oriented so as to be readable by an observer facing the structure. Local excavation turned up no trace of either a sub-altar cache or an accompanying stela. Its occurence without a stela partner and mounted on reused masonry blocks strongly suggests that it was found at a location of secondary placement.

ALTAR 11: SUMMARY OF CHRONOLOGY

A1	(9.9.0.0.0)	3 Ahau (3 Zotz)

COMMENT ON THE INSCRIPTION

This monument is similar to various of the early Giant Glyph Altars through the aspects of its large size, irregular oval shape and the scalloped border. Night lighting brought out traces of a dot without a bar at the right above the giant glyph. Symmetrical reconstruction of this dot as part of the coefficient allows readings of 2, 3 or 4. By comparison with the other Giant Glyph Altars, the glyph is reconstructed as Ahau. An examination of katun positions with SR coefficients 2, 3 or 4 Ahau within the carving period at Caracol yields the following results:

9. 2.0.0.0	4 Ahau	(too early?)	
9. 3.0.0.0	2 Ahau	Altar 4	
9. 9.0.0.0	3 Ahau	Altar 15	Stelae 5, 6 (?)
9.15.0.0.0	4 Ahau		
9.16.0.0.0	2 Ahau	Altar 17	
10. 2.0.0.0	3 Ahau		

On the theory that generally only one Giant Glyph Altar marked a given katun, the two 2 Ahau positions can be eliminated from consideration. The late 3 Ahau position would cause Altar 11 to postdate the very different Giant Glyph Altars 16 and 18 and can also be discounted. The early 4 Ahau position would require a backward extension of the known local carving period. However, this possibility cannot be ruled out since Altar 4 (9.3.0.0.0) is very similar to Altar 11. The position at 9.15.0.0.0 4 Ahau cannot be ruled out either, because both Altar 7 at 9.11.0.0.0 and Altar 3 at 9.18.0.0.0, the two known Giant Glyph Altars that bracket 9.15.0.0.0, are similar in many regards to Altar 11.   9.9.0.0.0 3 Ahau might seem to be negated as a possibility since it is marked also by the fragmentary Altar 15. However, our postulated reconstruction of the DD's of Stelae 5 and 6 would place them at the half-katun 9.8.10.0.0 and the katun end 9.9.0.0.0. The Short

Count hypothesis allows a Giant Glyph Altar to dedicate any date within the ongoing katun. Thus, if both Stelae 5 and 6 were to be paired with Giant Glyph Altars, they would both require a coefficient of 3 on those altars. The 9.9.0.0.0 3 Ahau position is therefore favored since it allows us to pair stelae and altars most economically. It should be kept in mind that this solution is presently one of convenience more than one of fact.

ALTAR 12

Location:	The disturbed fragments were found in a group visible at the ground surface in front of Structure B5. The center of the group is about 4.50 m. north and about 1.00 m. east (left) of the center of the *in situ* butt of Stela 19
Associations:	Stela 19?; Altar 13?
Dedicatory Date:	9.19.10.0.0 8 Ahau 8 Xul
Style Date:	9.17.0.0.0 ± 3 katuns
Condition:	In 6 fragments and incomplete; carved surfaces vary between fair and very poor preservation
Photographs:	Fig. 42a Satterthwaite 1954:Fig. 36
Drawings:	Fig. 23
Other References:	Satterthwaite 1954 Riese 1980:18-19
Carved Areas:	Altar Class 1: T
Material:	Limestone
Shape:	Flattened round
Dimensions:	Max. W: 1.58 m. Th: ca. 0.46 m. Min. W: 1.56 m.

GENERAL REMARKS

Altar 12 was found on the surface with its surviving fragments in approximate alignment. However, the monument was discovered resting upside down. Local excavation failed to recover all the fragments of the altar at this locus.

Examination of this stone revealed that the sides were finished to only about 10 cm. below the top surface. Below this and on the bottom, Altar 12 was rough-hewn and very irregular. Presumably it was intended to be set into a floor where the unfinished portions would be hidden. It bears close similarities to Altar 13 nearby and the later Altar 10. These three monuments are altars which, unlike others at Caracol, bear figural carving surrounded by a hieroglyphic text.

It appears unlikely from the size of the altar that it was turned over by other than human action. It might conceivably have been flipped for ease of transportation; the flat upper surface would work more easily with wooden rollers than would the undulating bottom. Altar 12 is similar to the nearby Altar 13 in date, in "scenic" layout and in the fact that the latter stone was also left unfinished on the sides and bottom. It therefore seems most reasonable to assume that Altar 12 was located originally somewhere in the general area of Altar 13, probably within Plaza B1.

ALTAR 12: GLYPH CLASSIFICATION AND CHRONOLOGICAL DECIPHERMENT

(Order of reading: Main panel, reconstructed as clockwise beginning with Blocks 1 and 2;
left-right and downward in double column in the L-shaped Panel Y;
downward in vertical Panel Z. Number of blocks: 39 + 7 + 22 = 68)

Main Panel

A	(?. ?. ?. ?. ?)	1-2	CR date; coefficients of 13 and 8 (day name is lost; the month name is largely lost but may be Uo or Zip)
		3-13	11 non-calendrical glyphs, badly damaged ("imix-comb-imix" *bacab* title at 13, presumably follows a name phrase)
SS1?	———— ?. ?	14-16	Possible SSIG at 14 followed by 2 nearly lost blocks
		17	1 non-calendrical, damaged
B	(?. ?. ?. ?. ?)	18-19	CR date; SR coefficient of 12, main sign lost; 11 Mol
		20-29	10 non-calendrical glyphs, damaged
		30-32	Name-title phrase; probable ruler name at 30, Caracol Glyph at 31 (see page 115) and "imix-comb-imix" *bacab* title at 32
		33	SSIG
SS2	———— ?. 3.14	34-35	14 (kins), 3 uinals, ? tuns (possible trace of tun-coefficient 2)
C	(?. ?. ?. ?. ?)	36-39	4 lost blocks; presumably carried CR date and may also have contained a katun term for the SS

Panel Y

SS3?	———— ?	yA1-yA2	3 lost blocks which may have marked an SS (inferred from the CR that follows)
D	(9.19. 9.17. 0)	yB2-yC1	1 Ahau 8 Zec (1 Ahau and 1 dot of the month coefficient are restored)
		yD1	1 non-calendrical glyph (possible event glyph; carries lunar "event" suffix)
		yC2-yF1	4 non-calendrical glyphs (probable name phrase; yC2 similar to zA3, yF1 reconstructed as a Caracol Glyph)
		yE2	SSIG
SS4	———— 1. 0	yF2	0 (kins), 1 uinal
		yG1	1 non-calendrical glyph (largely eroded)
E	(9.19.10. 0. 0)	yH1-yG2	8 Ahau 8 Xul (Ahau details restored)
		yH2	T710 "hand scattering" glyph
		yG3	1 non-calendrical glyph
		yH3	Half-period glyph
		yG4-yH5	4 non-calendrical glyphs (probable name phrase; *Mah K'ina* title at yG4 (Lounsbury 1974), Caracol Glyph at yG5, "imix-comb-imix" *bacab* title at yH5)

Panel Z

		zA1-zA7	7 non-calendrical glyphs (T74.184 *Mah K'ina* title at zA3)

ALTAR 12: SUMMARY OF CHRONOLOGY

1-2	Date A	CR	(?. ?. ?. ?. ?)	13 <u>?</u> 8 <u>?</u>
14-16		SS1?	?. ?	
18-19	Date B		(?. ?. ?. ?. ?)	12 <u>?</u> 11 Mol
33-35		SS2	?. 3.14	
36-38	Date C		(?. ?. ?. ?. ?)	<u>?</u> <u>?</u> <u>?</u> <u>?</u>
yA1-yB1		SS3	?	
yB2-yC1	Date D		(9.19. 9.17. 0)	1 Ahau 8 Zec
yE2-yF2		SS4	1. 0	
yH1-yH3	Date E		(9.19.10. 0. 0)	8 Ahau 8 Xul, "hand scattering," 1 non-calendrical glyph, half-period glyph

COMMENT ON THE INSCRIPTION

ORDER OF READING

The arrangement of text in three separate panels allows a number of options in reconstruction of the order of reading. It is indeed possible, and not at all unlikely, that each glyph panel was intended to be read as a separate text. The course taken here follows a middle road by reading the two panels that bear chronological information as a single continuous text while reading the entirely non-calendrical Panel Z as a separate statement.

It is difficult under the circumstance of incomplete preservation to state definitely which panel was to be read first or to know exactly where to begin the reading of the circular panel around the perimeter. The only dates which can be nailed down with any security are the two that remain in Panel Y. In that place there appears a CR of 8 Ahau 8 Xul which can be placed at 9.19.10.0.0 with confirmation from a "hand scattering" and a half-period glyph that follow. The statement that involves this CR thus has an appropriately final aspect to it which would be correct for the final clause of a text. While this does not prove the order of reading, it is at least in full agreement with known ancient Maya practice.

Having more or less established Panel Y as the second-read of the two chronological panels, the circular Main Panel must be examined for a starting point to the entire statement. From the SS at glyphs 33-35, we know that the reading was clockwise. By comparison, Altar 14 at Tikal, which begins with an IS, opens at the top of the circular band a little to the left of the vertical axis of the interior design (a large Ahau glyph). Stela 16/Altar 5 from Tikal present a slightly different starting point. There, if we follow Morley's rather than Spinden's reconstruction, the DD on the stela is read before stepping back in time to Date A on the altar which begins the circular text at a point just a bit to the right of the vertical axis.

Unfortunately, all the glyphs at the top of the circular Main Panel of Caracol Altar 12 that are in the vicinity of the vertical axis are lost. Examination of the glyphs to either side of this lost area reveals a CR date just to the right, and part or the whole of an SS just to the left. If this SS and its following CR were to be represented in the circular panel before the reading shifts to Panel Y, then the lost clause would take probably three of the lost glyph blocks by comparison to the appearance of the preserved Date E. In that place, the CR is separated from the preceding SS by a single non-calendrical glyph. Examination of the first part of Panel Y reveals four lost blocks followed by the VYr portion of a CR. Thus the opening four blocks contain just the right amount of room for a short SS on the pattern of: SSIG/SS (kin and uinal only)/non-calendrical glyph/SR. A reading which proceeds from what is here labeled SS2 on to Panel Y must therefore place the CR of Date C into the lost blocks of the top of the Main Panel. Further, if any sort of statement were to accompany that date (although it is possible that the SS2/Date C clause was entirely calendric) then it is almost mandatory that all the lost glyph blocks short of the CR of Date A be considered part of that same clause. For this reason the SR of Date A occupies the position of glyph Block 1 in our organization of labeling.

An alternative starting point for reading the Main Panel might be taken as at glyph Block 33. This condition could obtain if the altar were to be read as a part of a continuous text that began elsewhere. A start at the corner of the panel would mimic the opening of the clause on Altar 13 at an interior corner.

A preliminary system of labeling the glyphs of Caracol Altar 12 was utilized by Thompson in his *Catalog* (1962). That system was based on field photographs of unfitted fragments and has been superseded. A table of concordance between the old provisional system and the new one follows:

Altar 12: Correlation of final glyph block designations to a preliminary set used by Thompson (1962)

Main Panel
1-14 : (2,2–2,15)
15   : ––
16-19 : (3,1–3,4)
20-34 : (1,1–1,15)
35-38 : ––
39   : (2,1)

Panel Y
yA1-yA2 : (B1-B2)
yB1-yB2 : (C1-C2)
yC1-yC2 : (D1-D2)
yD1-yD2 : (E1-E2)
yE1-yE2 : (F1-F2)
yF1-yF2 : (G1-G2)
yG1-yG2 : (H1-H2)
yH1-yH2 : (I1-I2)

Panel Z
zA1-zA7 : (X1-X7)

CHRONOLOGICAL ANALYSIS; DEDICATORY DATE

The glyph classification table shows the locations of five lettered dates. These may have been recorded with four SS's forming a complete "chain." However, with one of the two sure SS's incompletely known, and with two others completely lost or illegible, only dubious alternative reconstructions of Dates A, B and C can be made.

As noted earlier, the only reliable date that can be read by inspection is Date E (yH1-yG2) which records 8 Ahau 8 Xul. The "hand scattering" glyph that follows leads us to suspect a PE marking, and this is confirmed at yH3 by the appearance of a half-period glyph. The only real possibility for this date is 9.19.10.0.0 if we take into account all these factors. Immediately preceding Date E is a short SS of 1.0 which indicates that Date D should record (9.19. 9.17. 0) 1 Ahau 8 Zec. At yC1 the damaged main sign and half of the coefficient are preserved and confirm the possible reading of 8 Zec.

A gap of eight glyph blocks separates Date D from the next readable glyph. At the anterior end, this gap is bounded by part or the whole of an SS (SS2). The destroyed glyph blocks should have included a CR (Date C) and a connecting SS (SS3) if the hypothesized continuous reading of the Main Panel and Panel Y is correct.

The date that SS2 hypothetically leads from is presumably marked at Blocks 18 and 19 of the Main Panel by a CR of 12 ? 11 Mol. This date unfortunately cannot be placed into the LC. The possible remains of an SSIG appear four blocks ahead of Date B. The reconstructed SSIG is followed by two well eroded blocks that obscure chronological linkages.

Decipherment of the opening date of the text is also blocked. Date A offers fairly clear coefficients of 13 and 8 for the SR and VYr respectively. Details of the main signs are entirely lost although the VYr sign might be that of Uo or Zip by gross outline. With no reliable information as to the reading of these signs, and lacking a connecting SS, this date, as also Dates B and C, cannot be reconstructed.

ALTAR 13

Location: At surface in front of Structure B5, possibly *in situ*. Center of monument is about 7.27 m. to the right (NW) of the *in situ* butt of Stela 19

Associations: Possibly Stela 19

Dedicatory Date: 10.0.0.0.0   7 Ahau 18 Zip ?

Style Date: Ca. 9.19.0.0.0

Condition: Broken into fragments; relief details of carving preserved, fine details lost through erosion

Photographs: Fig. 42b
Satterthwaite 1954:Fig. 27

Drawings: Fig. 24

Other References: Satterthwaite 1954
Willcox 1954
Riese 1980:19-20

Carved Areas: Altar Class 1: T

Material: Limestone

Shape: Irregular round

Dimensions: Max. W: 1.60 m.   Max. Th: 0.35 m.
Min. W: 1.30 m.

GENERAL REMARKS

Altar 13 was found near but not necessarily in association with Stela 19 to the southeast and Altar 12 upside down to the east. It sat right side up and fragmented, with its pieces closely packed in proper alignment. All the bits of the monument were recovered or accounted for by excavation at the locus. It appears from this that Altar 13 probably was broken in place by natural agencies. The lower portion of the periphery was left unfinished as on Altar 12, so the monument was apparently intended to be set into a floor.

Local excavation around Altar 13 revealed no sub-altar cache although it did demonstrate that the altar was set into a somewhat eroded floor. Thus the stone was probably *in situ* where found, despite a somewhat pecular orientation. Digging was not extensive enough to absolutely rule out the possibility that a stela may have once been located nearby. Alignment of the altar's design was found to deviate from a straight line drawn to the nearby Stela 19 by about 21°. The front-back axis of Stela 19 deviated from the vertical axis of the Altar 13 design by about 69°, so that they were not even close to being parallel in orien-

tation. Similarly, the alignment of the altar varied from the apparent axis of Structure B5 by about 10°. Out-of-line position and especially the unusual orientation suggest that the altar, apparently in original position, might have been planned as a complete unit, without a stela.

However, there is nothing to preclude the possibility of re-setting of Altar 13. Indeed, there is some suggestion that the altar was intended to be read as a continuation of a stela text, as will be noted later. In Plaza B1 there is another anomaly formed by Stela 18. This stela was found on its side and lacking its butt portion. Possibly, the stela and Altar 13 were carved and erected as a pair (in the locus of the altar or elsewhere) and the stela was subsequently broken and moved across the plaza. Another search for the stela butt might resolve this issue. Such a pairing would allow us to hypothesize that Stela 19/Altar 12 marked the half-katun 9.19.10.0.0 and that Stela 18/Altar 13 then marked the katun end 10.0.0.0.0. Unfortunately, this appears to be the sort of speculation that will continue to beg resolution because evidence that could affirm or deny simply does not exist.

ALTAR 13: GLYPH CLASSIFICATION AND CHRONOLOGICAL DECIPHERMENT

(Order of reading: Main panel, clockwise; Panels V, W and X, left-right;
Panel U, left-right and downward; Panels Y and Z, downward. Number of blocks:
32 + 4 + 2(?) + 3 + 3 + 6 + 4 = 54)

Main Panel

A	(?. ?. ?. ?. ?)	1-2	CR date 9 _?_ 6-10 _?_ (details of day and month signs lost)
		3-12	10 non-calendrical glyphs (presumably contains a name phrase since this section ends with a Caracol Glyph at Block 11 and an "imix-comb-imix" *bacab* title at 12)
		13-17	5 non-calendrical glyphs, eroded
B	(?. ?. ?. ?. ?)	18-19	CR date 7-8 _?_ 18 _?_ (details of day and month signs lost)
		20-32	13 non-calendrical glyphs (details of most lost through erosion)

Panel U

		uA1	SSIG
SS1	_?. 4.19_	uB1	19 (kins), 4 uinals (possible continuation of SS1 into Panel X)
C	(9.19.10. 0. 0)	uB2-uB3	8 Ahau 8 Xul (Ahau and part of Xul reconstructed)

Panel V

		vA1-vB1	2 lost or eroded glyphs, presumably non-calendrical
SS2?	_10. 0. 0_	vC1	10 tuns (dubious reconstruction of tun sign without preceding SSIG)

Panel W

D	(10. 0. 0. 0. 0??)	wA1-wB1	7 Ahau 18 Zip (day and month signs reconstructed)
		wC1	1 eroded glyph, presumably non-calendrical

Panex X

		xA1-xB1	2 eroded or lost glyphs, presumably non-calendrical

Panel Y

		yA1-yA6	6 eroded blocks, all apparently non-calendrical

Panel Z

		zA1-zA4	4 eroded blocks, all apparently non-calendrical

ALTAR 13: SUMMARY OF CHRONOLOGY

1-2	Date A	CR	(?. ?. ?. ?. ?)	9 _?_ 6-10 _?_
18-19	Date B	CR	(?. ?. ?. ?. ?)	7-8 _?_ 18 _?_
uA1-uB1		SS1	_?. 4.19_	
uB2-uB3	Date C		(9.19.10. 0. 0)	4 Ahau 4 Xul
vC1		SS2?	_10. 0. 0_	
wA1-wB1	Date D		(10. 0. 0. 0. 0??)	7 Ahau 18 Zip

COMMENT ON THE INSCRIPTION

GLYPH BLOCK DESIGNATION; ORDER OF READING

Altar 13 offers a number of scattered glyph-bearing panels that have no obvious spatial relationship to each other. This and the paucity of SS's that lead neatly from CR to CR give rise to confusion over the proper order of reading. The obvious starting point might be taken as the long continuous statement in the four-lobed panel that encloses the scene. From its size and prominent position, this panel has been labeled as the Main Panel. Blocks within this group have been numbered simply 1 through 32 beginning with a likely starting point at the upper left.

Following the Main Panel, the other pieces of text have been labeled Panels U through Z. In this labeling, the practice of naming the panels with calendrical information before those containing only non-calendrical glyphs has been followed. Thus Panel U opens with an SS which presumably leads to a CR date. Panel V then might possibly be counting forward from that to a CR date in Panel W. Panel X is arbitrarily labeled next, although it should be noted that it appears likely that it is actually only an extension of Panel U. Panel U probably formed a T-shaped block of dates reading five glyphs across the top and then down the two glyphs of the CR. Unfortunately, the surface between Panels U and X has been lost from the stone and the two sets of glyphs have to be labeled separately. The final two blocks of glyphs appear to the left of the left-hand figure (Panel Y) and to the right of the right-hand figure (Panel Z). This proximity to these two characters suggests some association with the people represented, perhaps their names. Unfortunately, erosion is heavy, and confirmation for this speculation is difficult to find.

CHRONOLOGY RECORDED ON ALTAR 13

A full chronological decipherment of Altar 13 is hampered by the erosion of details of almost all of the main signs involved in dates and by the lack of connecting SS's. In the Main Panel there appear two CR's which might be taken as starting points for the text. Date A appears in Blocks 1-2 at the upper left corner, and Date B appears in a diametrically opposite position at the lower right corner (Blocks 18-19). Careful scrutiny of the eroded glyph blocks that separate these two dates allows us to say with certainty that no SS's exist to connect them. Date A bears coefficients of 9 for the day sign and 6-10 for the month sign. The form of the VYr main sign suggests that it might be read as Uo, Zip, Zec, Chen, Yax, Zac or Ceh. Coefficients of Date B are clearer than those of Date A. The SR has a reasonably certain SR coefficient of 7-8 and the VYr a coefficient of 18. At present, these dates cannot be placed into LC positions. A further point might be made about the symmetrical layout of the text within the Main Panel. In addition to the two CR dates falling at diametrically opposite interior corners, duplicate glyph groups (in layout, in any case) likewise fall in symmetrical positions at the upper right (Block 9) and lower left (Block 25). It is curious that these latter two glyphs as well as the two CR's all occupy positions at the opening blocks of each "lobe" of the text.

Panel U opens with an eroded but nonetheless clear SSIG (uA1), followed by an SS of at least 4.19. If indeed Panel X originally formed a part of Panel U, then the count may have been larger by some tuns or katuns. The date to which this SS leads (Date C) is a CR which by inspection

reads 8 ? 8 Xul. This date can be reasonably reconstructed by comparison with the dates on the nearby monuments Altar 12 and Stela 19 as 9.19.10.0.0 8 Ahau 8 Xul. Counting back the 4.19 of SS2 gives a hypothetical starting point for the count of 9.19.9.13.1 13 Imix 9 Pop. If the count was intended to proceed backward in time rather than forward, then it would lead from the LC position 9.19.10.4.19 3 Cauac 7 Zac. Neither of these CR dates could possibly be recorded on the altar. The beginning date for the count of SS2 was thus apparently only implied on the monument.

The only other date recorded on Altar 13 appears at the far right of the carving in Panel W. It takes the form of 7 ? 18 ? , with the second coefficient being slightly reconstructed. Examination of PE's around 9.19.10.0.0 reveals that the CR of 10.0.0.0.0 is 7 Ahau 18 Zip. If this is postulated to be the LC position of Date D, then a possible connective with Date C might be found in Panel V. There, at vC1, an eroded glyph carries a prefix of two bar-like elements. This might be very tentatively read as an SS of 10.0.0, although it lacks a characteristic SS subfix and is not preceded by any apparent SSIG.

From this discussion, it is apparent that our interpretation of the chronology recorded on Altar 13 can only be confused at best. The CR dates of the Main Panel appear to be unrelated to other dates on the stone by SS's. Even if we postulate that Dates A and B marked tun ends no obvious solution presents itself. The nearest such tun ends might be 9.17.14.0.0 9 Ahau 8 Muan for Date A and 9.18.4.0.0 8 Ahau 18 Ceh for Date B. And the VYr main signs as preserved by no means resemble particularly either Muan or Ceh. Glyphs of the Main Panel are best regarded as a separate text, or perhaps two separate texts beginning with CR's. SS 2 in Panel U has no starting point recorded on Altar 13. It was thus either implied or perhaps found on a stela that paired with the altar. In the latter case, a tentative assignment might be made to match Altar 13 with Stela 18 found across the plaza.

If the position of Date D at 10.0.0.0.0 is accepted, then it must by normal rules represent the DD. The marking of a baktun end might also have been depicted on this altar by the layout of the text of the Main Panel into the form of a "zero" sign to symbolize completion.

ALTAR 14

Location:	In Court A1 on the north-south axis; near but not associated with Stela 8
Associations:	Near Stela 8: lying over a fragment of Altar 15
Dedicatory Date:	9.5.0.0.0 11 Ahau
Style Date:	Undetermined
Condition:	Broken into three large fragments; surface pitted by erosion although the carving still largely legible
Photographs:	Fig. 42c Satterthwaite 1954:Fig. 33
Drawings:	Fig. 25a Satterthwaite 1954:Fig. 40
Other References:	Satterthwaite 1954 Riese 1980:20
Carved Areas:	Altar Class 1: T
Material:	Limestone
Shape:	Irregular round
Dimensions:	Max. W: 1.82 m. Th: ca. 0.35 m. Min. W: 1.72 m.

GENERAL REMARKS

Altar 14 lay misoriented near Stela 8 and just to the east of the north-south centerline of Court A1. It was broken into three large fragments, apparently by natural causes. Beneath the west edge of Altar 14 was found a well carved fragment of Altar 15 resting face up. This fragment sat in a layer of small limestone and stone fragments that supported Altar 14. There was apparently no cache below Altar 14, although the fragment of Altar 15 might be construed as such.

ALTAR 14: SUMMARY OF CHRONOLOGY

A1	Date A	CR	(9.5.0.0.0)	11 Ahau (18 Zec)

COMMENT ON THE INSCRIPTION

DEDICATORY DATE

Under the Short Count katun-naming hypothesis, Altar 14 should mark a date during or at the end of either the katun that ends at 9.5.0.0.0 or 9.18.0.0.0. The SR of 11 Ahau is also marked by the Giant Glyph Altar 3. As has been discussed (see Altar 3, "Comment on the Inscription") Altar 3 appears to be perhaps later than Altar 14 and is postulated to have marked the later katun 11 Ahau at 9.18.0.0.0. Altar 14 is thus considered to have marked 9.5.0.0.0, at which position it might have originally paired with Stela 16.

ALTAR 15

Location:	In Court A1 on north-south axis
Associations:	Found below Altar 14; near but not with Stela 8
Dedicatory Date:	9.9.0.0.0 3 Ahau ?
Style Date:	Undetermined
Condition:	A small fragment from the upper left of the monument is all that has been recovered; carving on this bit well preserved
Photographs:	Fig. 42c
Drawings:	Fig. 25b
Other References:	Satterthwaite 1954
	Riese 1980:20-21
Carved Areas:	Altar Class 1: T
Material:	Limestone
Shape:	Undetermined
Dimensions:	Max. W: ca. 2.06 m. (reconstructed) Th: 0.35 m.
	Min. W: ca. 1.72 m. (reconstructed)

GENERAL REMARKS

As noted earlier (see Altar 14, "General Remarks"), the known fragment of Altar 15 was found face up beneath the west edge of Altar 14. The recovered piece is well carved and nicely preserved. The stone was found set into a layer of small limestone and stone fragments that supported Altar 14.

ALTAR 15: SUMMARY OF CHRONOLOGY

A1	Date A	CR	(9.9.0.0.0)	3 Ahau (3 Zotz)

COMMENT ON THE INSCRIPTION

DEDICATORY DATE

Although Altar 15 is known only from a fragment, enough remains to allow reconstruction of its date and probable dimensions. In size, it is comparable to the large Altar 6 which is dated to 9.7.0.0.0 by our reconstruction. The coefficient can be confidently read as 3, which gives the practical choices of 9.9.0.0.0 and 10.2.0.0.0 as DD for Altar 15. A late position would stretch the known carving period for Giant Glyph Altars by a katun and would be difficult to reconcile with the use of the known fragment of the altar as part of the fill below Altar 14. The earlier position gives more time for the altar to have been broken up as obsolete. Supporting the selection of the early position for Altar 15 is the use of the scalloped frame which appears on other early Giant Glyph Altars (Altars 1, 3, 4, 19).

STELA PAIRING

Reconstruction of the DD's of the stelae places Stela 6 at perhaps 9.8.10.0.0 and Stela 5 at 9.9.0.0.0 in the LC. There are suggestions of a disturbed cache before the *in situ* Stela 5 which raises the possibility that Stelae 5, 6 and 7 all originally paired with altars. A hypothetical pairing would match Altars 15 and 11 with Stelae 5 and 6 (see also Altar 11, "Comment on the Inscription"). The geographical distance between these stelae and Altar 15 is not great. The final stela of the set, Stela 7, has been very tentatively placed at 9.9.10.0.0 where it may have paired with Altar 19.

ALTAR 16

Location:	Isolated at the base of the south slope of Structure B19 rising from Court B3
Associations:	None apparent
Dedicatory Date:	10.0.0.0.0 7 Ahau
Style Date:	Undetermined
Condition:	Upper right and lower left edges are broken away; carving largely preserved, although details of the Ahau are gone
Photographs:	Fig. 43a
Drawings:	Fig. 25c Satterthwaite 1954:Fig. 38
Other References:	Satterthwaite 1954 Riese 1980:21
Carved Areas:	Altar Class 1: T
Material:	Limestone
Shape:	Round
Dimensions:	Max. W: 1.07 m. Th: 0.30 m. Min. W: 1.03 m.

GENERAL REMARKS

Altar 16, the smallest Giant Glyph Altar, was found partially buried on the south slope of Structure B19. It rested on and among some small limestone construction blocks. The monument sloped and its center axis was 90° off the center-line of Structure B19. Thus it was presumably not in a position of intentional placement. Probably it had fallen from a placement higher on the structure. The lower left and upper right edges have fractured off. Preservation is good except that the details of the presumed Ahau have not survived erosion.

ALTAR 16: SUMMARY OF CHRONOLOGY

A1	Date A	CR	(10.0.0.0.0)	7 Ahau (18 Zip)

COMMENT ON THE INSCRIPTION

DEDICATORY DATE

As noted earlier for Altar 6, both that altar and Altar 16 mark 7 Ahau (see Altar 6, "Comment on the Inscription"). Because of the presence of some presumed earlier traits on Altar 6 and their lack on Altar 16 it has been assumed that a period of time separated their carving and that Altar 6 is the earlier. Accordingly, Altar 16 has been assigned to the commemoration of 10.0.0.0.0 and Altar 6 to 9.7.0.0.0.

ORIGINAL PLACEMENT; STELA PAIRING

Since Altar 16 was found fallen partway down the side of a structure, any association with another monument that may have existed higher up the structure has been lost through natural architectural collapse. However, the locus atop Structure B19 is improbably high for stela placement, considering the locations of other stelae at Caracol. It seems that Altar 16 must either have been sited atop Structure B19 without a stela pair, or was secondarily moved there from a hypothetical original accompanying stela.

At this point in time it is difficult to suggest a possible stela complement to Altar 16. Dates during or at the end of the katun 10.0.0.0.0 are marked by Stela 19, Altar 12, Altar 13 and possibly Stela 18. Thus there appears to be a surfeit of altars for the possible number of stelae erected during this katun. A possible solution would be to consider the two Scene Altars 12 and 13 to be independent monuments. However, this hypothesis would contradict the need for an accompanying monument for Altar 13, as is demonstrated by the "hanging" SS1 on that stone.

ALTAR 17

Location:	Resting on edge near the top of Structure A2
Associations:	None apparent
Dedicatory Date:	9.16.0.0.0 2 Ahau ?
Style Date:	Undetermined
Condition:	Missing the lower left edge; remainder fragmented and heavily eroded in areas
Photographs:	Fig. 43b
Drawings:	Fig. 25d
Other References:	Satterthwaite 1954
	Riese 1980:21
Carved Areas:	Altar Class 5: TFLRB
Material:	Limestone
Shape:	Rectangular
Dimensions:	Max. W: 1.36 m. Th: 0.32 m.
	Min. W: 1.08 m.

GENERAL REMARKS

Altar 17 was discovered resting on edge on the east slope of Structure A2 only about 5 m. from the top of the ruined structural debris. A large piece of the lower part of the monument had fragmented off. Flaking had destroyed a strip of carving between the glyph coefficient and the centerline of the altar. Erosion blurred much of the remaining carving. The position of the altar may have come about as the result of sliding down from a higher point, as was probably the case with Stela 16. However, there is a possibility that it was purposely erected on edge. As found, the design was upright and in position to be read by a viewer approaching Structure A2 from Court A1.

ALTAR 17: GLYPH CLASSIFICATION AND CHRONOLOGICAL DECIPHERMENT

(Order of reading: Unknown. Number of glyph blocks: 12 + 1 = 13)

Panel Y

	y1-y12	12 badly eroded or lost glyph blocks, some bearing remains of coefficients

Panel Z

A	(9.16. 0. 0. 0)	zA1	2, 7 or 12 Ahau (2 Ahau reconstructed)

ALTAR 17: SUMMARY OF CHRONOLOGY

zA1	Date A	CR	(9.16. 0. 0. 0)	2 Ahau (13 Zec)

COMMENT ON THE INSCRIPTION

DEDICATORY DATE

As has been noted (see Altar 2, "Comment on the Inscription") Altar 2 and Altar 17 share a number of features that distinguish them as a set distinct from other Caracol monuments.

The spot glyphs of Altar 17 are largely destroyed although there are traces of numerical coefficients at Block y1 and possibly y5. The bits that survive of the large central glyph suggest that it may have been a full-figure glyph. The coefficient that accompanies this glyph displays two clear dots separated by a feather filler. The right edges of the elements of the coefficient are scaled off along with the area immediately to their right. There is thus a certain amount of space between the known elements of the coefficient and the reconstructed left edge of the cartouche of the main sign. One or two numerical bars of the coefficient could have fitted into this zone, and this has been indicated on the drawing. However, an examination of the height to width ratios of the cartouches of the main signs of other Giant Glyph Altars at Caracol severely contradicts the possibility of bars in the prefixed coefficient. To allow space for bars, the ratio of height to width for the cartouche of Altar 17 must be about 0.80. This may be compared with a figure of about 0.71 for Altar 4, the tallest among all other Giant Glyph Altar cartouches. Altar 2 gives a ratio of 0.62. Applying the proportion derived from Altar 2 causes the main sign cartouche of Altar 17 to fill the entire space to the right of the two preserved dots of the coefficient.

Possible LC positions for Altar 17 are listed below, allowing for the presumably thin chance that the coefficient may have been 7 or 12 rather than the more likely 2:

Altar 17

9. 3.0.0.0   2 Ahau (marked by Altar 4)
9. 7.0.0.0   7 Ahau (marked by Altar 6)
9.11.0.0.0 12 Ahau (marked by Altar 7)
9.16.0.0.0   2 Ahau
10. 0.0.0.0   7 Ahau (marked by Altar 16)
10. 4.0.0.0 12 Ahau

Economy of monuments as well as the clear differences between Altar 17 and other Giant Glyph Altars allows the elimination of those LC positions already known to be marked. The late 12 Ahau date at 10.4.0.0.0 not only disagrees with the preferred reading of 2 Ahau but falls beyond the local monument carving limit of 10.1.0.0.0 for the well dated Stela 17/Altar 10 or 10.3.0.0.0 for the not so certain position of Stela 10. The LC position of 9.16.0.0.0 appears (granted the assumptions underlying our methods of date elimination) to be a fairly secure date for Altar 17. As has been argued for Altar 2 (see the "Comment on the Inscription" for that monument) it is reasonable to postulate that Altar 17 was also intended to stand alone instead of paired with a stela.

ALTAR 18

Location:	On south slope of Structure B6
Associations:	None apparent
Dedicatory Date:	10.1.0.0.0 5 Ahau ??
Style Date:	Undetermined
Condition:	Only two fragments of the upper right portion of the monument were recovered. What was found is heavily eroded
Photographs:	None
Drawings:	Fig. 26a
Other References:	Satterthwaite 1954
	Riese 1980:21-22
Carved Areas:	Altar Class 1: T
Material:	Limestone
Shape:	Undetermined
Dimensions:	Max. W: ca. 1.60 m. (reconstructed) Th: 0.25 m.
	Min. W: ca. 1.56 m. (reconstructed)

GENERAL REMARKS

As known, Altar 18 consists of two large fitting fragments found together on the sloping surface of Structure B6. This position probably reflects a combination of disturbances by both natural and human agencies. As with Altar 16, Altar 18 in all likelihood paired with a stela somewhere in a plaza or courtyard at ground level.

The two recovered fragments of Altar 18 account for rather more than half of the weathered top surface and about half of the periphery. The larger right fragment showed no remaining signs of sculpture, but the left displayed traces of a bar over a cartouche.

ALTAR 18: SUMMARY OF CHRONOLOGY

A1	Date A	CR	(10. 1. 0. 0. 0)	5 Ahau (3 Kayab)

COMMENT ON THE INSCRIPTION

DEDICATORY DATE

Difficulty in the assignment of an LC position arises from the poor state of preservation of this monument. Fortunately, the carving that did survive on Altar 18 is in the area of the superfixed coefficient. There, enough remains to reconstruct the number as a single bar with no dots. The bar could not have been divided longitudinally without making the resultant two bars disproportionately narrow. Traces of an incised line within the bar probably represent the remains of interior decoration such as found on other Giant Glyph Altars at Caracol. Carving on Altar 18 differs from that of other Giant Glyph Altars by being incised without relief. Further, there is no evidence of an enclosing border or frame around the periphery of the top.

Altar 18 presumably marks either 9.8.0.0.0 or 10.1.0.0.0 by the reconstructed 5 Ahau reading. The early date is marked by the securely dated pair of Stela 1/Altar 1. Similarly, the late position is dedicated by Stela 17/Altar 10 of equally certain date. Thus neither date can be preferred on the basis of economy of marking by monuments. The alternative seems to be that Altar 18 marked a date (with a presently unknown stela) during the current rather than the lapsed katun, perhaps at the half-katun preceding the katun end.

Altar 18 was found in the structural grouping that contained Altar 16, Altar 12, Altar 13, Stela 18 and Stela 19. All of these (with the possible exception of Stela 18) are monuments of demonstrably late date (9.19.10.0.0 for Altar 12 and Stela 19; 10.0.0.0.0 for Altar 6, Altar 13, and possibly Stela 18). Location thus seems to argue rather strongly for the late 10.1.0.0.0 rather than the early 9.8.0.0.0 date.

Lack of an enclosing frame is different from the situation on Altar 1 as is the lack of relief carving on Altar 18. In size and shape, Altar 18 conforms generally to the pattern of Altar 1 rather than to the late Altar 16. If the late position is preferred for Altar 18, then the feature of large irregular shape postdates as well as predates the relatively round and small Altars 7 (9.11.0.0.0) and 16 (10.0.0.0.0). This is by no means unlikely since large size and irregular round shape may still have been standard down to 9.10.0.0.0 and present but not universal thereafter. Altar 3 seems to confirm this latter possibility, falling as it does at 9.18.0.0.0 between Altars 7 and 16 yet still being relatively large and irregular round in shape. To avoid placing Altar 18 chronologically near to Altar 1 which differs in the only two stylistic details that can be discerned, the late date during or at the end of the katun 10.1.0.0.0 is preferred despite the similarities in shape and size of the two stones.

ALTAR 19

See "Stela 11/Altar 19" for a discussion of this monument

STONE 28

Location: At northwest base of Structure A18; presumably rolled down from original placement
Associations: None apparent
Dedicatory Date: None
Style Date: Undetermined
Condition: Weathered but clear
Photographs: Fig. 43d Satterthwaite 1954:Fig. 31 (photograph reversed)
Drawings: Fig. 28a, b, c
Other References: Satterthwaite 1954
Carved Areas: Front
Material: Limestone
Shape: Roughly wedge-shaped
Dimensions: Height: 0.50 m.
                     Width: 0.40 m.
                     Depth: 0.94 m.

GENERAL REMARKS

Stone 28 was found on the surface near Structure A18 in 1951 by Ascensión Alfaro. During excavation, it was noted that this stone rested on two or three flat pieces of limestone without any evidence of solid placement. It seems unlikely that it was intended to be viewed from this position because the sides and back are only roughly shaped. A more likely postulate is that the stone was intended to be fitted into a masonry surface. In this manner it could possibly have served as a column altar or, less probably, as a horizontally placed decorative element.

IV: SUMMARY
STELA AND ALTAR PLACEMENT AND PAIRING

Chronological ordering of the monuments of Caracol has proven to be a difficult task. Poor state of preservation of many of the stones has precluded positive dating. However, DD's have been suggested for many otherwise undated monuments by a combination of spatial proximity and locational evidence. Table 1 presents in an abbreviated form the conclusions reached in the preceding monument descriptions.

Some assumptions have been utilized throughout this text to assist with the reconstruction of DD's of damaged monuments. It has been assumed that monuments generally marked ending days of either the katun or half-katun. This rule is contradicted by only one sure example: Stela 3, which apparently bears a DD of 9.10.4.7.0. Another important postulate is that the stelae and altars generally formed pairs in their original placements. Finally, the hypothesis has been applied wherever possible that any one katun or half-katun end was marked by a single stela with but one altar. None of these assumptions appears to be absolutely correct. However, they are well supported in a general way by the following evidence from monuments at Caracol that are readable and/or in original placement. Stelae 1, 13, 14, 16, 17 and 21 all carry katun or half-katun ending DD's. No two of these mark an identical DD. The likely erection of Stelae 13, 14 and 16 at sequent katun ends in Court A2 further suggests that the stelae were intended to mark different dates. The primary associations of Stela 1/Altar 1, Stela "X"/Altar 3 and Stela 17/Altar 10 along

with the appearance of probable subaltar caches in front of Stelae 5 and 14 suggest that a pattern of regular stela/altar pairing was followed.

Altar 4 seems to be the earliest monument known from Caracol. It was found in close proximity to Stela 9 but was apparently not originally placed at that spot. Stela 9, although badly damaged, appears to be similar to the late Stelae 8 and 11 nearby. Altar 4 on the other hand seems most like the earlier of the Giant Glyph Altars. Thus the clear 2 Ahau on the altar allows its placement in or at the end of the Katun 9.3.0.0.0. Application of the above assumptions regarding stela and altar pairing permits us to suggest the existence of a presently unknown stela of the same age as Altar 4. Since Altar 4 is apparently at a locus of secondary erection, the precise area where monuments began to be erected at Caracol is unknown.

The earliest known scene of monument activity was on Platform A1 (Court A2) for the four katun ends from 9.4.0.0.0 to 9.7.0.0.0. Stelae 13, 16, 14 and 15 in that order marked these katun ends. All four stelae were probably erected in a line paralleling the approximate east-west axis of Court A2. They faced roughly south toward the center of Platform A1. Stela 13 preserves parts of a long inscription on its back with two SS's that probably count backward from an IS/LS of 9.4.0.0.0. Its butt was found *in situ* and apparently marks the western extension of the stela row. Stela 16 was found broken beneath the floor that the secondarily placed Altar 7 was set into. This stela shows an IS/LS of 9.5.0.0.0. Stela 14 carries an IS of 9.6.0.0.0. Like Stela 13, it had broken away from an *in situ* butt and lay above the final flooring of the court. Slate Stela 15 is the least well preserved of the set despite its clear IS of 9.4.16.13.3. Following the assumptions that the DD of Stela 15 is later than its IS (there are traces of more than one SS preserved) and that the stela formed a part of a coherent set with the other three stelae found in Court A2, the DD has been reconstructed as 9.7.0.0.0. Stela 15 was broken and buried before the placement of Altar 7 at this locus, since a piece of the stela turned up directly beneath the altar.

In the section describing the altars, it is suggested that Altars 14, 5 and 6 found buried in the debris of Court A1 marked the current or expired Katuns 9.5.0.0.0, 9.6.0.0.0 and 9.7.0.0.0 respectively. If this was the case they were probably originally paired to Stelae 16, 14 and 15 respectively in accordance with one of the above-given assumptions. An apparent sub-altar cache found disturbed in front of Stela 14 and below the cache associated with Altar 7 suggests that an altar was indeed placed there prior to Altar 7. This hypothetical pairing of monuments leaves Stela 13 unpaired. From this fact, it can be considered likely that an early 13 Ahau altar exists,

possibly buried in the debris of Court A1 where Altars 14, 5 and 6 were located.

With the advent of Katun 9.8.0.0.0 5 Ahau, the area of monument placement shifted southward. Stela 1/Altar 1 were erected at the base of the apparent reverse slope of Structure A1. These two monuments form the best preserved Stela/Giant Glyph Altar pair. Stela 1 has a single IS date of 9.8.0.0.0, and its altar carries a clear 5 Ahau.

Following the erection of Stela 1/Altar 1, monuments began to be placed even farther south. Stelae 5, 6 and 7 were erected in an approximate north-south line at the west base of Structure A13, facing west. None of these three *in situ* monuments carries a certain preserved DD. A single glyph-bearing frame was preserved on the right side of Stela 5. On Stela 6 the entire right side has survived, but nothing of the left side. On Stela 7 almost nothing has remained. Preserved glyphs on Stelae 5 and 6 are apparently from the first halves of the respective texts. Thus possibilities exist for later DD's now lost. Stela 5 records a katun end at 9.9.0.0.0 at one point. The latest date preserved on Stela 6 marks 9.8.10.0.0. By assuming that the three monuments marked sequent or identical katuns or half-katuns, possible DD's can be suggested for them. Three options have been suggested:

	I	II	III
Stela 6	9.8.10.0.0	9.9. 0.0.0	9.9.0.0.0
Stela 5	9.9. 0.0.0	9.9.10.0.0	9.9.0.0.0
Stela 7	9.9.10.0.0	9.10.0.0.0	9.9.0.0.0

Option I means that the latest katun or half-katun marked must have been the DD. It avoids multiple marking of the same DD and allows us to tentatively pair the Giant Glyph Altars 11, 15 and 19 (3, 3, 1 Ahau) to Stelae 5, 6 and 7. It has the disadvantage that it would cause Stela 7 to postdate the postulated death of Lord Water to whom Stela 6 is probably dedicated (see pages 114-130). Under Option I the three stelae might not have formed a coherent set as regards subject matter. Option II would be even further out of line in that regard and also would leave one of the two 3 Ahau altars (Altars 11 and 15) as well as either Stela 6 or 7 unpaired. Option III would bring all three DD's into the reign of Lord Water by plac-

ing them all at the same date. This would be unusual for this time at Caracol, since other dates prior to this seem to be marked by only a single stela. Also, III would leave one of the stelae unpaired by any known monument, since there exist only two altars marking Katun 3 Ahau. It would also mean that Altar 19 would be unpaired by any known stela during the Katun 1 Ahau ending at 9.10.0.0.0. Considering the fact that the stelae form a spatial set and that they can thus be presumed to have had a common subject, Options I and III are favored. For economy, Option I might be slightly preferred since it allows us to pair all the known stelae and altars of the period. Following this option, Stela 7 (which would postdate the death of Lord Water) might have been planned as commemorative to the deceased ruler. All this speculation may of course prove to be fruitless if future investigations at Caracol bring to light other monuments dating to this same period.

After the hypothetical 9.10.0.0.0 date of Stela 7 there are no known *in situ* monuments until perhaps 9.18.0.0.0. The earliest monuments known after 9.10.0.0.0 are Stela 3 and its possible Giant Glyph Altar complement Altar 7 (12 Ahau). Stela 3 marks 9.10.4.7.0 as its latest date, which falls into the katun that ends at 9.11.0.0.0. It was found in two pieces widely separated in two different areas of the site. Altar 7 turned up in presumed secondary placement in Court A2 in front of Stela 14 dating to 9.6.0.0.0. Installation of Altar 7 at this location must postdate the breakage and burial of Stelae 15 and 16 since pieces of those monuments were, as noted earlier, discovered directly below the altar.

Postulated Court A2 Giant Glyph Altars (Altars 14, 5, 6) must have been moved and Stelae 15 and 16 cast down sometime before the disturbance of Altar 7 from its location and its movement to Court A2. The destruction of the two stelae presumably happened after the initial erection of Stela 15 at perhaps 9.7.0.0.0; (although Stela 16 may have been broken earlier, this can be considered unlikely). If a katun of use is allowed as a minimum before breakage, then the Court A2 monument disturbance dates to 9.8.0.0.0 — ?. If we allow a katun of use for Stela 3 and Altar 7 also as a minimum, their breakup and movement would not have occurred until at least 9.12.0.0.0.

Following movement from original loci of erection, the majority of the "early" Giant Glyph Altars found themselves in Court A1. Altar 1 was not moved at all, Altar 7 was set on Court A2 only a short distance up Platform A1 from Court A1 and Altar 11 wound up far away at the base of Structure B2. Altars 5 and 6 were discovered unassociated with any monuments at the north extremity of Court A1. Altars 4, 14 and 19 were found near but unaligned with Stelae 9, 8 and 11 respectively. A fragment of Altar 15 was found beneath Altar 14. The positions of these latter four altars in front of Stelae 8, 9 and 11 suggest that their movements may have occurred around the time of placement of the three stelae at about

9.19.0.0.0. It seems most economical to hypothesize that the destruction and movement of the "early" stelae and altars happened during a single short period of monument disturbance. There is, however, no way to pin down the upper end dates for dispersal of the monuments. All that can be stated with assurance is that the disturbance of Altar 15 occurred during or before the disturbance of Altars 14, 5 and 6 and Stelae 15 and 16, all of which happened sometime before the disturbance of Stela 3/Altar 7 after 9.11.0.0.0.

One monument bears a date in the gap that exists between Stela 3 at 9.10.4.7.0 and the two "spot-complex" Altars 17 and 2 at 9.16.0.0.0 and 9.17.0.0.0. Almost exactly in the middle of this spread fits the date of the fragmentary Stela 21 at 9.13.10.0.0. The original place of erection of Stela 21 is unknown and no possible Giant Glyph Altar pair has been discovered.

Two extraordinary monuments in separated locations apparently marked katuns 9.16.0.0.0 2 Ahau and 9.17.0.0.0 13 Ahau: Altars 17 and 2, the "spot-complex" altars. Altar 2 appears to be in secondary placement in Plaza A3 through the action of human agencies. Altar 17 may have slid down from a placement further up on Structure A2 or may possibly have been intentionally placed on edge facing Court A1. Its position on Structure A2 quite likely represents movement from wherever it was primarily deposited.

Altar 3 and the fragment of slate stela butt labeled Stela "X" might have been placed at 9.18.0.0.0 in Court A1 in front of Structure A1. The altar, on legs, and the stela butt are apparently *in situ*. Comparison of the slate butt with recovered slate stelae suggests that Stela 4 actually was the upper portion of Stela "X." The three fragments of Stela 4 were recovered in Plaza A3.

Around the time of the Katun 9 Ahau ending at 9.19.0.0.0, three stelae might have been erected in Court A1. Stela 9 (almost destroyed by erosion and truck passage) was discovered in the exact center of Court A1. Stela 11 was located on the north-south axis of the court about halfway between Stela 9 and Structure A3 to the north. Stela 8 was erected on the north-south axis in a complementary position to the south. Possibly at this time the disturbance of Altars 4, 14, 15 and 19 took place. As is the case with Altars 2 and 17, these three stelae as a set are most similar to each other and differ from any others at Caracol.

All three have a wide flat front surface, only one carved face and a wide border. Furthermore, they have a common figural layout of a dominant central character with diagonal serpent bar with a "dwarf" to the lower left. This basic arrangement is also found on Stelae 1, 21 and the front side of Stela 6 at earlier dates. However, these earlier stelae as well as all the others of which we now know that precede 9.18.0.0.0, bear their main texts in large continuous blocks, or (for Stelae 5 and 6) in regular glyph panels on the sides. Stelae 8, 9 and 11 on the other hand bear their inscriptions in irregular panels of glyphs that are scattered about the figural carving.

After the 9.18.0.0.0. DD of Stela 8, monument activity seems to have moved east. Stela 19 in Plaza B2 was *in situ* but badly damaged. However, a CR date provides a possible DD of 9.19.10.0.0 8 Ahau for the monument. The same date seems to be recorded on Altar 12 nearby. The similar Altar 13 with a DD of 10.0.0.0.0 lay nearby. Stela 18, a peculiar monument, rests also in Plaza B1 and may have dated to around the same period. A case might be made for a pairing of Stela 19 with Altar 12 and Stela 18 with Altar 13. But another plausible suggestion might be that the two scene altars actually paired with each other. The displaced Giant Glyph Altar 16 could then have coupled with Stela 19 and possibly Altar 18 with the unreadable Stela 18 at 10.0.10.0.0 or 10.1.0.0.0.

Katun 5 Ahau at 10.0.0.0.0 was marked by the stela/scene altar pair of Stela 17/Altar 10 at a point somewhere outside the zone of major constructional activity as we know it. Stela 17 carries only a CR notation and is crudely executed.

Altar 10 is also crudely done and carries a largely eroded glyphic notation. This monument pair is far to the southeast of Group B, apparently far from any other monuments.

A possible final monument at Caracol appears two katuns after Stela 17/Altar 10. Stela 10 was erected on the north-south axis of Court A1 a little to the north of Stela 9. It presents a crudely carved purely glyphic inscription. The appearance of the glyphs is similar to those on Stela 17. Its notation appears to be in CR's concluding with an eroded 1 Ahau that presumably marks the DD at 10.3.0.0.0. This date is uncertain.

As summarized above, the calendric record of Caracol presents many gaps. Monuments that we know of were all located by surface survey. It appears likely from the experiences at other sites that many other stelae and altars were wrecked and buried one way or another and may now lie concealed beneath rubble tailings at the margins of tumbled structures. A more thorough clearing of these structures is needed to determine this. It may well develop that the apparent gap in monument activity that we now note between 9.11.0.0.0 and 9.16.0.0.0 is simply due to the accident of recovery. Indeed, the position of Stela 21 in the middle of this gap suggests that this is the case.

Three tables that summarize many of the details presented already in the preceding descriptions of individual monuments and discussion conclude this summary. The first, Table 1, presents details of the stelae. Table 2 then summarizes features of the Giant Glyph Altars. Finally, a reconstructed chronological ordering of monuments is essayed in Table 3.

TABLE 1
SYNOPSES OF STELAE
Asterisk indicates reconstructed dimension

Monument Label	Carved Areas	Morley Designation	Starting Point of Text	Figure Facing/ Feet Facing	Height of Carving	Width of Stela
Stela 1	C1 1: F	(M7)	F	L/L	2.08	0.88
Stela 2	C1 3: FLR?	(M3)?	?	F/?	?	0.90*
Stela 3	C1 2: FB	(M1)	B	?/L	2.65*	0.89
Stela 4	C1 2: FB	(M1)	?	?/F	2.60*	0.74*
Stela 5	C1 3: FLR	(M3)	L	L/F	3.02	1.22
Stela 6	C1 4: FLRB	(M2)	R	L/F	3.13	0.74
Stela 7	C1 3: FLR?	(M3)?	?	?	?	0.65
Stela 8	C1 1: F	(M7)	F	L/?	2.55*	0.46*
Stela 9	C1 1: F	(M7)	F	L/?	1.96*	1.25
Stela 10	C1 1: F	(M5)	F	–	2.00	1.04
Stela 11	C1 1: F	(M7)	F	L/	3.25*	1.15
Stela 12	Plain	–	–	–	1.90*	1.00*
Stela 13	C1 2: FB	(M1)	B	L/L	1.95	0.82
Stela 14	C1 1: F	(M7)	F	L/FS	2.45	0.80
Stela 15	C1 1: F	(M7)	F	?/L	1.85	0.62
Stela 16	C1 2: FB	(M1)	B	L/	2.10	0.74*
Stela 17	C1 3: FLR	(M3)	F	R/FS; L/FS	2.34	0.85*
Stela 18	C1 1: F	(M1)	F	R		0.75*
Stela 19	C1 3: FLR	(M3)	?	?		1.10*
Stela 20	C1 1: F	(M–)	F	R/RS; L/LS		0.75
Stela 21	C1 1: F	(M7)	F	L/F	2.10*	0.85

TABLE 1

Method of Recording DD	Style Date	Number of Glyph Blocks	Present Location	Material
IS	9. 5. 0.0.0 ± 3K (TP)	36	Belize	Limestone
?		?	Caracol	Limestone
IS	9. 6. 0.0.0 K (TP)	164	Denver	Limestone
?		?	Philadelphia	Slate
PE	9. 9. 0.0.0 ± 2K (TP)	220	Philadelphia	Limestone
IS	9. 8.15.0.0 ± 1.25K (TP)	154	Philadelphia	Limestone
?		?	Caracol	Limestone
IS		13	Caracol	Limestone
?		17	Caracol	Limestone
PE		14	Caracol	Limestone
PE	9.16. 0.0.0 ± 2K (TP)	28	Caracol	Limestone
—		—	Caracol	Limestone
IS		64	Caracol	Limestone
IS		48	Caracol	Limestone
IS		88	Philadelphia	Slate
IS	9. 4. 0.0.0 K (TP)	75	Philadelphia	Limestone
PE		29	Philadelphia	Limestone
?		8	Caracol	Limestone
PE		44	Caracol	Limestone
?		51	Caracol	Limestone
IS		19	Belmopan	Slate

TABLE 2
SYNOPSES OF CARACOL GIANT GLYPH ALTARS
BY SUGGESTED LC POSITIONS
Scene Altars 10, 12 and 13; Plain Altars 8, 9 not included in this tabulation

Katun ends	Altars	Border or Frame	Giant Glyph Cartouche	Central Pedestal Element	Decorated Coefficient?
9. 3.0.0.0 2 Ahau	Altar 4	Frame; scalloped	Notched	T-shape	?
9. 4.0.0.0 13 Ahau					
9. 5.0.0.0 11 Ahau	Altar 14	Frame; scalloped	?	Ovoid	No
9. 6.0.0.0 9 Ahau	Altar 5	U-shaped panel?	?	?	?
9. 7.0.0.0 7 Ahau	Altar 6	Border; scalloped	?	T-shape	Yes
9. 8.0.0.0 5 Ahau	Altar 1	Frame; scalloped	Notched	T-shape	Yes
9. 9.0.0.0 3 Ahau	Altar 11	Border; scalloped	?	?	?
	Altar 15	Frame; scalloped	?	T-shape	Yes
9.10.0.0.0 1 Ahau	Altar 19	Frame; scalloped	Notched	T-shape	No
9.11.0.0.0 12 Ahau	Altar 7	Border; scalloped	Notched	T-shape	Yes
9.12.0.0.0 10 Ahau					
9.13.0.0.0 8 Ahau					
9.14.0.0.0 6 Ahau					
9.15.0.0.0 4 Ahau					
9.16.0.0.0 2 Ahau	Altar 17	Border; simple	Simple	?	?
9.17.0.0.0 13 Ahau	Altar 2	Border; simple	Simple	Simple	?
9.18.0.0.0 11 Ahau	Altar 3	Frame; scalloped	Simple	T-shape	No
9.19.0.0.0 9 Ahau					
10. 0.0.0.0 7 Ahau	Altar 16	Border; simple	Simple	U-shape	No
10. 1.0.0.0 5 Ahau	Altar 18	No border or frame	?	?	Yes?

TABLE 2

Filler	Maximum Diameter	Shape	Supports (if any)
None	1.77 m.	Irregular round	—
Crescent	1.82 m.	Irregular round	—
?	1.93 m.	Irregular oval	—
"Feathers"	2.25 m.	Irregular oval	Tripod
—	2.07 m.	Oval	
?	1.67 m.	Irregular oval	Blocks
—	2.00 m.	Irregular round	
"Feathers"	1.81 m.	Flattened round	
"Feathers"	1.38 m.	Round	
"Feathers"	1.36 m.	Oblong	
?	1.17 m.	Square	
Crescent	1.78 m.	Irregular round	**Tripod**
Crescent	1.07 m.	Round	
—	1.60 m.	Irregular round	

TABLE 3
LONG COUNT POSITIONS BY KATUN ENDS
FOR CARACOL STELAE AND ALTARS
Asterisks indicate original stela/altar pairs. Superfixed numerals
mark stelae and altars found secondarily paired.

Katun ends	Stelae (date)
9. 0.0.0.0 8 Ahau	
9. 1.0.0.0 6 Ahau	
9. 2.0.0.0 4 Ahau	
9. 3.0.0.0 2 Ahau	. . . .
9. 4.0.0.0 13 Ahau	Stela 13 (9.4.0.0.0)
9. 5.0.0.0 11 Ahau	Stela 16 (9.5.0.0.0) . . . .
9. 6.0.0.0 9 Ahau	Stela 14 (9.6.0.0.0)[1] . . . .
9. 7.0.0.0 7 Ahau	Stela 15 (9.4.16.13.3 + ?) . . . .
9. 8.0.0.0 5 Ahau	Stela 1 (9.8.0.0.0)* . . . .
9. 9.0.0.0 3 Ahau	Stela 5 (9.9.0.0.0 ?); Stela 6 (9.8.10.0.0 ??) . . . .
9.10.0.0.0 1 Ahau	Stela 7 (9.9.10.0.0 ???) . . . .
9.11.0.0.0 12 Ahau	Stela 3 (9.10.4.7.0) . . . .
9.12.0.0.0 10 Ahau	
9.13.0.0.0 8 Ahau	
9.14.0.0.0 6 Ahau	Stela 21 (9.13.10.0.0)
9.15.0.0.0 4 Ahau	
9.16.0.0.0 2 Ahau	. . . .
9.17.0.0.0 13 Ahau	. . . .
9.18.0.0.0 11 Ahau	Stela "X"/4? (9.18.0.0.0 ???) . . . .
9.19.0.0.0 9 Ahau	Stela 8 (9.19.0.0.0 ?); Stela 11 (9.18.10.0.0 ??),[2] Stela 9 (ca. 9.19.0.0.0 ?)[3]
10. 0.0.0.0 7 Ahau	Stela 19 (9.19.10.0.0) . . . .
10. 1.0.0.0 5 Ahau	Stela 17 (10.1.0.0.0)* . . . .
10. 2.0.0.0 3 Ahau	
10. 3.0.0.0 1 Ahau	Stela 10 (10.3.0.0.0 ??)
10. 4.0.0.0 12 Ahau	

TABLE 3

Giant Glyph Altars	Spot-Complex Altars	Scene Altars
Altar 4[3]		
Altar 14		
Altar 5		
Altar 6		
Altar 1*		
Altar 15; Altar 11		
Altar 19[2]		
Altar 7[1]		
. . . . Altar 17		
. . . . Altar 2		
Altar 3		
Altar 16 . . . . Altar 12 (9.19.10.0.0);		
		Altar 13 (10.0.0.0.0 ?)
Altar 18 . . . . Altar 10*		

V: THE RULERS OF CARACOL

This final portion of the report presents a study of the non-calendric pieces of the Caracol inscriptions. The technique of research employed is one that might be labeled "clausal comparison." Using this approach, several investigators have discovered information about the lives of rulers and related characters at Maya sites (Proskouriakoff 1960, 1961, 1963, 1964; Kelley 1962; Coggins 1975; Jones 1977; Matthews and Schele 1974). The procedure involves examination of "clauses" of similar date or epigraphic content in order to recognize the meaning of glyphs by their repetitive contexts and to isolate probable events and people involved. Success of these tactics varies in direct proportion to the quantities of legible inscriptions at a given site.

Caracol displays a dearth of chronologically overlapping clauses on its monuments. It is therefore difficult to substantiate new readings at this site. Rather, research must utilize advances made at other sites to interpret the bits of remaining texts. The outline of dynastic history that follows is based on a series of single readings generally without confirming texts. As a result, the discussion makes no claim to be the final interpretation. The analysis that led to the conclusions that follow has evolved and been modified through ongoing discussion with Christopher Jones.

Dynastic information on the Caracol monuments has already been the subject of some earlier research. Berlin (1973) was the first to note the name phrases and birth dates of two of the Caracol personalities. At about the same time Satterthwaite became aware of the T740 "up-ended frog" that marks "birth" statements on

Stela 3 which he had originally added to the discussion of that stone for this report. Later, an outline of the material presented here appeared (Beetz 1980). Recently, an undergraduate course at the University of Texas, Austin, taught by Linda Schele, studied the Caracol inscriptions by means of the University of Pennsylvania drawings. This led initially to a short preliminary article dealing with Caracol rulers (Sosa and Reents 1980). In this case the interpretation differs rather dramatically from that presented here. Since the writing of this section, another paper by Stone, Reents and Coffman was read at the 1980 Palenque conference. Unfortunately the new interpretations could not be worked into the current essay. However, the authors of that work have apparently reconsidered many of the conclusions and terminology of the first paper. For this reason, the Sosa and Reents 1980 article will not be extensively considered here.

In the present thesis, the labels that are applied to various nominal glyphs are based upon rough English translations of the meanings of component glyphs where this information is known. Berlin has applied names to Caracol personalities that vary from those used in this paper. His labels have been replaced because they are letter designations which imply an order and closure which may not hold true under further scrutiny. Berlin's "Car. V" is equivalent to the personality labeled here as God C Star, and his "Car. W" is the same as that designated as Lord Storm-water Moon. The labels used by Sosa and Reents are, in addition to being somewhat inelegant, partially ambiguous. For example, "Antennatop" is not only an uncomfortable label for application to a people of the Maya's technology, but is also not sufficiently descriptive to allow the reader to identify the glyph group in question.

Study of the dynastic information recorded on the Caracol monuments soon raises key questions. How can personalities be identified? More to the point, how can the nominative phrases of rulers be recognized? The basic problem rests in the proper identification of clauses. The system used here is that proposed by Kubler (1973) in which a clause begins with a calendric notation and ends with the last glyph preceding the next calendric record. Kubler noted some flexibility in the creation of clauses by the separation of the CR from the Distance Number (1973:153-159). This seems to occur frequently at Caracol, most notably on Stela 6.

Work at other sites demonstrates that clauses may be divided into the following general order: "(Date)/Event Phrase/Person #1/Relationship/ Person #2/Relationship/Person #3" (Schele, Matthews and Lounsbury 1977). The event phrase can be recognized by affix or by position immediately following the date (either a DN or CR). Relationship statements usually precede the nominative phrases. Comparative evidence from other scholars is relied on here to identify relationship glyphs. Name phrases can thus be sorted out partly by exclusion (as glyphs that are neither events nor relationship markers) and by position (glyphs that conclude a clause or "sub-clause" between relationship markers). It is notable that while chains of relationships may divide a clause into subclauses, to date it has not been demonstrated that two event phrases can exist within a single clause (save perhaps for the separated CR statements as noted by Kubler).

To verify the assumption that certain nominative phrases refer to actual rulers rather than to other characters calls for other criteria. The first marker to be recognized was that of association with the EG of the site. It is not certain that a name accompanied by an EG necessarily represents membership in a ruling lineage, yet there is some similar close relationship between the two factors. This link is expressed by Proskouriakoff (1964:190) in a discussion of a character at Yaxchilan, "His name usually ends with Yaxchilan emblem glyphs, which suggests that he was of the ruling family."

In order to use the criteria of an EG to indicate members of a ruling family, an EG must first be identified. Berlin (1958) provides the basis for the recognition of proper EG's. They must have a main sign peculiar to a locale with a T168 "ben-ich" superfix and a T36, T37, T38, T39 or T40 prefix. Berlin was not certain about the EG's meaning. He hypothesized that it was a representation of something uniquely associated with a particular locale, a titular deity for a site or perhaps a family marker. He noted the EG's common occurrence before an SS, which we can reinterpret as falling at the end of a clause. At Caracol there appears a glyph group that corresponds in all particulars to Berlin's definition. This occurs on Caracol Stela 3 at A9b, B10b, A16a and D12a only with one personage's name (God C Star) and at Naranjo on Lintel 1 (Graham 1978[2]:105) again in association with God C Star's name. Such a limited distribution argues that it cannot be the sole one for Caracol, if indeed it refers to Caracol at all.

There is another glyph group that appears to function in a manner similar to an EG at the end of certain Caracol nominal phrases immediately preceding SS's. This group is displayed on Stelae 1, 3 and 6 and possibly on Stela 11 and Altars 10, 12 and 13. The compound, henceforth called the "Caracol Glyph," is made up of the glyphs T32/ 33, T281, T58/59 and T74 with a fifth glyph which may be T513. This group does not comply in all particulars with Berlin's definition of an EG and thus is not specified to be such. It appears also at Naranjo, Guatemala on Lintel 1 and on the Hieroglyphic Stairway but only with the name phrases of the Caracol rulers Lord Water and Lord Storm-water Moon. It is possible that the Caracol Glyph represents a title peculiar to the lords of Caracol rather than an EG. It does however utilize the water group and Kan cross elements that are parts of a normal EG. The important point for the purposes of this study is that it appears regularly in an EG position within clauses with the names of characters who appear to be rulers.

Sovereigns might also be expected to be identifiable by some particular title or titles. A compound glyph identified at Palenque (T74:184) seems to be specially associated with the nominal phrases of lords there. The title has been read phonetically as *Mah K'ina* which translates roughly as "Lord" (Lounsbury 1974). It appears that the

T74:184 compound occurs affixed to a ruler's name or title or sometimes to a deity name. This affix is thus taken to be one of the surest indicators of rulership at Caracol.

ALTAR 4, STELA 13 AND STELA 16

The earliest Caracol monument known is Altar 4, a Giant Glyph Altar. Since its entire carved face is taken up by a huge 2 Ahau, there is obviously no possibility of reading dynastic information from it. Two katuns later, Stela 13 marks the date 9.4.0.0.0. However, this text is too eroded to discern nominal or event phrases.

Stela 16 then marks the Katun 9.5.0.0.0. Following the IS and LS on this monument is an inscription sixty glyph blocks in length. Portions of the text are unreadable through breakage or erosion. Ignoring a doubtful SS at B9-B11, we can detect no calendric notation to separate the text into clauses. It is conceivable that an SS may once have occupied the space represented by the eroded blocks C7-D8. By Kubler's definition of clauses, this text might be said to represent one single long clause.

A sub-clause does seem to be marked off between B16 and A18. This begins with an "*u*-completion of haab" glyph at B16 and ends at A18 before a T126.534:670 "female parent indicator." Following the "completion of haab" marker are three portrait glyphs (Thompson 1962:14), the middle of which (B17) carries a T74.184 affix. The three glyphs thus probably represent the name of a Caracol ruler, most likely the one in office at 9.5.0.0.0. Of these, the portrait glyph with the T74.184 affix is an animal head, possibly a dog or jaguar variant (T752). It differs from other jaguar representations on Stela 16 at A16 and D16, but is similar to the jaguar portrait represented at zA6 of Tikal Stela 26. Without further comparative evidence B17 cannot be surely identified as the "name" glyph. But, for convenience of discussion during this presentation, this ruler will be labeled "Lord Jaguar" of Caracol.

The bulk of the text is undivided by either dates or obvious relationship glyphs. A pattern of presentation may however be noted. In at least four places in the text there are sets of three consecutive portrait glyphs: A14-A15, A17-A18, D10-D11 and D15-D16. The first set follows a symbolic glyph group with a prefix of three dots at A13. This glyph block is similar to the Palenque

Triad Introductory Glyph (Berlin 1963:Fig. 6 nos. 7-8) and might in some way be enumerating the following portrait glyphs. The first block contains T1036b, a vulture head. The second displays a "*ben-ich*" and God C head(?), and the third the head of God GI from the Palenque Triad, the "feather serpent" (Kelley 1965, Schele 1977). Another symbolic glyph in the form of a "sky" glyph with "*ich-ben*" (T168:561:23) and bars prefixed and superfixed appears before a jaguar head glyph. The reason for the appearance of these three portraits at this point in the text is uncertain. It is possible that they represent gods providing mythological ancestry or titles to Lord Jaguar much as the gods of the Palenque Triad do (Schele 1977).

The second set of three portrait glyphs is that which includes Lord Jaguar's glyph as the middle member, as noted earlier. The "female parent indicator" (Jones 1977; Schele, Matthews and Lounsbury 1977) that follows at B18 unfortunately is the last clear glyph before a long unreadable section of text. Thus the name of the mother of this early ruler labeled Lord Jaguar is unknown. Legible carving begins again at C10 with another "sky" glyph compound (T168:561:23) preceding the third set of three portraits. The first portrait is T1013, and the second is T1040, the death god's head. The third, at D11, is similar but not the same as the God GI representation at A15. It is uncertain how the glyphs that follow relate to this statement.

Included in the fourth "three-portrait glyph" presentation (D15-D16) are a possible GI variant, T1013 and a jaguar's head. Again the glyphs that follow have not been related to the portrait phrase.

The pattern of the known nominative expression at A17-A18 may give a clue as to the reading of the rest of the carving. This "name phrase" consists of a series of three portrait glyphs, the middle of which carries a T74.184 prefix. By extrapolation we might tentatively suggest that other occurrences of three portrait glyphs on Stela 16 could similarly represent names. Such a situation would be in agreement with the assessment of the Stela 16 text as a single long clause following a solitary date at the beginning of the inscription. As a single clause, the entire inscription can be regarded as carrying only name phrases and relationship markers after presentation of an event glyph (possibly once at B8?).

Shortly after the break in the inscription that follows the VYr marking are the very eroded remains (A10-A11) of what may be three portrait glyphs. If the groups of three portrait glyphs are to be regarded as name expressions, then this badly weathered set could well mark the actual protagonist of Stela 16. However, the next set of three portraits (A14-A15) follows the Palenque Triad Introductory Glyph simulacrum at B13 with no obvious intervening relationship glyphs and is best interpreted as deity names or titles. These are then followed shortly by the three portraits of Lord Jaguar's name (A17-A18), which immediately precede a female parent indicator (B18). Despite the three portraits at A10-A11 it seems best to interpret the non-calendrical text up to A18 as referring to the names and titles of Lord Jaguar. Under this explanation the three eroded portraits at A10-A11 could well depict deity titles as are presented later on in the same phrase at A14-A15.

Erosion and flaking have removed the name of the mother of Lord Jaguar from Stela 16. Proceeding to the second double column of text brings to consideration a portrait glyph at D5. On the assumption that this is part of a name, it cannot be determined whether this is a component of the mother's name or whether it might be part of a postulated name of the father to Lord Jaguar. If the father's name did appear, it could well have continued into the eroded portion of text that

exists at C6-C9. Following this gap there is a damaged block with "sky" sign (C10) succeeded by three portrait glyphs. These, in the absence of any obvious event or relationship glyphs might be postulated to represent a predecessor to Lord Jaguar. If so, the fact that the T74.184 title is attached to the middle glyph of Lord Jaguar's three-portrait set causes us to focus on the skull glyph at C11 as the possible "name" glyph of this person. The final recognizable three-portrait glyph set occurs at D15-D16. In this group, the center glyph is T1013, which had been presented earlier as the first glyph of a three-portrait set at D11-D12. Among the glyphs that intervene between the last two possible names marked by three-portrait sets there is an apparent female name as indicated by T1000 at D13. A block that incorporates the "up-ended bone" glyph (T571) immediately precedes this female name. This glyph again appears later near the end of the text as part of a block at C17, immediately after the presentation of the final three-portrait glyph statement. Possibly then, T571 is serving to mark female relationship.

Overall, the pattern of presentation of Stela 16 may begin with mention of the names and titles of Lord Jaguar up until A18 including three-portrait sets at A14-A15 as well as the postulated set at A10-A11. Parents then seem to be mentioned. Another name, as marked by a set of three portrait glyphs appears at D10-D11 followed by a possible female relative at D13. A final name could then be recorded at D15-D16 along with another possible female relative at D17-C18. Stela 16 might thus record a contemporary ruler of Caracol along with at least two generations of ancestry.

STELA 6 AND STELA 14

Stela 6 displays the name of the next identifiable Caracol ruler at A4, B9, A12 and B21. The first three occurrences of his name bear the T184.74 suffix indicating rulership. At A4, B9 and B21 the whole compound (T125.168:513: 130.184.74) precedes the Caracol Glyph. A similar compound appears on Yaxchilan Lintel 37 in a series of differing name phrases which might suggest that it be read as a title. Although that may indeed be the case at Yaxchilan, this possibility is contradicted at Caracol by its appear-

ance as the sole member of a nominative phrase at B9 on Stela 6. This circumstance allows identification of this glyph group as the "name" of the ruler. In the paper by Sosa and Reents (1980) the existence of this ruler was postulated, but the name glyph was not identified. Because of the prominent Muluc glyph (T513) in his name, the sovereign is now labeled "Lord Water."

Lord Water appears as the prominent character in the preserved portion of the Stela 6 text. Unfortunately, exactly one-half of the text is missing because of erosion (the entire left side). It is possible therefore that another person was introduced in the missing portion of the text.

Preserved text begins with an IS of 9.5.19.1.2 9 Ik 5 Uo. In the event glyph position following the IS there is a symbolic glyph with unidentified main sign, T178 subfix and possibly T181?? postfix. Events marked at other sites are commonly accession to office, birth and very rarely death. A "death event" seems to be ruled out by the mention of Lord Water in successive clauses on this monument. A reading of "accession" for the glyph might be slightly favored over one of "birth" by the relatively greater frequency of inauguration statements to birth notations at other sites. (Despite the fact that it is recognized that T740 "up-ended frog" probably represents an event shortly after birth, for convenience of discussion hereafter this event will be referred to as birth).

Following the event glyph is apparently a profile head with T228 prefix. Over T228 is a tiny "caterpillar," like the upper element of T53. At A4-B4 is the name of a ruler, Lord Water, and the Caracol Glyph. These are followed by three unclear glyphs which complete the initial clause. A T1 "*u*-bracket" prefix is borne by the first of these glyphs. The second is a portrait glyph. An EG may then be the last of these three eroded glyphs. By the position of these three glyphs after Lord Water's name phrase we can suggest that they should be a relationship statement according to what is presently known of the nature of clauses on Maya monuments. On the first glyph a T1 affix corresponds with the construction of known relationship glyphs and thus could be part of a male or female parent indicator. Next, the portrait glyph might be part or the whole of a nominative statement, since such glyphs are commonly part of name phrases. Emblem Glyphs, like the one that may exist at B5, often terminate nominal phrases as indeed this one might. Thus, the opening clause of Stela 6 can be safely interpreted as an event occurring with Lord Water and a relationship phrase for that same ruler. Comparison of the name of Lord Water's relative as preserved at B5 with that of Lord Jaguar at B17 on Stela 16 at Caracol reveals that the two are similar in preserved details of form although lacking the *Mah K'ina* on Stela 6. From this, it may be tentatively proposed that the two glyphs be identified

as representing the same character. And, from the position of the name of this person in the relationship phrase on Stela 6 it can further be postulated that he, Lord Jaguar, was the father of Lord Water.

At C5, the next clause opens with an SSIG, the SS and the date (9.6.0.0.0) 9 Ahau. Inserted between the SS and the CR there are at B6-C6 two glyphs. The first (B6) has a main sign similar to that of the event of B3 and might possibly be counting the time forward from that initial event to the date 9 Ahau. The subfix is lost, but the postfix appears much larger than that for the group at B3. An eroded glyph follows. After the VYr is an unclear glyph group that may include T712 (B7b).

A CR unaccompanied by any SS opens the subsequent clause, marking the position (9.7.0.0.0) 7 Ahau. Following the CR is a "hand scattering" glyph and the same glyph compound that terminated the previous clause (T712?? main sign). Another CR (C8a-C8b) then marks the beginning of another clause at 9.8.0.0.0. A "hand scattering" glyph is followed in this case by Lord Water's name and a Caracol Glyph at E9-F9 in the lower right corner of the third frame.

A long compound clause or pair of clauses accompanies the next date (9.8.5.16.12 at A10-C15). It might be noted that this entire clause fits neatly into two of the glyph frames with no overlap. Several glyph blocks separate the CR from the SS, causing the whole to resemble two separate clauses in some ways. Following an SS of 5.16.12 is a katun glyph with eroded coefficient which could be seen as an "isolated katun" relating to a period of time independent of the SS. However, it is possible that the katun actually was a part of the SS and counted the SS forward from the last recorded SS at 9.6.0.0.0. Both clauses that intervene between the SS's are CR statements with no attached distance numbers. If this interpretation is correct, then the coefficient of the katun glyph at A11 should be 2. After the katun notation is a symbolic glyph with the same main sign as the event glyph at E3 but with different affixes. A "caterpillar" over T228.168.518 appears in the next block. Then, preceding the CR, is a phrase of six glyph blocks in length. Lord Water's name is the first of these. The next glyph is unidentified but may be a part of a nominal expression for Lord Water. At C12 the third glyph appears to be T747, the vulture. Such a glyph is noted by Thompson (1962:334) as a possible substitute for the sign of the day Ahau. In this appearance it might represent a title similar to Ahau for Lord Water. Preceding the CR are three unrecognized glyphs. The second of these (E13) is nonetheless an interesting glyph. It appears to show a mask of the "jester god" (Schele 1974) tied over the face of a person or god. A possible interpretation of this glyph reads it as Lord Water donning the mask of the "jester god." In some way it appears to be marking a change of state for this character.

A portion of this clause or perhaps a new one seems to be separated off by the CR at A14-B14. Prefixed to the day sign is a T53 affix. Block C14 appears again to be a near duplicate of the event glyph of B3. Infixing of a strip of cross-hatching along the left side of the main sign is the only difference noted. Following this is a glyph with "caterpillar" over T228, and a T168 superfix as is found also at C11. The main sign is totally unfamiliar. At F15 the clause or sub-clause ends with a Caracol Glyph. Just ahead of it appears a peculiar compound that, by position, should be a name. Apparently this glyph consists of a flaming Ahau prefixed to a serpent head (in profile) with knot, curl and black dot superfixed. For purposes of identification this name will be referred to as "Ahau-serpent."

An SSIG at D16 begins the final calendrical statement readable on Stela 6. The SS of this clause brings the count forward to 9.8.10.0.0. Between the SS and CR are inserted two blocks of unknown significance. That at A17 may share the same main sign with the event glyph of B3, although this is not certain. Its subfix and the "inverted Ahau" postfix are in any case clearly different from B3. Next is a glyph carrying a full T53 prefix of T228 prefixed to a portrait head.

Affix T53 is again attached to the day glyph of the CR at C17-C18. A "hand scattering" glyph and half-period marker follow. A long phrase completes a sub-clause that ends at A22 with a Caracol Glyph. Ahau-serpent's name appears at A20. Lord Water's name occurs further along (B21). It is without the usual T184.74 postfix but is followed by a portrait head which may in some way represent a variant title. Two blocks before Lord Water's name (C20) is a record of three katuns. This could refer to the fact that Lord

Water was in his third katun of life at 9.8.10.0.0 which would indicate his birth to have occurred between 9.5.10.0.0 and 9.6.10.0.0. From B22 to C24 there appears a second sub-clause. Understood rules of presentation discussed earlier would seem to indicate that this sub-clause is a relationship statement. If so, the relationship marked is not understood. The glyph at B22 has been interpreted by Kelley (1976) as referring to marriage, but that is speculative. The presence of the Caracol Glyph at the end of the sub-clause indicates a name immediately before it. However, no glyph block or blocks appear as obvious nomenclature.

Two of the dates marked on Stela 6 are also recorded on Stela 14 at Caracol. The IS of 9.6.0.0.0 marks the beginning of one clause, and an SS leading back to 9.5.19.1.2 marks another. Most of the text of this monument is unreadable because of erosion. An event glyph should lie at perhaps B7, immediately after the IS. A glyph with possible lunar "event" suffix does indeed fill that space. Glyphs of this form have been interpreted as indicating accession to rule. It seems unlikely that this particular glyph could be interpreted in that way, since the odds are very much against an accession actually falling on the katun end. It might, however, very well mark the first katun end immediately after an accession date. Near the end of this same clause occurs mention of Lord Water without T74.184 affix or the Caracol Glyph (C8). Following the SS, no event glyph is discovered (it may have existed at the now eroded block F2). But, again near the end of the clause (E8), Lord Water's name occurs without T74.184 or the Caracol Glyph.

Uncertainty derived from inability to read event glyphs on Stela 6 obviously creates difficulty in interpretation. The earliest date recorded with Lord Water's name is 9.5.10.1.2 both as IS for Stela 6 and as Date B for Stela 14. As mentioned earlier, birth and accession to office seem to be the two best candidates for interpretation of the event glyph following the IS on Stela 6. Although accession seems slightly favored statistically, both options must, for the time being, be kept open.

Before discussing the interpretation of Stelae 6 and 14 at Caracol details of one further monument must be brought in. Naranjo Lintel 1 opens its text with a clause that marks the birth date of a later Caracol ruler, Lord Storm-water Moon. At

F3 of this clause, Lord Water's name occurs, followed by the Caracol Glyph and preceded by a 4 *"ben-ich"* katun notation. Schele (n.d.: 6) notes, ". . . the observation that in most cases where the notations can be compared to known birth and death dates, 'numbered katuns' appear to refer to 'katuns of life.'" Lord Storm-water Moon's possible accession date from Stela 3 at Caracol (and thus the likely upper end date for Lord Water's death) was 9.9.4.16.2. Extrapolation back four katuns from this point allows a range from 9.5.4.16.2 to 9.6.4.16.2 as the possible time of birth for Lord Water. This actually does not help to pinpoint Lord Water's birth date since the three-katun statement of Caracol Stela 6 indicates that he was born after 9.5.10.0.0 while his appearance in the first clause of the monument shows that he was alive at 9.5.19.1.2. Thus these last two dates actually demarcate the range of time during which Lord Water was born. The four-katun statement of Naranjo Lintel 1, if counted forward from this range, suggests that Lord Water died between 9.8.10.0.0 and 9.9.19.1.2. This is at least in agreement with Lord Storm-water Moon's putative accession date of 9.9.4.16.2.

We are still not able to eliminate either birth or accession as possible interpretations for the event at B3 of Stela 6. However, if it does represent accession to office, then Lord Water could have been no more than about nine years old when he came into power. The clause that opens with the IS on Stela 6 concludes, after mention of Lord Water, with a relationship statement that has tentatively been interpreted to name Lord Jaguar as the father of Lord Water.

Following the IS statement, two clauses intervene before Lord Water's name again appears. These two, and the third clause in which Lord Water's name does appear, mark in an abbreviated way the passage of three katun ends. The next clause (A10-C15) is a long compound statement that mentions Lord Water without the Caracol Glyph in the first half, and Ahau-serpent with the Caracol Glyph in the second half following the CR. If the opening event of Stela 6 is interpreted as birth, then this clause could well be construed as marking his accession to power. The

Ahau-serpent name would then be merely a new name acquired with rulership. Donning of the "jester god" mask at B13 could then symbolize this assumption of power. On the other hand, this could equally well symbolize the acquisition of a new title if the opening event is read as accession. Alternatively it might represent the birth of an heir if Ahau-serpent is to be read as a separate individual from Lord Water. Another long compound remark is the final clause that is preserved on Stela 6. Nothing obvious is offered for interpretation in the two-block long first portion. Again following the CR, the second part is much longer but similarly uncomprehended. The Ahau-serpent name appears here four blocks before Lord Water's name (A20) with no known relationship glyphs intervening. This clause evidently marks some non-crisis (that is to say not birth, accession or death) event in the life of Lord Water. During the course of the statement, Lord Water is declared to be in the third katun of life (C20).

In sum, Stelae 6 and 14 mention at least one Caracol ruler as demonstrated by the T184.74 title and the accompanying Caracol Glyph. An unlikely possibility exists that a second character is mentioned by the name of Ahau-serpent. Economy and the pattern of statement in the last known clause of Stela 6 argue against that interpretation. On the basis of the slightly greater prevalence of accession dates over birth dates elsewhere in the Maya area, a favored interpretation would suggest that Lord Water was born between 9.5.10.0.0 and 9.5.19.1.2 as the son of the current monarch, Lord Jaguar. Upon the death of his father, he acceded to power at 9.5.19.1.2 at a very young age. The father-son relationship between Lord Jaguar and Lord Water may find confirmation in a female parentage statement on Stela 1 at Caracol, as will be discussed shortly. Three katuns passed during Lord Water's rule without any notable change in his life. A major event occurred at 9.8.5.16.12 which led to the acquisition of an important new title. Finally, the last readable clause of Stela 6 begins with the marking of the first PE after the acquisition of title, at 9.8.10.0.0.

STELA 1 AND STELA 3

Despite the temporal priority of the DD (9.8.0.0.0) of Stela 1, it is better first to consider

Stela 3 which opens with an IS of 9.6.12.4.16. After the VYr date is a slightly eroded but clear "up-ended frog" glyph (T740.181:126) at A8b. Next are two eroded glyphs (B8a-B8b) followed by a third that is a representation of God C with a "star" postfix (T1016?.510:23). This latter glyph has previously been identified by Berlin as ruler "Car. V" (1973). Next comes a glyph with an EG that uses a T518 "Muluc variant" main sign. The EG signals that a name has been mentioned. For convenience, since there is no single constant glyph that represents this character's name, the head with the star affix will be used to label the person as "God C Star." After the EG, the clause continues with a female parent indicator at B9a followed by a T1000 compound at B9b. Proskouriakoff (1961) has noted that T1000 occurs as a marker of female names. Block A10a is then a glyph of a bird looking left over its right shoulder with its tail curled underneath. This glyph might compose part of the lady's name from B9b (cf. Tikal Stela 13: A7 also with a woman's name) allowing us to name this person as "Lady Bird." Glyph block B11a contains a male parent indicator (T?:536:?) followed by another EG. Process of elimination perhaps more than anything else leads to the postulate that the male parent is referred to at A10b upper half—A10b lower half or possibly just to the right of the Ahau. The second clause of the monument is largely eroded, running from A11a to A13b.

In the next clause (B13a-A16a) appears an event glyph (T713.181:24?) of arguable interpretation. It is similar, but not identical, to one proposed as accession (Schele, Matthews and Lounsbury 1977). It appears somewhat like the vestiges of the hypothetical accession glyph at B3 of Stela 6. The bulk of the clause after this glyph is filled with a nominative phrase for God C Star. However, later on in the same inscription the same or similar event glyph appears at C11b with God C Star again being mentioned immediately after the event. In this latter instance the clause, with some interruption from breakage, goes on to mention a later ruler, Lord Storm-water Moon. The occurrence of the same event with God C Star apparently the referent in both cases seems to argue against accession at either point. Another fact that makes the identification of the event at B14b as accession disturbing is that on Stela 3, as on other Caracol monuments, there is the pattern of a ruler's name being accompanied by the T74.184 affix. God C Star never appears with this title either on Stela 3 nor anywhere else. This fact does not negate the possibility that God C Star could have been a ruler, but is a part of a weight of cumulative evidence that makes identification of this person as at least a sovereign of Caracol uncomfortable. Another difficulty with the identification of God C Star as a Caracol ruler is that the evidence from Stela 6 suggests that Lord Water was comfortably in power until at least 9.8.10.0.0. Indeed the "fourth katun of life" statement from Naranjo Lintel 1 causes us to believe that Lord Water lived and ruled at least until 9.8.10.0.0–9.9.19.1.2, which is well past a putative accession date for God C Star at 9.7.10.15.8 on Stela 3. It is speculated that the importance of God C Star arose not from direct rulership at Caracol but from relationship to someone else who did rule there.

A new clause at 9.7.14.10.8 then starts at A16b and continues until A18b. Another birth marker (T740.181:126) occurs as the event at B17a. There is then a single glyph occupying the nominative position before a full-scale version of the Caracol Glyph at A18. The name represented is postulated to be a "pre-rulership" name or title for Lord Storm-water Moon who appears later in the text. This equivalence is validated at C4a-C4b by the occurrence of the two nominative glyphs (those of B17b and of Lord Storm-water Moon) in the same clause side by side preceding the Caracol Glyph. There is no possibility that a relationship or other glyph fits between them. This pre-rule form of Lord Storm-water Moon's name is here labeled "Yellow Storm" from a rudimentary translation of the kan element as "yellow" and of the tiny superfixed cauac element as "storm." Yellow Storm is mentioned again at A20a dating to 9.7.19.13.12. The event is not understood, and the end of the clause is lost at C1-D1. It is interesting to note that at the end of the readable portion of this clause there appears a 4 katun statement followed by a glyph group with "*ich-ben*" superfix. It has been discussed how a similar 4 katun statement on Naranjo Lintel 1 referred to Lord Water and seemed to indicate that he died in the fourth katun of life. The 4-katun record on Stela 3 could similarly refer to Lord Water. As an historical document dating to a much later date (9.10.4.7.0) it would be referring to Lord Water as a deceased rather than an existing monarch.

Blocks C2a-C3b carry the highly eroded SS of the next clause. However, there is a clear 10 Ik at C3a. The date marked by the 10 Ik must fall between 9.7.19.13.12 (Date E) and 9.9.5.13.8 (Date G). Calculation for the suppressed Date O at the end of the text allows us to suggest 9.9.4.16.2 10 Ik 0 Pop as the position for Date F on the basis of a presumed identity between the two dates. Following the eroded Date F is another ruined clause (D3a-D4b). As noted earlier, however, a ruler's name appears at C4a as marked by a T184:74 suffix. Comparison with other records of the ruler allows identification of his name as T351:774:184:74. The superfix is actually made of a small cauac and a small muluc sign. Sign T774 is not identical to the lunar sign T683, but is close enough to allow creation of the label "Storm-water Moon." The nominative phrase of this lord continues with the previously observed name of Yellow Storm and ends with a Caracol Glyph at D4. This date (9.9.4.16.2) is interpreted as the accession date for Lord Storm-water Moon. Berlin (1973) pointed out the existence of this ruler elsewhere on Stela 3 and at Naranjo (his ruler "Car. W"). Sosa and Reents were first to draw attention to the probable occurrence of the accession event at this time (as accession of their "Antennatop II"; Sosa and Reents 1980). It is significant that in this clause Lord Storm-water Moon appears for the first time in the text with the T74.184 title. Interpretation of the event of this clause as accession is in agreement with the death of Lord Water in his fourth katun of life (9.8.10.0.0—9.9.19.1.2).

Erosion makes the two succeeding clauses largely unreadable. The second (D7a-D9b) may show Lord Storm-water Moon's name at D8a. A long clause (A10a-D14a) follows an SS leading to the date 9.9.9.10.5. The second appearance of the T713.181? event glyph is at C11b followed by a nominative expression that includes God C Star's name (D11a-D12a). This date marks the latest known appearance of God C Star. Preceding the God C glyph is a compound of T575:819:?. Thompson (1962:386) notes that T819 appears at Copan between the heads of death gods; T575 is found in a glyph group identified by Proskouriakoff as marking death (1963:163). This perhaps hints that the death of God C Star is referred to here. Such an interpretation is of course highly speculative. Also appearing with the name-title phrase of God C Star is a T571 at D11b upper

half. In the discussion of Stela 16 it was noted that this glyph might precede the names of two female characters there. Immediately after the EG of God C Star appears Proskouriakoff's "rodent" glyph (T757) with a T181 postfix. Proskouriakoff (1968: 249) suggests that T757 is an introducing glyph with a meaning similar to, " 'Here is portrayed (or recorded) . . . ,' 'In commemoration of . . .'." Glyph T757 could well bear such a meaning in this position since it occurs two blocks before Lord Storm-water Moon's name. There then appears a sequence of clauses (D14b-C16b; D16a-D18a: D18b-D20b; E1-F5) which record a series of closely occurring events. Lord Storm-water Moon is mentioned in the first three of these clauses, but not in the fourth. The subsequent clause (E6-E8) marks 9.10.0.0.0 and may show Lord Storm-water Moon's name at F7b. A purely calendric SS leads to 9.10.4.7.0 before the ultimate clause counts back to the possible accession date of Lord Storm-water Moon at 9.9.4.16.2. His name may appear in this clause at F10b upper half. God C Star's name then appears in the last block of the text, possibly only as a parent.

Stela 3 thus displays prominently two persons. Lord Storm-water Moon was almost certainly a Caracol ruler. The other, God C Star, probably was not. No clear statement of relationship between the two can be found. They do appear twice together in common clauses on Stela 3. On Naranjo Lintel 1, in the clause that follows the incomplete record of Lord Storm-water Moon's birth date, the ruler and God C Star are mentioned together a third time. This clause also contains Lord Water's name further on. Again no clear relationship statements are found. It should be noted that a second clause on the Naranjo Lintel counts forward to 9.10.0.0.0 and again mentions Lord Storm-water Moon's name. The organization of the first clause of Naranjo Lintel 1 parallels the expected order for a relationship clause with God C Star in the female parent position and Lord Water in the male parent position. Unfortunately, none of the glyphs that intervene between the characters' names can be identified with any known relationship markers.

On the front of Stela 3 (and Stela 1) appears a figure that seems to conform to Proskouriakoff's description of women on monuments (1961). It is felt, however, that her criteria in this case (beaded skirt and short cape) are too broad to assuredly identify the Stela 3 portrait as female. Until studies of iconography allow more certain definition of female-male differences in Maya art it is probably best to consider it equally likely that the Caracol Stelae 3 and 1 portraits represent males or females.

Stela 1 bears a portrait on its front that is nearly identical to that on Stela 3. Since Stela 1 carries the earlier DD it is reasonable to say that Stela 3 was copied from the prior monument. The inscription of Stela 1 bears a single date represented by the IS of 9.8.0.0.0. The text that follows has three Caracol Glyphs indicating three locations of the name of a member or members of the "royal lineage." An event glyph at C2 carries the T181 postfix but cannot be recognized as a known event. Following this, in nominative position, is a glyph that is not recognizable from other monuments. This probable name glyph is given the label "Serpent-head." Two unread glyphs precede a "hand scattering" glyph at F1. Between this and the Caracol Glyph at E3 are two glyphs which should represent a name. The first at E2 is unclear but bears a bar-and-dot prefix of 7. The next, at F2, is a profile head that bears the same T125 prefix attached to Lord Water's name on Stela 6. Since Lord Water was apparently ruling at 9.8.0.0.0 and might justifiably be expected to be mentioned on a contemporaneous text of that date, this glyph might thus be tentatively identified as a head-variant form of Lord Water's name. This identification would be strengthened if the "name" glyph of Serpent-head was also similar to the putative Lord Water name at F2. This is unfortunately not the case, and the suggested congruence of the head-variant at F2 with Lord Water must remain speculative.

Continuing, a female parent indicator (T?.I: 606) at F3 is followed by two portrait glyphs naming a female, "Lady Jaguar." The first portrait is T1000 with a lunar postfix supported by a T184:74 subfix. Block H1 seems to be a head (jaguar?), G2 is unclear and H2a is a katun glyph. Block G3 then carries Lord Storm-water Moon's name with possible postfixed T184.74 followed by a Caracol Glyph.

Identification of the names carved on Stela 1 is difficult. That at D2, after the event glyph, is not recognizable. At E2-F2 the name might be identified with Lord Water particularly since he should have been ruling at 9.8.0.0.0. A female

parent indicator at F3 should relate Lady Jaguar to the preceding person mentioned (Lord Water?) or it might relate her to Lord Storm-water Moon at G3. This latter character was only five years old at 9.8.0.0.0, and some time away from acceding to power. The katun notation at H2a could refer to the fact that Storm-water Moon was in his first katun of life at 9.8.0.0.0. Sosa and Reents (1980) identify the character at G3 as being actually an earlier ruler who used the same name glyph as Lord Storm-water Moon on Stela 3. There is no reason, however, to assume that there were two characters using the same name at the same point in time since the future lord was already alive by 9.8.0.0.0.

With regard to Lady Jaguar's name, it can be noted that the second part (H1) is extremely similar to the portrait head that represents Lord Jaguar on Stela 16. In accordance with the already mentioned tentative postulate that Lord Jaguar was father to Lord Water, the woman's name could be taken to represent also the wife to Lord Jaguar if we accept the idea that the name at F2 is indeed representing Lord Water. Some support for this speculation might well be derived from the use of the portrait head of Lord Jaguar's name as a component for Lady Jaguar's name.

Thus the relationship statement following the "hand scattering" glyph at F1 of Stela 1 (E2-H1) might be transliterated, "Lord Water of Caracol, child of female parent, woman of royal lineage, wife of Lord Jaguar." The final four blocks which include a mention of the later Lord Storm-water Moon in the first katun of life (as indeed he was at 9.8.0.0.0) then represent an apparent disjunction from the preceding parentage statement. It is possible that this mention of Lord Storm-water Moon is something of an aside which is intended to verify the intended line of descent. Alternatively it might be seen as an integral part of the relationship phrase of which Lord Water appears to be the subject. This phrase could then be tying Lord Water to his mother and to his son(?) in a pair of prepositional phrases.

Storm-water Moon's name also appears repeatedly on the Naranjo Hieroglyphic Stairway. The blocks of the stair are not articulated and the order of the text is confused. Thus the context of occurrence of Storm-water Moon's name on this stairway must await more detailed reconstruction and analysis of the text.

STELA 21

At present Stela 21 is the only monument which carries a date that falls into the gap between the time of Stela 3 (DD 9.10.4.7.0) and Stelae 8, 9 and 11 (all circa 9.19.0.0.0). Unfortunately, the inscription of this slate monument has been subjected to breaking and erosion. The IS/LS of the opening clause has itself had to be reconstructed as 9.13.10.0.0. At A3b, immediately after the presentation of Glyph A of the LS, is a partially destroyed glyph that once appeared to be of the form of an "up-ended frog" (T740). But, further examination makes such a reading unsubstantiable. Two glyphs follow this possible event marker before an SSIG at C3a. Despite damage it is nonetheless evident that neither glyph represents an EG and that little of the dynastic matters of Caracol can be gleaned from Stela 21.

STELA 8, STELA 9 AND STELA 11

Problems of textual erosion become yet more acute when dealing with the Late Classic monuments of Caracol. Stela 8 preserves a bit of the opening date at the upper left of the front face, but the bulk of the carving is lost. Stela 9 displays only the bare outlines of carving. Even the date of Stela 9 must be guessed at from its similarity to Stelae 8 and 11.

Stela 11 retains the best preserved text of these similar and temporally and spatially proximal stelae. Unfortunately, due to the circumstances of discovery (under a tree in the last week of work), Stela 11 is the least well recorded of the three. Some details can be made out. No obvious event glyph follows the CR of the IS at A2 of the Main Panel. The five glyph blocks between the CR and the half-period glyph at B4 are all heavily eroded.

After the half-period glyph, at A5, there appears another eroded block that precedes a possible damaged female parent indicator (T122.534: 670:?) at B5. The female name that should follow at A6 is again almost lost although the outlines of what may be the Caracol Glyph are visible at B6. The text conceivably passes on to Panel Y which is in poorer condition than the Main Panel. Most of the blocks of Panel Y are unreadable even as to form. However, the final two blocks at yA4-yB4 appear to be the Caracol Glyph and the "imix-comb-imix" *bacab* title (Schele n.d.). The name of a ruler of Caracol therefore presumably precedes these two glyphs somewhere on Panel Y, but the inscription there is too badly eroded for identification.

STELA 19, ALTAR 12 AND ALTAR 13

Altars 12 and 13, both scene altars, were found close by each other and near the fractured Stela 19. Their proper arrangement and associations are not however understood, since Altar 12 at least was disturbed by human action and Altar 13 was located unaligned with Stela 19.

Most of the carving has spalled off of Stela 19 and its text is therefore largely unknown. What little is known of the inscription appears in side glyph panels and in the remains of two front panels. Although these panels are the most fragmentary, it is here that the only solid bit of dynastic information is preserved. The surviving portion of Panel Y opens at yA1 with an eroded glyph and apparent prefixed numerical 3. Study of night photographs indicates that this glyph may be a portrait head with a smaller glyph infixed into the area of the mouth, similar to the glyph at D11a on Stela 3 at Caracol in the name-title phrase of

God C Star. Following an assumed order of reading of left-right and downward in double column, yB1 should be read next. This block shows the remains of a peculiar main sign with T122 prefix. The main sign displays a definite vertical band without cartouche or framing. Examination of Thompson's *Catalog* (1962) indicates that there are few possible reconstructions of this block if the sign is not peculiar to Caracol. A variant of the "toothache" glyph T684 would seem to be the most obvious candidate. But the glyph at yB1 does not show the characteristic knot element over the main sign. An alternative consideration is that it might represent the T559 glyph that serves as the main sign of the Quirigua EG. This identification is far from validated.

Block yA2 carries a glyph composed of a main sign with horizontal banding and eroded subfix and postfix. Affixes are too eroded to read. Panel

Y terminates at yB2 with a glyph utilizing a grotesque head as a main sign, possibly with a superfix and with a partially eroded but nonetheless reasonably clear T74.184 prefix. This T74.184 title probably marks the glyph as some part of the name phrase of a ruler of Caracol. Indeed, it might be suggested that the four glyphs of Panel Y all function as portions of the name of that same ruler. At this point it is impossible to make out the animal or god head in block yB2. Therefore for the time being a final name cannot be assigned to this character. For purposes of discussion, the putative ruler identified by this T74.184 affix in Panel Y of Caracol Stela 19 will be labeled as "Provisional Character Z" (PCZ) of Caracol. The letters of this series of provisional characters bear no necessary relation to temporal order. The designation will be dropped and replaced with a more permanent name when the person can be more adequately identified.

Following a possible CR date at zA1-zA2 on the side panel of Stela 19 are six known non-calendrical glyphs. None of these glyphs can presently be identified as a known event or title. At zC2-zD2 appears another CR date which is presumably the beginning of a clause. The glyphs that came after this date (9.19.10.0.0) are again of unrecognized meaning, although the block at zD3 is similar in its prefix to the form of an EG. A final consideration is the trace of figural carving on the front of the stone. Much of this is lost, but at the upper reaches, just below the glyph band of Panel X, appear the remains of the headdress —a peculiar turban-like hat displaying an extension that dangles over the wearer's face. Comparable examples are seen at Caracol on Altar 12 on the right-hand figure and on Stela 17 and Altar 10, again on the right-hand figures and possibly also on the left-hand figures.

Proceeding chronologically, the next known monument is Altar 12. The DD of 9.19.10.0.0 repeats the position of Date B and possibly also Date C of Stela 19. The text of Altar 12 opens with a CR of uncertain position beginning a clause now largely lost (Blocks 1-13). Block 13, the last of this first clause can be reconstructed as T502.25:502 which is read as the title *bacab* by Schele (n.d.). Presumably then, the blocks immediately preceding this title once described a ruler of Caracol.

A T502.25:502 title again terminates the subsequent clause (Blocks 14-32). In this instance the compound is preceded by an example of the Caracol Glyph. Immediately ahead of the Caracol Glyph is a grotesque head which possibly is identifiable with PCZ but lacks the T74.184 title.

Just after the start of the SS that begins it, the third clause is lost. Similarly, the beginning of the fourth clause in Panel Y is missing. Possibly the end of the third clause ran over into Panel Y. A Caracol Glyph terminates the fourth clause itself at yF1. Three blocks precede the Caracol Glyph, revealing no sure event or relationship glyphs. The next clause, the fifth of Altar 12 and the final one of the ongoing calendrical portion of the text, opens with an SS separated from its accompanying CR by a non-calendrical glyph at G1. This pattern is similar to that at Block 17 of the circular text in the second clause and to the presentation already noted on the much earlier Stela 6. After the CR of the fifth clause of Altar 12, a "hand scattering" glyph is separated from a half-period marker by a single glyph of undetermined significance. This clause then terminates with a nominal phrase for what must be a Caracol monarch. Block yG4 carries a glyph group with a T74.184 prefix (T74 is actually split into two halves—one above and the other below T184). The entire compound, which probably represents an important part of the name of the ruler, is T74.184.III:585:? with T585 ("quincunx") the main sign. The subsequent glyph is eroded and not identifiable with known name phrases from Caracol. After this, the name phrase and the clause terminate at G5-H5 with a Caracol Glyph and a T502.25:502 title. This lord, who will be referred to as "Lord Quincunx" of Caracol, appears to be different from PCZ on Stela 19 although the DD of that monument (9.19.10.0.0) is the same as that which is recorded in the very clause on Altar 12 that mentions Lord Quincunx. Panel Z concludes the glyphic inscription of Altar 12. It is spatially proximate to, and might therefore identify, the left-hand figure of the scene. Alternatively, this feature may just be an artifact of necessity derived from the need to fit so much text into the scene. At block zA3, T184 is prefixed to a portrait head with T1 superfix. It is possible that the title T74.184 was meant to be represented. The head itself is similar to that which forms the main sign of the name of PCZ, but the succeeding glyphs are similar to a name on Altar

13 and are here labeled "Provisional Character Y."

Altar 13 shows patterns of glyph presentation which are repeated within its own text and in those on Altar 12 and Stela 19. Altar 13 has been reconstructed to carry a DD of 10.0.0.0.0 although a CR for the position 9.19.10.0.0 is apparently also marked. The text seems to open with a CR date of unknown LC position at the upper left interior corner of the four-lobed inscription that encircles the scene (Block 1). The CR is followed immediately by a glyph which on the surface appears to be a possible female parent indicator. Its prefix is, however, definitely T1 rather than the expected T122 or T126. Also, unlike those female parent indicators recorded heretofore (Schele, Matthews and Lounsbury 1977), this glyph has a large subfix. Its position immediately after the CR would seem to argue against its use as a relationship glyph of any sort and for its use as an event glyph.

Glyph Blocks 5-7 of Altar 13 are similar in form to the last three glyphs of the name phrase of PCZ on Stela 19. Block 7, which by comparison with Stela 19 should carry the head with T74.184 title, does show a prefix which can be reconstructed as the title. But it also carries a superfix which cannot presently be made out at yB2 of Stela 19. The form of the glyph with its main sign and affixes actually resembles more the representation of Lord Quincunx, and thus will we so identify it. Altar 13 continues with an unrecognized glyph (Block 8) and a glyph (Block 9) that parallels one found on Altar 12 at yE1b. Both examples of this glyph are followed by the Caracol Glyph (Block 10 on Altar 13). Although erosion and limited distribution cause uncertainty, it seems likely that this glyph (yE1b on Altar 12, Block 10 on Altar 13) represents a title. Block 11 on Altar 13 then seems to conclude the suggested name phrase for Lord Quincunx with a post-EG title of T502.25:502, *bacab*. After this title, the clause itself continues for six more blocks before a new clause begins at Blocks 18-19 with a CR. Of the last six blocks of the first clause, three (Blocks 13-15) are comparable to examples seen behind the left figure on Altar 12 (zA4-zA6) and labeled PCY.

Beginning the second clause of Altar 13 is another CR of uncertain LC position (Blocks 18-19) without an SSIG. The glyph immediately after the

VYr date carries a T1 prefix as does that in comparable position after the CR of the first clause. The glyphs in the next blocks are of undetermined significance. Blocks 23-25 then duplicate in outline the three glyphs presented at Blocks 5-7 that have been suggested to mention Lord Quincunx. Following an unrecognizable glyph (Block 26) are two eroded blocks that may be reasonably reconstructed as a Caracol Glyph followed by a T502.25:502 title. The two subsequent blocks, 27 and 28, parallel those occurring after the same title in the first clause at Blocks 12 and 13 and labeled PCY. Thus, the altar seems to twice mention the Caracol ruler Lord Quincunx followed each time by another name phrase for the personage PCY.

The bulk of the remaining text of Altar 13 is too badly eroded to work with. Reconstruction of chronology has interpreted the order of presentation as running from Panel U (and probably Panel X) to Panel V and then to Panel W where a possible DD of 10.0.0.0.0 is recorded. Two panels of purely non-calendrical content then complete the hieroglyphic inscription. These two panels, Panel Y and Panel Z, may themselves form a separate continuous text. Block yA4 is similar to the first name glyph of PCY as identified at Blocks 13 and 30 of Altar 13 and at zA4 of Altar 12. Block zA1 then marks the same glyph that appears at Block 15 of Altar 13 and zA6 of Altar 12 also identified with PCY.

Looking over the information gleaned from Stela 19 and Altars 12 and 13, several name phrases have been provisionally identified. Stela 19 shows one at yA1-yB2 which has been labeled PCZ. The context of the appearance of this person's name is unknown. The T74.184 title does however occur in the name of PCZ which may indicate that he was a ruler. Altar 12 may also display the name of PCZ at two points (Blocks 11-13 and 30-32). A subsequent monarch, Lord Quincunx, is mentioned later on Altar 12 in a clause that marks the same DD (9.19.10.0.0) as Stela 19. Also on Altar 12 is a set of three glyphs at zA4-zA6 which is repeated on Altar 13 at Blocks 13-15, Block 30 and Blocks yA4 and zA1. These three glyphs have tentatively been considered to be portions of a name-title phrase for a person who is temporarily labeled PCY. A final personage mentioned on Altar 13 is that at Blocks 5-11 and Blocks 23-28. Despite the similarity of presentation of portions of this person's name-title phrase to that identified as PCZ on Stela 19, he will be identified rather with Lord Quincunx.

Relationship of these characters to each other and to rulership at the site of Caracol is at this moment difficult to determine. It appears from Altar 12 that Lord Quincunx was in power at 9.19.10.0.0. Provisional Character Z of Stela 19 may have preceded, succeeded, or been identical with him. The first possibility seems most likely. Passing to Altar 13, two references are made to a person who bears similar titles to those of PCZ. But an apparently different main sign is attached to the T74.184 marker of rulership. Indeed, the glyph with the postulated T74. 184 prefix (Blocks 7 and 25 of Altar 13) is much closer in outline to that of Lord Quincunx on Altar 12 (Blocks G5-H5). Thus the two are postulated to be a single person. To the left of the left-hand figure on Altar 12 comes reference to PCY of Caracol. Portions of this character's name phrase are repeated on Altar 13 in the same clauses that men- tion Lord Quincunx and in the internal Panels Y and Z. With the possible exception of the presentation on Altar 12, these glyphs do not appear with any of the markers of rulership, including the Caracol Glyph or the T502.25:502 *bacab* title. On Altar 12 at zA3 a glyph with T184 prefix precedes PCY's name. The relation of this glyph to the person's name is uncertain.

Without more information regarding relationships and dates a solid interpretation cannot be made. An intuitive explanation might however be constructed as follows: Lord Quincunx was in power at 9.19.10.0.0 and probably also at 10.0.0.0.0 A predecessor sovereign may have been that person identified as PCZ on Stela 19. The third personage, PCY, does not seem to have been a ruler but was important enough to be mentioned several times and possibly in two common clauses with Lord Quincunx. From this it might be deduced that PCY was a relative to Lord Quincunx.

STELA 17, ALTAR 10 AND STELA 10

Stela 17 and its paired Altar 10, two of the latest monuments known at Caracol, bear a surprisingly clear record of a person who can be reliably identified as a sovereign. The chronology recorded on the stela has had to be partially reconstructed because of at least one probable mistake in carving and because of weathering that makes it impossible to distinguish a decorative filler from a numerical dot in coefficients. There is, however, a coherency to the count as reconstructed that gives it reliability. The initial clause of Stela 17 opens with a CR date that is read as 13 Ix 17 Zec at the LC position 10.0.19.6.14. Succeeding the CR in the event glyph position is a glyph that is a peculiar montage of components with T1 prefix. Next is the compound T25:502:? which might be given the speculative phonetic reading of *cab-ah* (ca-b(a)-ah?). The subsequent glyph is unrecognized and the final glyph of the opening clause appears to record 3 haabs. If the subject of this clause is to be found marked within it rather than implied, it must lie at B3. At that point is a glyph that shows no particular attributes of a name, and appears only this once.

Opening the second, and apparently final, clause of the chronological portion of the Stela 17 text is an SS at B4. This is followed by a split block at C4 which carries an unidentified glyph group followed by a posterior date indicator. At B5a-B5b appears the CR itself as 5 Ahau 3 Kayab marking the LC position 10.1.0.0.0. A "hand scattering" glyph succeeds the CR at C5a followed by an unrecognized compound at C5b. Text then apparently jumps back to A4a where it commences a name-title phrase. The first glyph of this phrase is not recognized, but the second is an animal head with uinal glyph infixed in the area of the jaw, and a prefix of three apparently numerical dots. This same compound has been noted in use with the name phrase of PCZ on Stela 19 at yA1 dating to around 9.19.10.0.0 and on Stela 3 at D11a in the name phrase of God C Star. This sort of distribution over many years and with three different characters indicates that it fulfills a titular function. Terminating the final clause at A5a-A5b occurs a glyphic compound of T351: 506(:?) and the T502.25:502 *bacab* title. On the basis of this name phrase and another dealing with the same character on Altar 10, the T351: 506 compound is identified as representing the name of a ruler of Caracol whom we can label "Lord Storm-water Maize" from the component glyphs of his name.

As has been mentioned, Lord Storm-water

Maize's name also appears on Altar 10. There it occurs at zA1 in a short glyphic inscription between the middle and right-hand figures. In this instance, his name bears a prefix of which T178 may be a part. Following the name glyph is postfixed a T184.74 title of rulership. Immediately after this glyph group representing Lord Storm-water Maize's name is a block that is similar to an EG. It takes the form of T93?.168:518:130?. The T518 main sign is the same as is found in the unidentified EG that accompanies God C Star's name on Stela 3 much earlier. However, this latter occurrence on Altar 10 does not appear to meet the previously specified criteria for an EG since it lacks the proper prefixes.

At three points on Stela 17 and Altar 10 there appears a badly weathered glyph group that can be made out as T122 prefixed to a main sign with bar-like element across the top and a split or two-part superfix (Stela 17, xA1a and zB2; Altar 10, yB2). It may be recalled that a compound utilizing T122 as a prefix was a prominent part of the name-title phrases of PCZ and Lord Quincunx

on Stela 19 and Altar 13.

History that can be read from Stela 17 and Altar 10 is scant at present. Lord Storm-water Maize evidently celebrated the PE 10.1.0.0.0 in power as the ruler of Caracol. Significance of the date marked by the CR at the opening of the text (10.0.19.6.14) is not presently known. We might speculate however that the glyph in the event position is a seating variant, since accession seems to be the event most prominently marked in Maya inscriptions. Thus it might be suggested that Lord Storm-water Maize came to power at 10.0.19.6.14 and celebrated his first PE in office at 10.1.0.0.0. Association of this ruler with the EG simulacrum on Altar 10 creates a possible "wrinkle" regarding foreign ancestry for Lord Storm-water Maize. This line of inquiry cannot be further developed without more evidence.

The latest monument from Caracol is presently Stela 10 with an eroded and purely glyphic inscription. Its state of preservation is unfortunately just too poor to find any clues about dynastic information.

SUMMARY

During the preceding analyses, it has been noted repeatedly that much of our interpretation of the history recorded on the monuments of Caracol must be speculative. Only a few events and names can be read with minimal doubts. Bearing this in mind, this final section will attempt a synthetic interpretation of the dynastic information that is preserved on the stelae and altars of Caracol.

Recently, during the final re-drawing of several Caracol monuments, the presence of apparent "name" glyphs was noted on the fronts of stelae. Earlier, Stone, Reents and Coffman (1980) spotted the first of these on the back of Stela 6. That example appears as part of the headdress of a face that emerges from the left-hand mouth of an intertwined aerial serpent. The name in this instance is recognizable as that of Lord Storm-water Moon. Another name probably occurred in the right-hand serpent's mouth but is now eroded.

Unfortunately, there has not been sufficient time between the discovery of these name glyphs and the date of publication to allow consideration of exactly how the presence of these names might affect the interpretation of history presented here. Thus a simple cataloguing will have to suffice.

The earliest such name is on Stela 16 above the headdress of the main figure. Stela 5 shows the name of Lord Storm-water Moon attached to the headdress of a head that emerges from the left-hand serpent head of two that show behind the "dwarfs" that flank the main figure. A complementary head with name is largely eroded on the right side. Another pair of possible names, both unreadable in this case, occur in the headdresses of medially placed heads and torsos that flank the central figure. A final pair of names exists, again attached to headdresses of faces within serpents' mouths, at either end of the horizontal ceremonial bar. Lord Water's name is that on the right end of the bar. A pair of intertwined aerial serpents floats over the main figure of Stela 5. However, neither of the heads that rests within their mouths seems to carry a "name" glyph as part of the headdress.

The earliest recognizable Caracol ruler is that labeled Lord Jaguar on Stela 16 at 9.5.0.0.0. That monument's text is not understood, but seems to take the form of a single long clause. Under the rules of composition as presently understood, this indicates that the bulk of the Stela 16 inscription should be a series of relationship statements. Such an idea is to a certain extent borne out by the repeated pattern of groups of three portrait heads. The timing is approximately correct for Lord Jaguar to have been at least the predecessor in power if not the father to Lord Water. There are suggestions on Stela 6 and Stela 1 that the two lords were indeed father and son. As a final note to Lord Jaguar's career, the IS of the damaged slate Stela 15 (9.4.16.13.3) would represent a reasonable accession date for Lord Jaguar to be in rule at 9.5.0.0.0, although there is no textual evidence for this.

Several preserved clauses on Caracol and Naranjo monuments refer to Lord Water, the next known ruler of Caracol. His name appears twice on Stela 14 (C8, E8) with a DD of 9.6.0.0.0. Lord Water's name occurs at least four times on the preserved half of the Stela 6 text (D4, E9, D12, E21) with a possible DD of 9.8.10.0.0. At Naranjo, Lord Water finds mention on the later (9.10.0.0.0) Lintel 1 in a clause that discusses Lord Storm-water Moon. Although the actual birth date of Lord Water is unknown, it can be approximated to between 9.5.10.0.0 and 9.5.19.1.2. His accession to rulership at Caracol seems to have occurred at 9.5.19.1.2, a date that is represented on both Stela 6 (IS) and Stela 14 (SS). The time of Lord Water's death is also unrecorded but can be calculated to be between 9.8.10.0.0 and 9.9.19.1.2 by use of katuns-of-life records. Stela 6 records a second name in two common clauses with Lord Water, Ahau-serpent. Since the contexts of appearance are unclear, it can only be speculated that Ahau-serpent is either a relative of, or identical to, Lord Water.

Stela 1 and probably also Stela 15 were erected during the reign of Lord Water. As mentioned above, the latter stone is slate which has fractured and spalled extensively, and may very tentatively have recorded 9.4.16.13.3 as Lord Jaguar's accession date. Stela 1 bears a clear IS and DD of 9.8.0.0.0 followed by a clause that records four names. The first (Serpent-head) is not presently identified, but the second can tentatively be assigned to Lord Water on the bases of a common prefix and the fact that he was in power at 9.8.0.0.0. Text on Stela 1 also indicates that the mother of Lord Water was one Lady Jaguar, who by means of shared glyphs can be speculatively regarded as the wife of Lord Jaguar. A final four-block portion of inscription concludes with a citation of Lord Storm-water Moon in the first katun

of his life.

Text on Stela 3 begins with discussion of some events that occurred during the reign of Lord Water. The opening clause records the birth of a possibly female character (God C Star), the mother (Lady Bird), and the father. Later on, the text marks the birth of Yellow Storm, which is interpreted to be a pre-rule name for Lord Storm-water Moon. Such an identity is indeed demonstrated further along on Stela 3. Lord Storm-water Moon's accession to power is tentatively reconstructed as 9.9.4.16.2, which fits in well with the span calculated for Lord Water's death (9.8.10.0.0–9.9.19.1.2). Naranjo Lintel 1 bears the 9.7.14.10.8 birth date of Lord Storm-water Moon and also a marking of the katun end 9.10.0.0.0. God C Star and Lord Water are mentioned in the birth clause with Lord Storm-water Moon in an order that resembles a relationship phrase that may identify God C Star as the mother and Lord Water as the father. Lord Storm-water Moon was in rule as late as 9.10.4.7.0 but after that the record breaks.

Stela 21 seems to retain an event glyph marking birth at 9.13.10.0.0 but the subject glyph is well eroded. The three badly damaged and eroded Stelae 8, 9 and 11 follow Stela 21 after a long gap, apparently dating to around 9.19.0.0.0. Only Stela 11 at 9.18.10.0.0?? currently reveals any dynastic information. This message is limited to the reconstruction of a female parent indicator at B5 followed by an eroded block that probably carried a name that is itself succeeded by a Caracol Glyph. The text presumably passed to Panel Y which is too badly destroyed to reveal much, although the last two blocks can be read as a Caracol Glyph and *bacab*.

Subsequent identifiable rulers of Caracol are found on Stela 19 and Altars 12 and 13. The stela text is largely lost, but one small section of glyphs does record an apparent sovereign's name, as marked by the T74.184 title. Until he is more completely identified, this personage has been given the label of PCZ. Altar 12, in a clause marking 9.19.10.0.0, presents a monarch who has been identified as Lord Quincunx. Text on Altar 12 also seems to mark PCZ's name at two points. Yet a third character is marked on Altar 12 in an internal panel near to the left-hand figure. Because the form of this person's name is uncertain, the label of PCY has been applied. Altar 3, in an eroded text, seems to present twice Lord Quincunx and PCY in common clauses. Such an occurrence suggests relationship between the two.

Preserved dynastic information at Caracol reaches its chronological limit with the inscriptions on Stela 17 and Altar 10 dating to 10.1.0.0.0. Stela 17 offers two clauses which both apparently refer to a single monarch, Lord Storm-water Maize. Opening the text is a CR date that marks the LC position 10.0.19.6.14 which has been suggested as representing the date of accession for Lord Storm-water Maize. The DD of Stela 17, 10.1.0.0.0, would then mark this sovereign's first PE in office. Another character seems to be recorded on Stela 17 in the nearly destroyed secondary glyph panels that are found near the figures. Altar 10 is badly damaged over much of its surface; however, one small interior panel does bear a record of Lord Storm-water Maize followed by a glyph that bears many of the attributes of an EG utilizing a T518 main sign. In the absence of any information, a speculation that Lord Storm-water Maize succeeded Lord Quincunx as ruler of Caracol has been made. It is however perfectly possible that another ruler or rulers intervened between the last putative date known for Lord Quincunx' reign (10.0.0.0.0) and the postulated accession date for Lord Storm-water Maize at 10.0.10.6.14.

In conclusion, we can observe that a surprising amount of information can be gleaned from the eroded and broken stones of Caracol. Three rulers can be identified between 9.5.0.0.0 and 9.10.4.7.0 along with subsidiary characters representing parents of the monarchs. Following a long gap, which may be more a product of the accident of discovery than any actual cessation of monument carving, three more monarchs and other persons can be recognized from 9.19.10.0.0 to 10.1.0.0.0. It is to be hoped and expected that the gaps in the dynastic record will be filled in as fieldwork is carried out at Caracol and other monuments are discovered. With new information, many of the conclusions that are only tentatively drawn in the present paper can be verified or discarded.

BIBLIOGRAPHY

Anderson, A. Hamilton
1958 Recent Discoveries at Caracol Site, British Honduras. *Proceedings: 32nd International Congress of Americanists, Copenhagen 1953.*
1959 More Discoveries at Caracol, British Honduras. *Proceedings: 33rd International Congress of Americanists, San Jose 1958.*

Beetz, Carl P.
1980 Caracol Thirty Years Later: A Preliminary Account of Two Rulers. *Expedition* 22(3): 4-11.

Berlin, Heinrich
1958 El glifo "emblema" en las inscripciones mayas. *Journal de la Société des Americanistes* n.s. 47:111-119.
1963 The Palenque Triad. *Journal de la Société des Americanistes* n.s. 52:91-99.
1973 Beitrage zum Verstandnis der Inschriften von Naranjo. *Société suisse des Americanistes Bulletin* 37:7-14.

Beyer, H.
1931 Mayan Hieroglyphs: the Variable Element of the Introducing Glyphs as Month Indicator. *Anthropos* 26:99-108.

Coggins, Clemency C.
1975 *Painting and Drawing Styles at Tikal: An Historical and Iconographic Reconstruction.* Ph.D. dissertation, Harvard University. University Microfilms, Ann Arbor.

Graham, Ian
1978 *Corpus of Maya Hieroglyphic Inscriptions* (Vol. 2, Part 2). Peabody Museum of Archaeology and Ethnology, Cambridge.

Graham, John A.
1972 The Hieroglyphic Inscriptions and Monumental Art of Altar de Sacrificios. *Papers of the Peabody Museum of Archaeology and Ethnology* 64(2).

Haviland, William A.
n.d. Excavations in Residential Areas of Tikal: Group 7F-1, an Elite Residential Group. *Tikal Report No. 22.*

Jones, Christopher
1977 Inauguration Dates of Three Late Classic Rulers of Tikal, Guatemala. *American Antiquity* 42:28-60.

Kelley, David H.
1962 Glyphic Evidence for a Dynastic Sequence at Quirigua, Guatemala. *American Antiquity* 27:323-335.
1965 The Birth of the Gods at Palenque. *Estudios de Cultura Maya* 5:93-134.
1976 *Deciphering the Maya Script.* University of Texas Press, Austin.

Kubler, George
1973 The Clauses of Classic Maya Inscriptions. In *Mesoamerican Writing Systems,* edited by E. P. Benson, pp. 145-164. Dumbarton Oaks, Washington, D.C.

Lounsbury, Floyd G.
1974 Untitled note on p. ii, preceding Preface of *Primera Mesa Redonda de Palenque* (Part I), edited by M. G. Robertson. The Robert Louis Stevenson School, Pebble Beach.

Marcus, Joyce
1976 *Emblem and State in the Classic Maya Lowlands: an Epigraphic Approach to Territorial Organization.* Dumbarton Oaks, Washington, D.C.

Matthews, Peter, and Linda Schele
1974 Lords of Palenque—the Glyphic Evidence. In *Primera Mesa Redonda de Palenque* (Part I), edited by M. G. Robertson, pp. 63-76. Robert Louis Stevenson School, Pebble Beach.

Morley, Sylvanus G.
1920 The Inscriptions at Copan. *Carnegie Institution of Washington Publication* 219.
1937- The Inscriptions of Peten. *Carnegie Institu-*
38 *tion of Washington Publication* 437.

Proskouriakoff, Tatiana
1950 A Study of Classic Maya Sculpture. *Carnegie Institution of Washington Publication* 593.
1960 Historical Implications of a Pattern of Dates

at Piedras Negras, Guatemala. *American Antiquity* 25:454-475.

1961 The Lords of the Maya Realm. *Expedition* 4(1): 14-21. University Museum, U. of Pa.

1961 Portraits of Women in Maya Art. In *Essays in Pre-Columbian Art and Archaeology*, S. K. Lothrop et al, pp. 81-99. Harvard University Press, Cambridge.

1963 Historical Data in the Inscriptions of Yaxchilan. *Estudios de Cultura Maya* 3:149-167.

1964 Historical Data in the Inscriptions of Yaxchilan (part II). *Estudios de Cultura Maya* 4:177-202.

1968 The Jog and the Jaguar Signs in Maya Writing. *American Antiquity* 33:247-251.

Riese, Berthold

1980 Caracol—Dokumentation der Inschriften. *Materialien der Hamburger Maya Inschriften Dokumentation 4.*

Satterthwaite, Linton

1951 Reconnaissance in British Honduras. *University Museum Bulletin* 16:21-37.

1954 Sculptured Monuments from Caracol, British Honduras. *University Museum Bulletin* 18: 1-45.

1958 Five Newly Discovered Carved Monuments at Tikal and New Data on Four Others. *Tikal Report No. 4.*

Schele, Linda

1974 Observations on the Cross Motif at Palenque. In *Primera Mesa Redonda de Palenque* (Part I), edited by M. G. Robertson, pp. 41-62. Robert Louis Stevenson School, Pebble Beach.

1977 Accession Iconography of Chan Bahlum in the Group of the Cross at Palenque. In *The Art, Iconography and Dynastic History of Palenque* (Part III), edited by M. G. Robertson, pp. 9-34. The Robert Louis Stevenson School, Pebble Beach.

n.d. Post-Emblem Glyphs and Directional Titles from Classic Maya Nominal Phrases. Unpublished Manuscript.

Schele, Linda, Peter Matthews and Floyd G. Lounsbury

1977 Parentage and Spouse Expressions from Classic Maya Inscriptions. Unpublished Manuscript.

Smith, Robert E.

1955 Ceramic sequence at Uaxactun, Guatemala. *Middle American Research Institute Publication 20.*

Sosa, John, and Dorie Reents

1980 Glyphic Evidence for Classic Maya Militarism. *Belizean Studies* 8(3):2-11.

Stone, Andrea, Dorie Reents and Robert Coffman

1980 *Genealogical Documentation of the Middle Classic Dynasty of Caracol, El Cayo, Belize.* Paper presented at the Cuarto Mesa Redonda de Palenque.

Thompson, J. Eric S.

1931 Archaeological Investigations in the Southern Cayo District, British Honduras. *Field Museum of Natural History, Anthropological Series* 17:213-362.

1950 *Maya Hieroglyphic Writing: An Introduction.* University of Oklahoma Press, Norman.

1962 *A Catalog of Maya Hieroglyphs.* University of Oklahoma Press, Norman.

Willcox, Horace

1954 Removal and Restoration of the Monuments of Caracol. *University Museum Bulletin* 18: 46-72.

ILLUSTRATIONS

FIGURE 1

Stela 1: Front. 1:10
See photograph, Fig. 29a

FIGURE 2

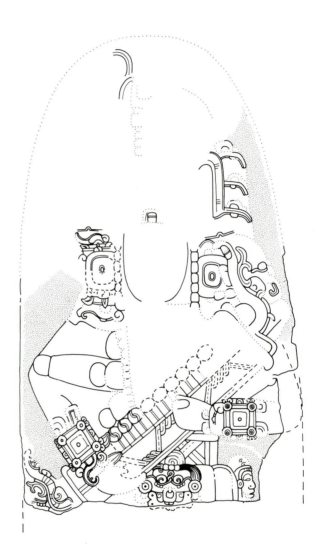

Stela 2: Front, upper half. 1:10
See photograph, Fig. 29b

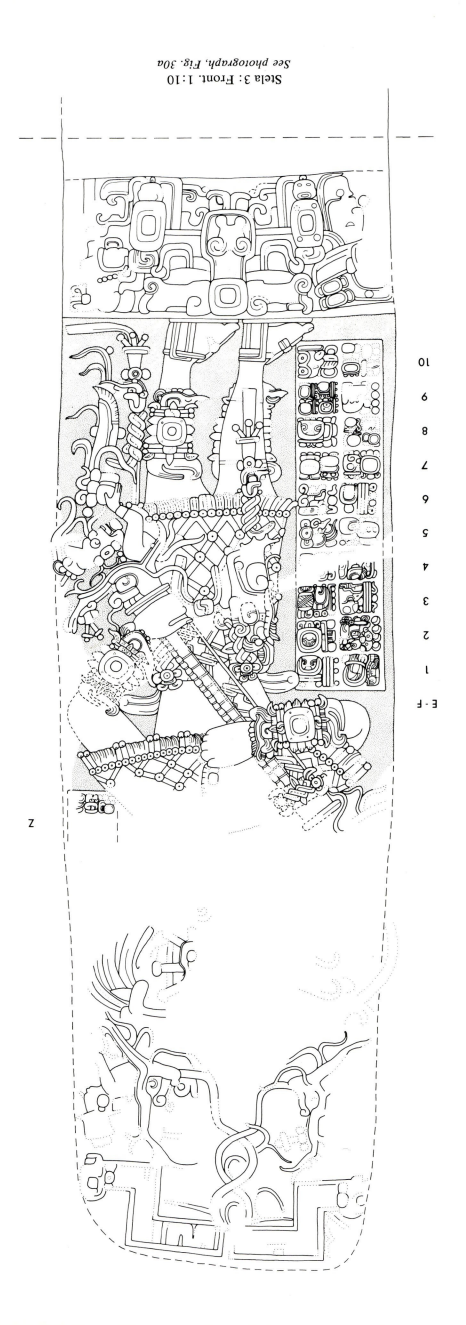

E–F

1 2 3 4 5 6 7 8 9 10

Z

FIGURE 3

FIGURE 4

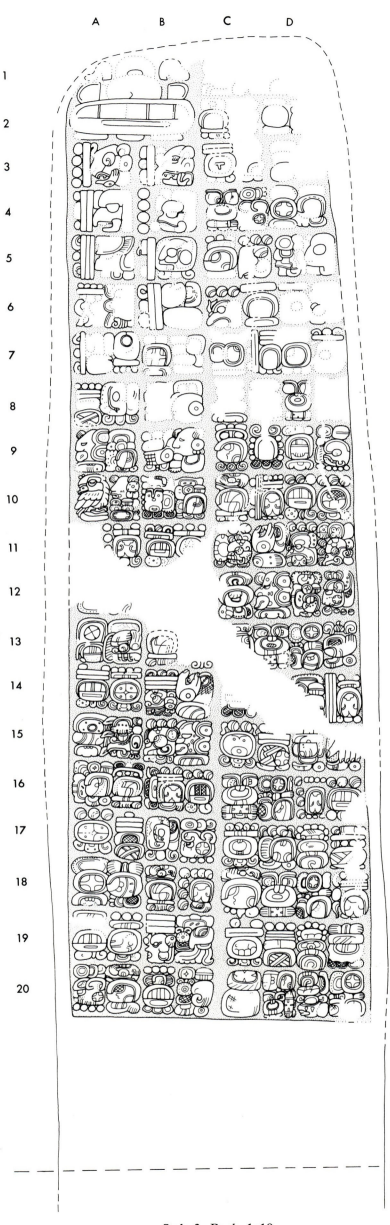

Stela 3: Back. 1:10
See photograph, Fig. 30b

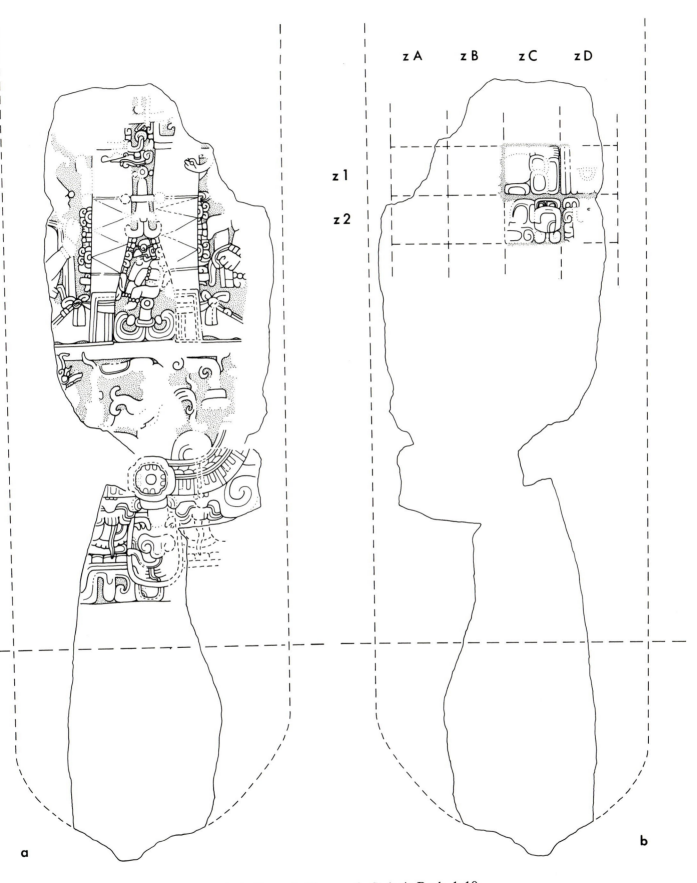

FIGURE 5

z A   z B   z C   z D

z 1

z 2

a

b

a. Stela 4: Front. 1:10
See photograph, Fig. 29c

b. Stela 4: Back. 1:10
See photograph, Fig. 29d

FIGURE 6

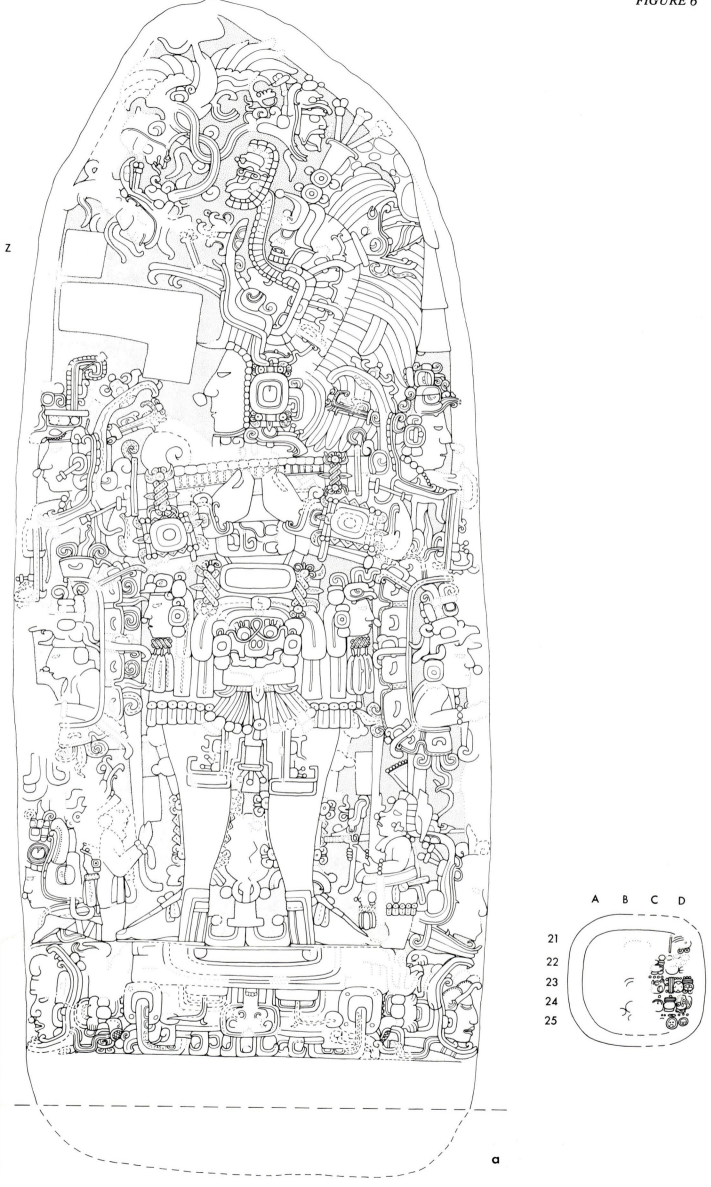

a. Stela 5: Front. 1:10   b. Stela 5: Lower right side glyph panel. 1:10
See photograph, Fig. 31a   *See photograph, Fig. 31b*

FIGURE 7

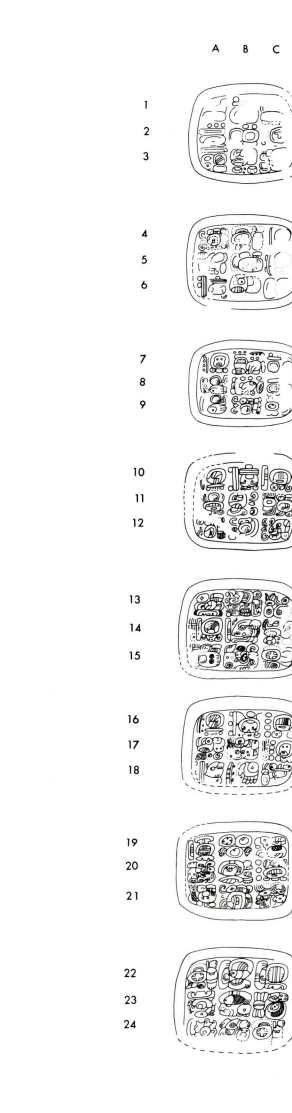

a. Stela 6: Front. 1:10

See photograph, Fig. 32a

b. Stela 6: Right side. 1:10

See photograph, Fig. 32b

FIGURE 8

Z

Stela 6: Back. 1:10
See photograph, Fig. 32c

FIGURE 9

W

X

Y

Z

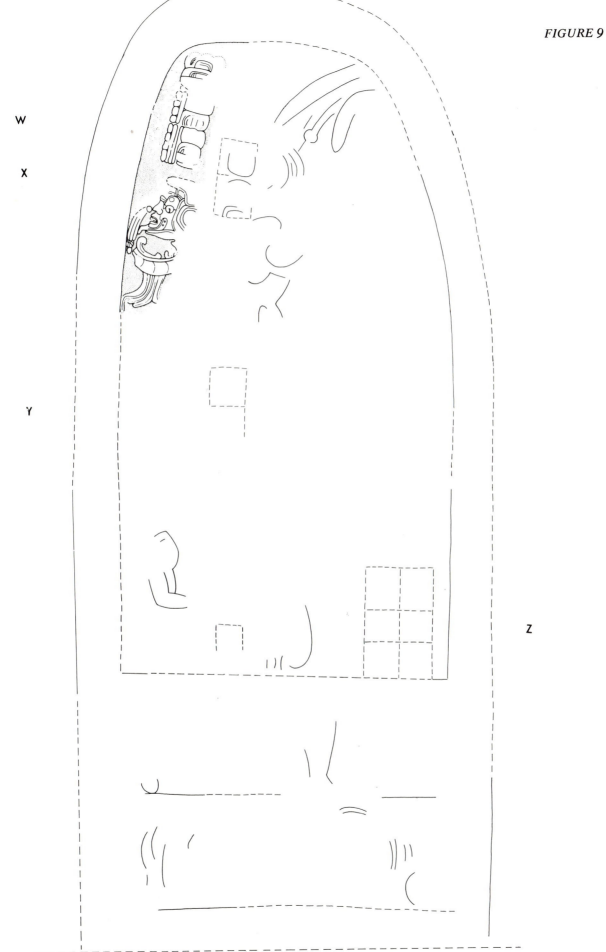

Stela 8: Front. 1:10
See photographs, Fig. 33a, b

FIGURE 10

W

Z

X

Y

Stela 9: Front. 1:10
See photograph, Fig. 34a

FIGURE 11

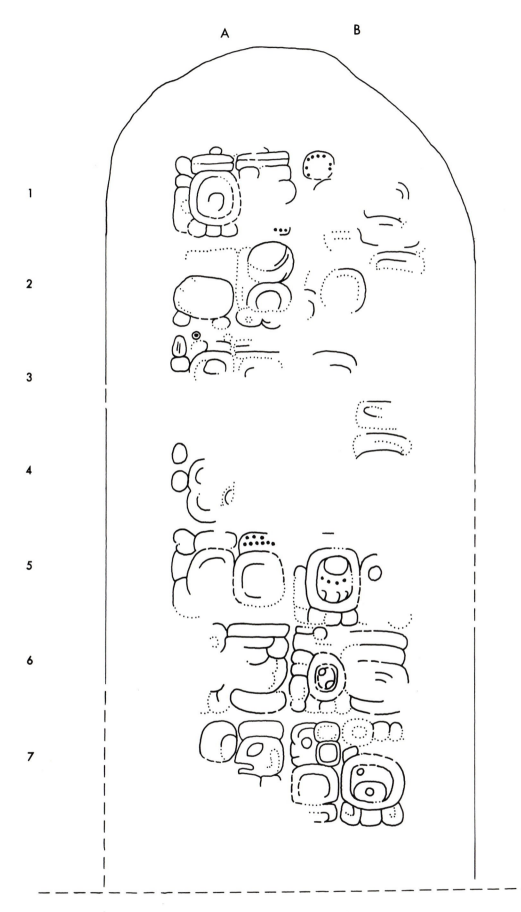

Stela 10: Front. 1:10
See photographs, Fig. 34b, c

FIGURE 12

Stela 11: Front. 1:10
See photographs, Fig. 35a, b

FIGURE 13

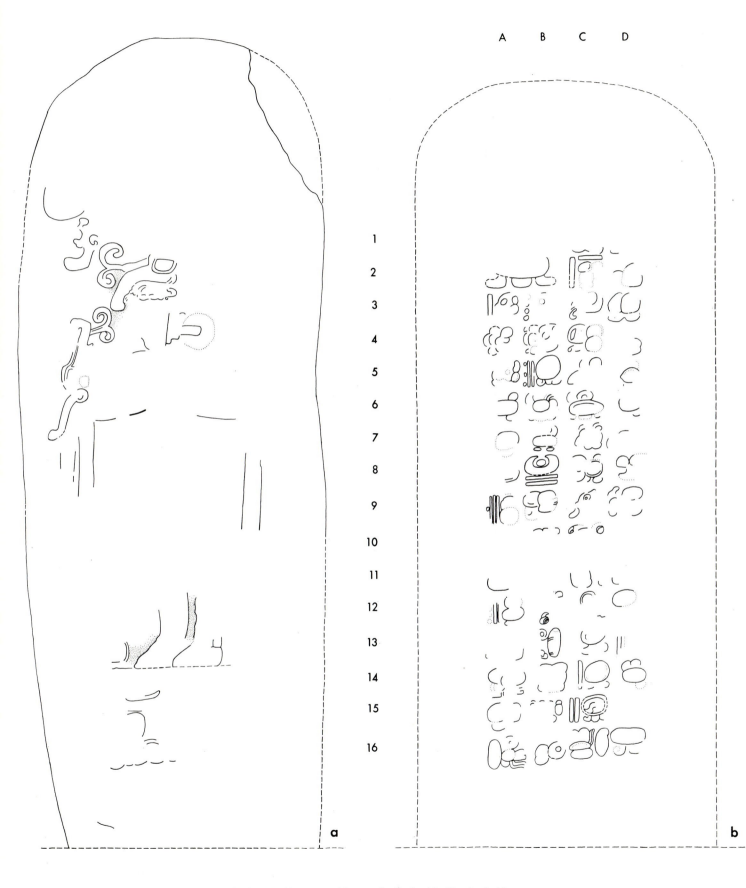

a. Stela 13: Front. 1:10
See photograph, Fig. 36a

b. Stela 13: Back. 1:10
See photograph, Fig. 36b

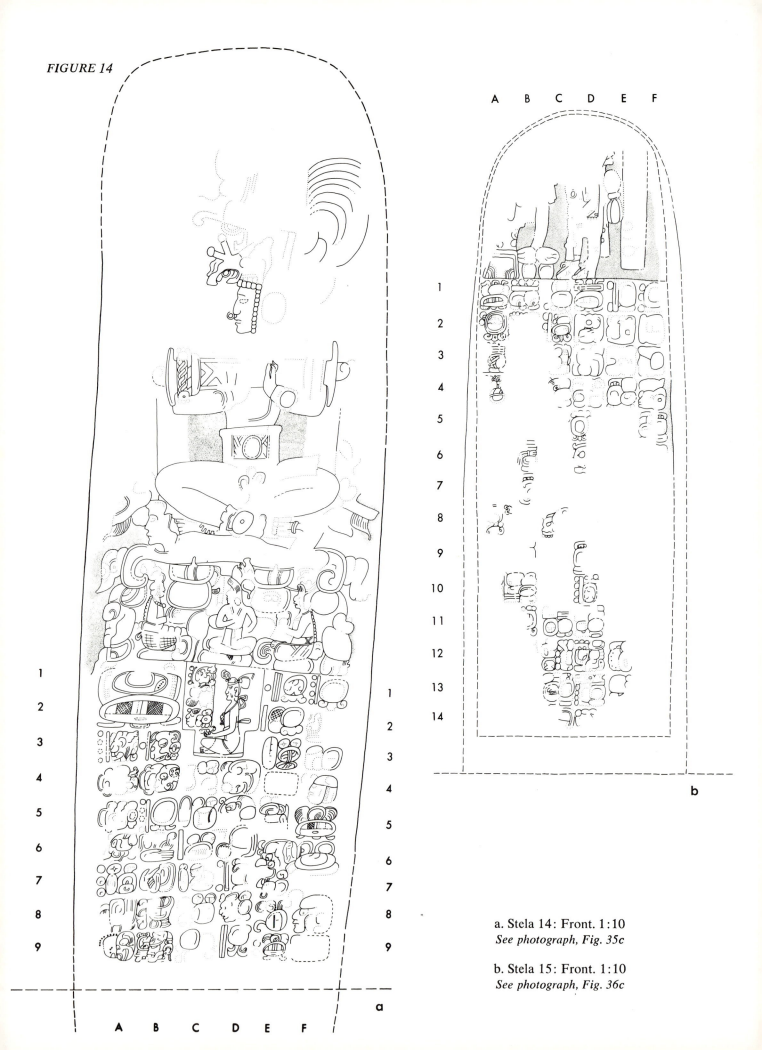

FIGURE 14

a. Stela 14: Front. 1:10
See photograph, Fig. 35c

b. Stela 15: Front. 1:10
See photograph, Fig. 36c

FIGURE 15

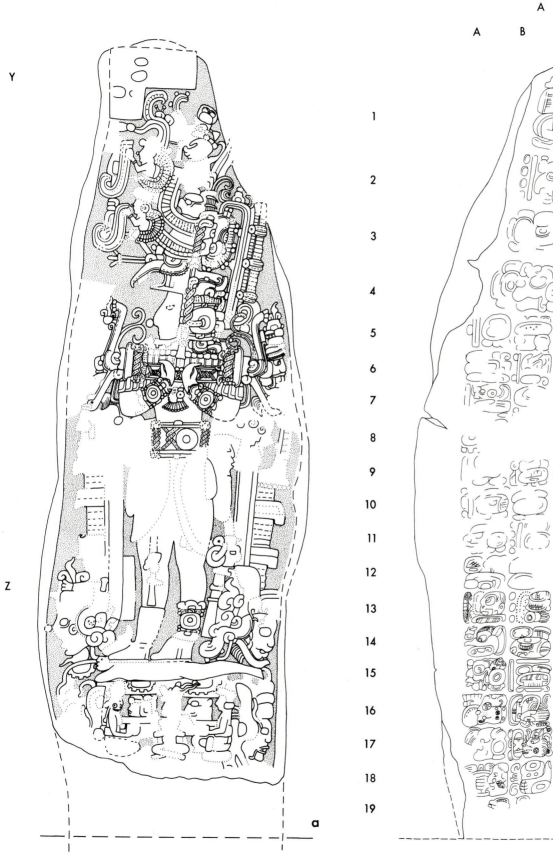

a. Stela 16: Front. 1:10
See photograph, Fig. 37a

b. Stela 16 Back. 1:10
See photograph, Fig. 37b

FIGURE 16

A B C

1
2
3
4
5
X
Y
Z

Y

Z

a

b

a. Stela 17: Front. 1:10
See photograph, Fig. 38a

b. Stela 18: Front. 1:10
See photograph, Fig. 38b

FIGURE 17

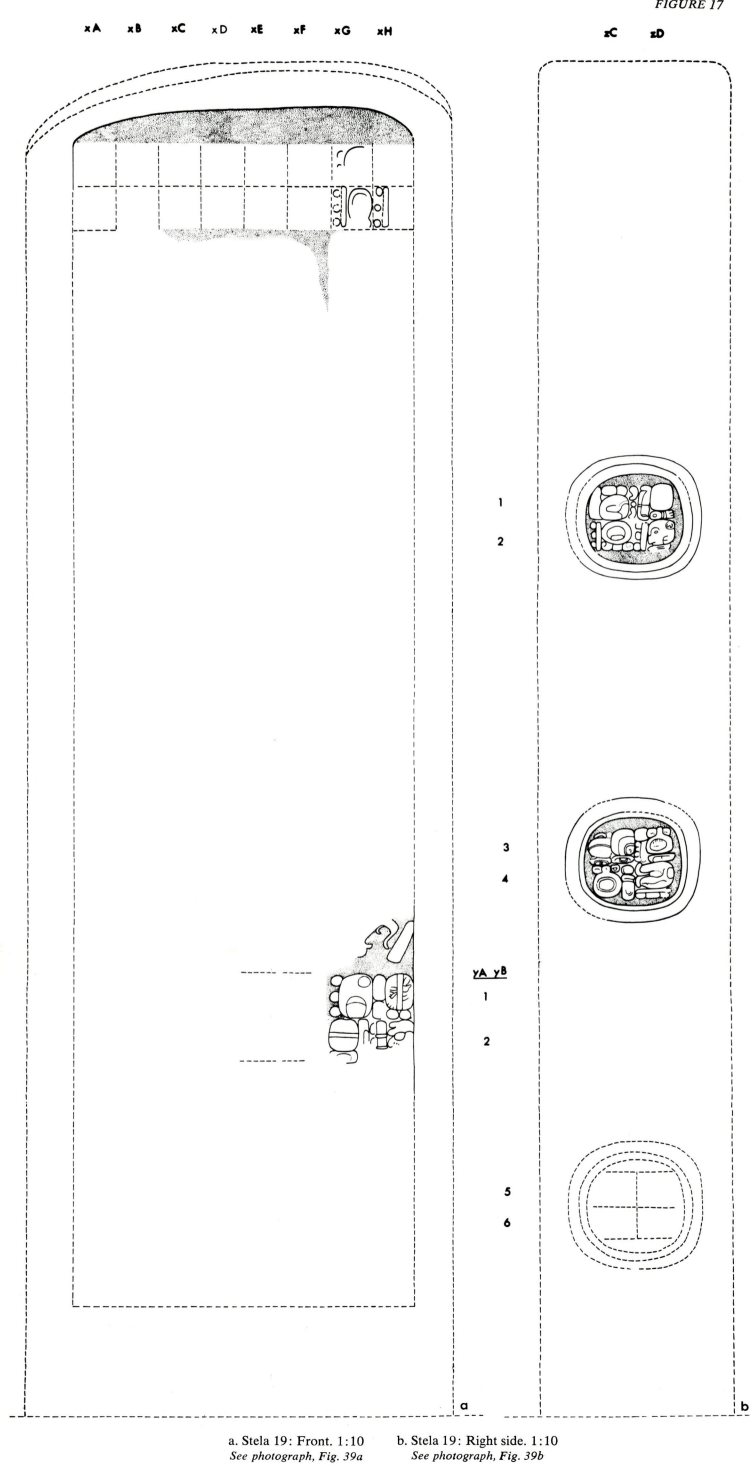

a. Stela 19: Front. 1:10　　b. Stela 19: Right side. 1:10
See photograph, Fig. 39a　　*See photograph, Fig. 39b*

FIGURE 18

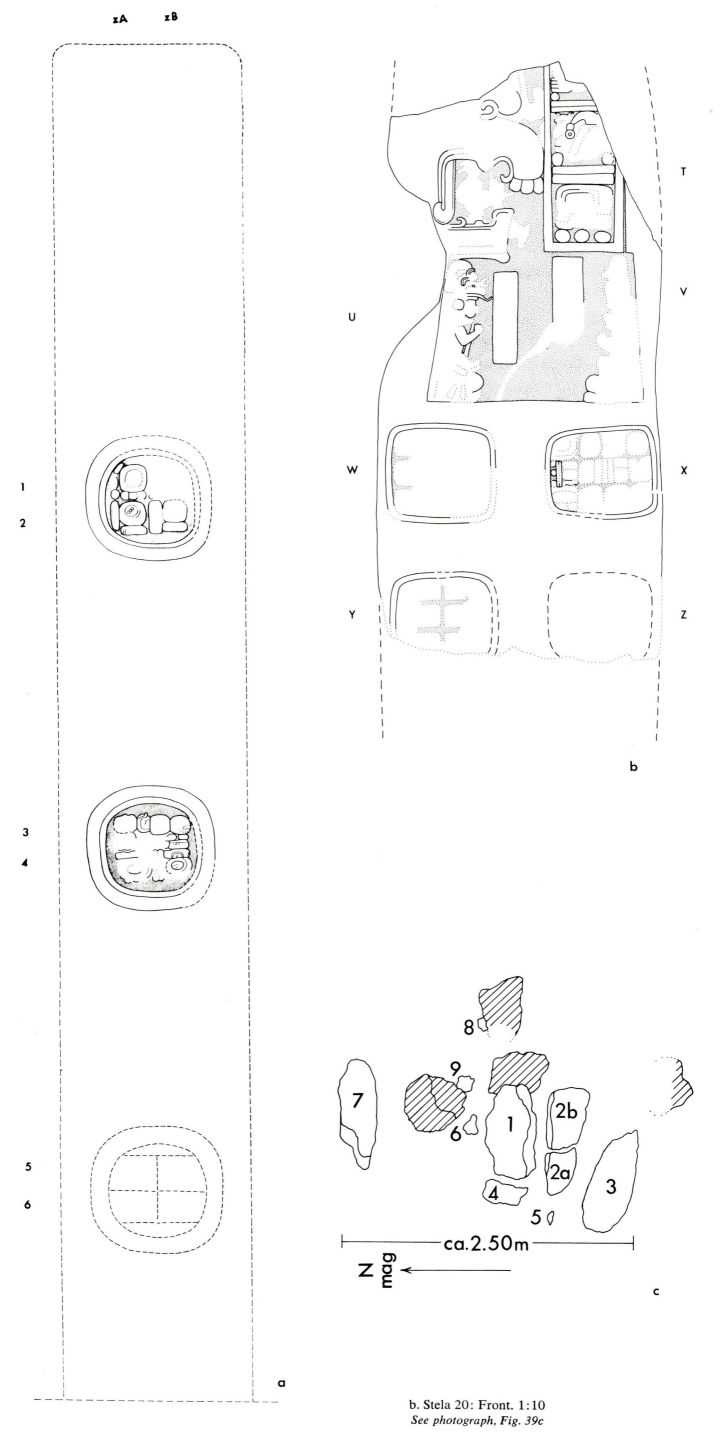

a. Stela 19: Left side. 1:10

b. Stela 20: Front. 1:10
See photograph, Fig. 39c

c. Schematic Diagram of Position of
Stela 4 Fragments as found

ca.2.50m

FIGURE 19

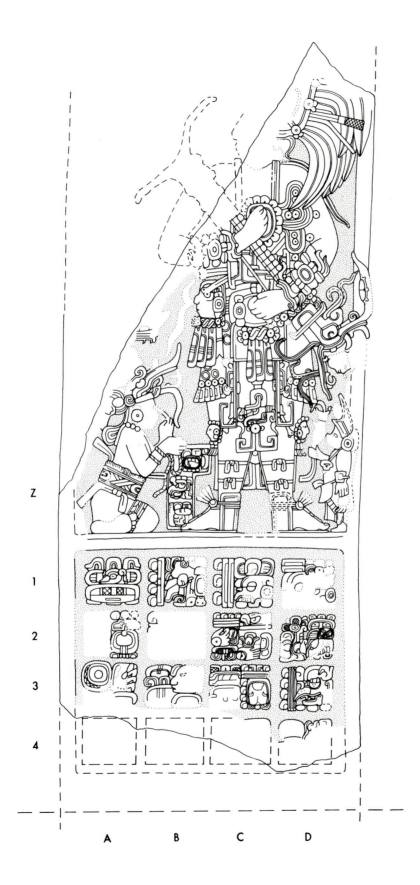

Z

1

2

3

4

A   B   C   D

Stela 21: Front. 1:10
See photograph, Fig. 39d

FIGURE 20

a

b

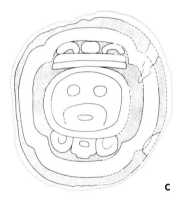

c

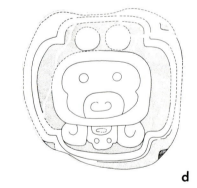

d

a. Altar 1. 1:40
See photograph, Fig. 40a

b. Altar 2. 1:40
See photograph, Fig. 40b

c. Altar 3. 1:40
See photograph, Fig. 40c

d. Altar 4. 1:40
See photograph, Fig. 40d

FIGURE 21

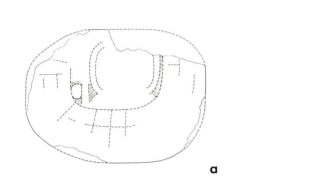

a

b

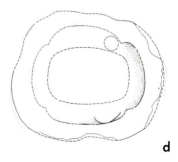

c

d

a. Altar 5. 1:40
See photograph, Fig. 41a

b. Altar 6. 1:40
See photograph, Fig. 41b

c. Altar 7. 1:40
See photograph, Fig. 41c

d. Altar 11. 1:40

FIGURE 22

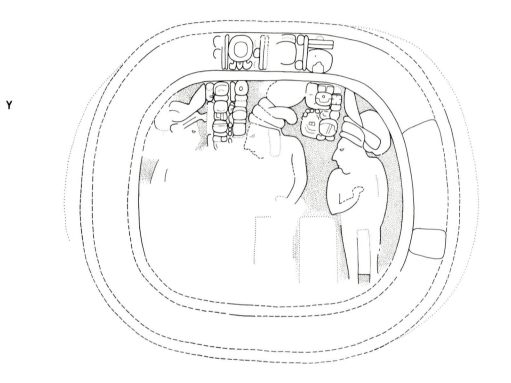

Altar 10. 1:10
See photograph 41d

FIGURE 23

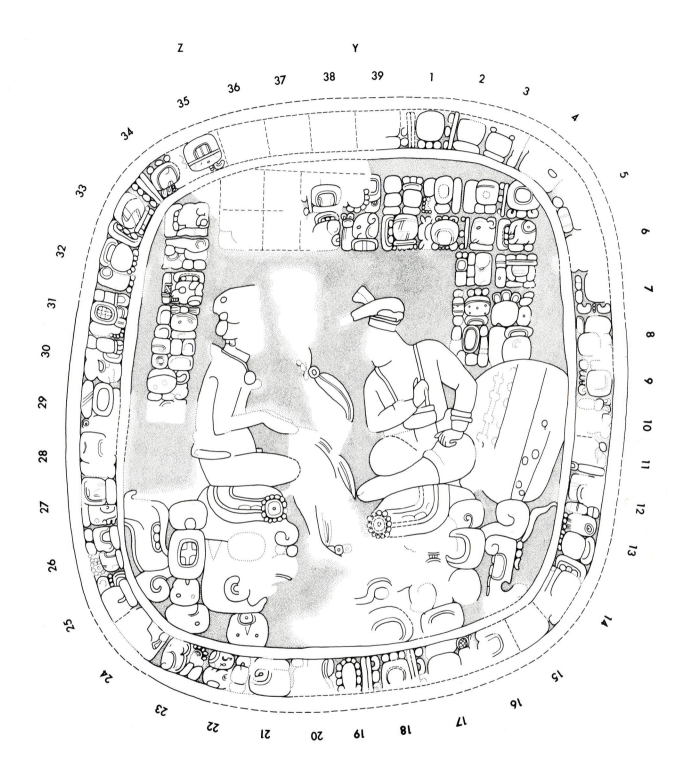

Altar 12. 1:10
See photograph, Fig. 42a

FIGURE 24

Main Panel

Altar 13. 1:10
See photograph, Fig. 42b

FIGURE 25

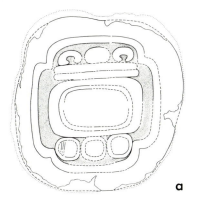

a

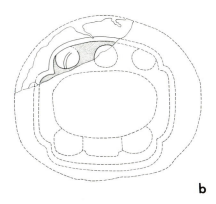

b

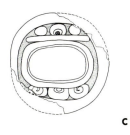

c

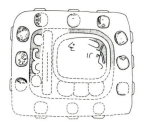

d

a. Altar 14. 1:40
See photograph, Fig. 42c

b. Altar 15. 1:40
See photograph, Fig. 42d

c. Altar 16. 1:40
See photograph, Fig. 43a

d. Altar 17. 1:40
See photograph, Fig. 43b

FIGURE 26

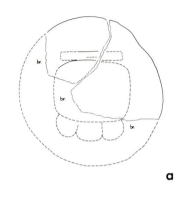

a

b

a. Altar 18. 1:40

b. Altar 19. 1:40
See photograph, Fig. 43c

FIGURE 27

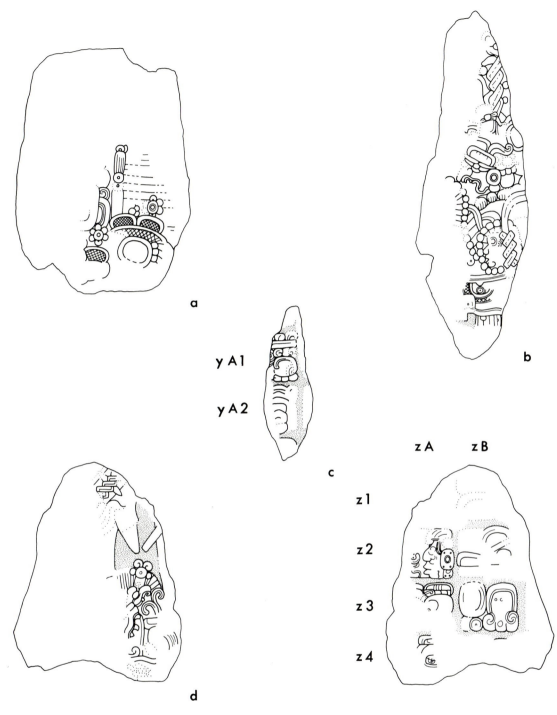

y A1

y A2

z A   z B

z 1

z 2

z 3

z 4

a. Stone Group 46
Reconstructed Fragment 1. 1:10

b. Stone Group 46/50
Reconstructed Fragment 2. 1:10

c. Stela 4 Fragment. 1:10

d. Stone Group 46
Reconstructed Fragment 3, Front. 1:10

e. Stone Group 46
Reconstructed Fragment 3, Back. 1:10

FIGURE 28

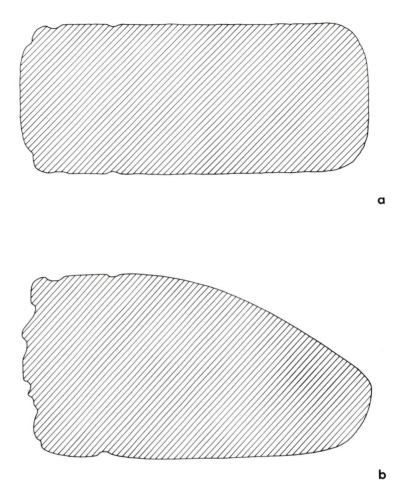

a

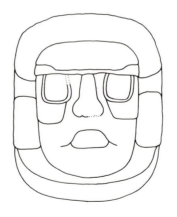

b

c

a. Stone 28: Top. 1:10

b. Stone 28: Right side. 1:10

c. Stone 28: Front. 1:10
See photograph, Fig. 43d

FIGURE 29

a. Stela 1 :Front
See drawing, Fig. 1

b. Stela 2: Front
See drawing, Fig. 2

c. Stela 4: Front
See drawing, Fig. 5a

d. Stela 4: Back
See drawing, Fig. 5b

FIGURE 30

a. Stela 3: Front
See drawing, Fig. 3

b. Stela 3: Back
See drawing, Fig. 4

FIGURE 31

a. Stela 5: Front   b. Stela 5: Lower right side glyph panel
See drawing, Fig. 6a   *See drawing, Fig. 6b*

FIGURE 32

a. Stela 6: Front
See drawing, Fig. 7a

b. Stela 6: Right side
See drawing, Fig. 7b

c. Stela 6: Back
See drawing, Fig. 8

FIGURE 33

a. Stela 7 *in situ* b. Stela 8: Front, upper half c. Stela 8: Front, lower half
See drawing, Fig. 9 *See drawing, Fig. 9*

FIGURE 34

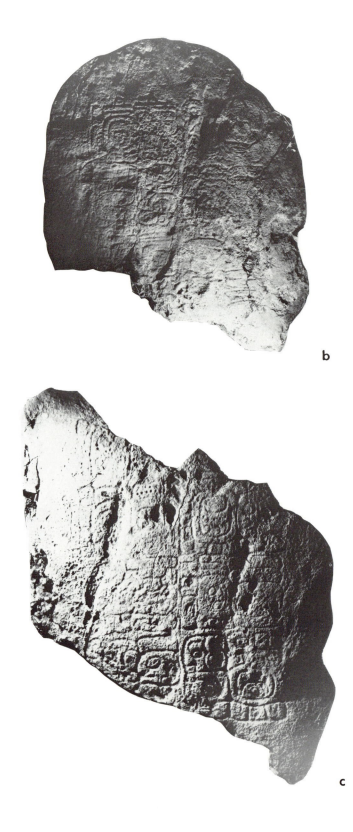

a. Stela 9: Front. Oblique
See drawing, Fig. 10

b. Stela 10: Front, upper half
See drawing, Fig. 11

c. Stela 10: Front, lower half
See drawing, Fig. 11

FIGURE 35

a. Stela 11: Front, upper half. Oblique   b. Stela 11: Front, lower half. Oblique   c. Stela 14: Front (cast)
See drawing, Fig. 12   *See drawing, Fig. 12*   *See drawing, Fig. 14a*

FIGURE 36

a. Stela 13: Front, upper half. Oblique   b. Stela 13: Back, upper half   c. Stela 15: Front
See drawing, Fig. 13a   *See drawing, Fig. 13b*   *See drawing, Fig. 14b*

FIGURE 37

a. Stela 16: Front   b. Stela 16: Back
See drawing, Fig. 15a   *See drawing, Fig. 15b*

FIGURE 38

a. Stela 17: Front   b. Stela 18: Front
See drawing, Fig. 16a   *See drawing, Fig. 16b*

FIGURE 39

a. Stela 19: Front, lower half
See drawing, Fig. 17a

c. Stela 20: Front
See drawing, Fig. 18b

b. Stela 19: Frame "IV"
See drawings, Fig. 17b, c

d. Stela 21: Front. Oblique
See drawing, Fig. 19

FIGURE 40

a

b

c

d

a. Altar 1. Oblique
See drawing, Fig. 20a

b. Altar 2. Oblique
See drawing, Fig. 20b

c. Altar 3
See drawing, Fig. 20c

d. Altar 4. Oblique
See drawing, Fig. 20d

FIGURE 41

a. Altar 5
See drawing, Fig. 21a

b. Altar 6. Oblique
See drawing, Fig. 21b

c. Altar 7. Oblique
See drawing, Fig. 21c

d. Altar 10
See drawing, Fig. 22

FIGURE 42

a. Altar 12   b. Altar 13   c. Altar 14 and Altar 15 Fragment. Oblique

See drawing, Fig. 23   *See drawing, Fig. 24*   *See drawings, Fig. 25a, b*

FIGURE 43

a. Altar 16. Oblique
See drawing, Fig. 25c

b. Altar 17
See drawing, Fig. 25d

c. Altar 19
See drawing, Fig. 26b

d. Stone 28. Oblique
See drawings, Fig. 28a, b, c